The Readable Thesis

A Guide to Clear and Effective Writing

Darrel Walters

THE READABLE THESIS
A GUIDE TO CLEAR AND EFFECTIVE WRITING

Published by: Avocus Publishing Inc.
4 White Brook Rd.
Gilsum, NH 03448
Telephone: 800-345-6665
Fax: 603-357-2073
email: pbs@monad.net
www.pathwaybook.com

Printed in the United States of America

ISBN 1-890765-02-3: 27.95 Softcover

To

MARCELLA O'CONNOR

for the wisdom to guide, the skill to teach,
and the fortitude to challenge

ACKNOWLEDGMENTS

From the time I printed the first bloated draft of this book, graduate students have been reading it, marking it, and talking to me about it—all for the betterment of the final copy. For scouring through the whole document, I am indebted to Cathie Ardrey, Eric Bluestine, Amy Chen, Glenda Cosenza, Ron Gerhardstein, Youngmee Kim, Alan Mudrick, Joe & Connie Showalter, Peter Stickney, Todd Westervelt, Eng-Cheng Wong, Jason Wroblewski, and Sheng-hwa Yu. Many others have given generous comments and suggestions about parts of the book over time, and dozens have contributed through our day-to-day working together.

Most examples in this book are from drafts of student work. I appreciate the good will and openness of graduate students I have worked with at Temple University—willing to talk freely about ways to improve writing and willing to share their work in seminars as fodder for discussion. This book is an extension of that work. Whatever insight it conveys is due in part to my association with those graduate students and with colleagues.

Many colleagues have read through earlier versions of this book and offered valuable comments. For their willingness to spend hours of valuable time I am deeply grateful, and only hope that over the years I can be of as much service to them as they have been to me. They are Richard Brodhead, Jeffrey Cornelius, Roger Dean, Cynthia Folio, Ed Flanagan, Steven Kreinberg, Eve Meyer, Stephen Willier, and Maurice Wright. I owe particular thanks to the dean of our college, Jeffrey Cornelius, for his time and encouragement. I owe particular thanks also to my good friend and department chair, Roger Dean, who has read numerous revisions and has been a constant source of encouragement.

Temple University colleagues from outside the college who have read drafts of the book and given help and encouragement are Scott Lee and Vice Provost Bill Tash. Both teach Intellectual Heritage, and both see *The Readable Thesis* as a valuable companion to the general studies of undergraduate students. I appreciate also the comments offered by Gayle Dulcey of Gwynedd Mercy College, Sharon Shapowal of SmithKline Beecham, and Patricia O'Connor. Patricia O'Connor is the daughter of the high school English teacher—Marcella O'Connor—who first showed me where writing standards should be and insisted that I never stop reaching for them. In the same vein, I owe much to Craig Thorn, of Avocus Publishing and Phillips Academy, for suggestions that have improved the book immeasurably, and to my good friend and colleague, Ken Bruscia, who brought Avocus and me together.

Finally, I thank my parents for the start they gave me, and my wife and daughters for their constant help and support. Two of my daughters, Jennifer and Johanna, read diligently through drafts of the book and marked them with a frankness that could have come only from those who know me best. Their comments were valuable. Meantime, my wife, Carol, has earned a medal for long-term tolerance of a husband's project. A bright and successful professional herself, and a constant support to me in my profession, she now deserves a respite from the fury that surrounds preparation of a manuscript.

CONTENTS

LIST OF FIGURES

Chapter 1

Appendix B—English Usage, Grammar, and Punctuation: A Primer

REFERENCES TO WRITING PRINCIPLES

1. 6, 22, 23, 33, 43, 44, 115, 152, 164, 168, 172, 175

2. 6, 15, 22, 97, 115, 180, 189

3. 6, 16, 17, 29, 30, 31, 37, 40, 43, 44, 115, 152, 164, 165, 181, 185, 207, 209, 242

4. 7, 20, 32, 189, 209, 239

5. 7, 34, 38, 54, 55, 111, 174, 178

6. 7, 25, 42, 45, 49, 53, 102, 109, 115, 162, 165, 167, 172, 173, 178, 181, 231, 245

7. 7, 30, 35, 40, 44, 45, 47, 48, 53, 102, 108, 115, 154, 157, 159, 163, 165, 167, 168, 172, 174, 175, 177, 178, 181

8. 8, 18, 29, 159, 160, 164, 165, 175, 179, 209

9. 8, 18, 19, 45, 94, 97, 98, 99, 100, 113, 115, 122, 140, 155, 157, 158, 159, 162, 163, 165, 170, 172, 173, 178, 179, 180, 181, 186, 209, 242

10. 8, 16, 40, 113, 115, 165, 208

11. 8, 104, 105, 106, 107, 115, 158, 167, 173, 179, 180

12. 8, 109

13. 9, 16, 37, 38, 40, 44, 45, 47, 159, 170, 174, 175, 177, 186, 187, 207

14. 9, 23, 42, 43, 100, 108, 115, 140, 152, 181, 242

15. 9, 32, 40, 107, 153, 179

16. 9, 26, 40, 41, 48, 115, 117, 124, 152, 154, 170, 180

17. 9, 95, 97, 115, 131, 135, 136, 170, 172, 175, 180, 193

18. 9, 15, 18, 32, 35, 36, 38, 45, 48, 52, 53, 55, 56, 115, 117, 131, 135, 155, 157, 158, 159, 160, 162, 167, 168, 169, 173, 175, 177, 178, 179, 242

19. 10, 33, 43, 45, 110, 111, 112, 113, 114, 115, 135, 153, 158, 162, 170, 186, 209

20. 10, 17, 31, 32, 169, 175, 250, 256

21. 10, 16, 17, 18, 55

22. 10, 24, 33, 100

23. 11, 33

24. 11, 106, 173, 195

25. 11, 27, 115, 157, 168

26. 11, 33, 34, 140–149, 155, 159, 169, 173

HOW TO MAKE GOOD USE OF THIS BOOK

1. Perspective

This book will be useful to almost anyone wanting to write more effectively. Its prime audience is the college and university population: graduate students and their thesis advisers, undergraduate students, and instructors of all subjects who want students to write more readable prose. Others who may find *The Readable Thesis* useful are professional persons across all disciplines and advanced high school students—students who have won the struggle with basic writing problems.[1] Whatever the population, the book will serve well as a writing-class text, a writing-seminar supplement, or a writing companion for individual use.

The subject of *The Readable Thesis* is readability in formal writing: research reports, scientific articles, monographs, theses, dissertations, and other such documents. If you associate that list with laborious reading you are not alone. Long-winded, tangled writing tortures all of us—more frequently than we like to think. The only sensible response is to commit ourselves to write in a style that others can read efficiently. If enough of us do that, in time the fog may begin to lift.

Advice for writers comes in several forms. Style manuals foster uniformity (APA; Chicago; MLA), technical manuals foster correctness (Fowler; Hacker; Kramer, et al.), and other books guide writers in broader ways (Strunk and White; Lanham; Zinser). In *The Readable Thesis,* I use actual writing examples and revisions as the core of a practical guide to producing more readable writing. Most examples come from ten years' worth of student writing that I collected as a thesis and dissertation advisor, but some are from other writings, published and unpublished. I use some nonstandard terms in writing about writing, and I offer only a limited account of the rules of grammar and punctuation; I suppose that makes my approach unconventional, and it certainly makes *The Readable Thesis* a supplement rather than a replacement for other books you

---

[1] A parallel writing companion for general high school use is planned for release soon.

turn to for writing advice. *The Readable Thesis* amounts to one college professor's extensive account of student writing problems, along with solutions that have helped many students write dramatically better. You will have to decide the extent to which that approach suits you.

While teaching and advising graduate students, I see the same writing problems time and time again. That is not surprising, because the questions that writers of formal papers and documents need to ask themselves are fundamental and universal. Here are a few:

- What belongs in this paragraph, and what is the best order?
- How can I emphasize what is most important?
- Can I write this sentence more clearly?
- Is this a proper use of that word?
- Which word is more precise here?
- How can I make this stronger?
- How can I hold the reader's interest?

Of course questions of content, organization, and form are also important—and you will find some insight into those broader issues in Chapters 7 and 8—but the principal purpose of this book is to help you root out writing gremlins and improve page-by-page readability. The diligence with which you ask yourself the kinds of questions listed above and the choices you make in answering them will influence greatly the readability of your writing.

2. Organization of this Book

I have organized the chapters of this book around aims of a good writer (clarity, precision, brevity, strength) and around examples that show the damage wrought when those aims are not met. To help you transfer the lessons of this book to your own writing, I have associated the examples with a concise set of writing principles, some unique and others echoing writing principles from across the ages. You will see those writing principles listed on a laminated moveable page labeled BOOKMARK, and you will read about them in "Writing Principles Described" immediately following this Introduction. Those principles are not meant as inflexible dictums that homogenize individual style out of existence: you may legitimately bend some of the principles at times, and you may violate others intentionally to create a specific effect. On the other hand, keep in mind that the principles shown on the BOOKMARK were born as reactions to writing practices that commonly impede readability. To put yourself in control of your own writing, study the principles and practice writing within them—then decide where individual circumstances call for you to write differently.

In the body of this book, the examples of flawed writing and suggestions for revision sit side by side in shaded columns. Most are followed by written comments and linked to writing principles by bold face numbers enclosed in wavy brackets **{ }**. You will see a boxed **R** placed next to examples whose research-related language might confuse nonresearchers. Depending on the type of writing you are doing, you may want to either scan those examples for usefulness or pay particular attention to them.

The organization of this book makes it easy to use in a variety of ways. You might read straight through, you might refer to particular chapters or particular writing problems within chapters, you might follow a particular writing principle through the book (see References to Writing Principles following the Table of Contents), or you might use the book as a reference. Whenever and however you use *The Readable Thesis,* keep the BOOKMARK close. You will want to refer to it periodically.

Following is a skeletal account of the eight chapters and three appendices contained in *The Readable Thesis.*

Chapter 1	Clarity and Precision in Construction
Chapter 2	Clarity and Precision in Word Choice
Chapter 3	Length, Strength, and Grace
Chapter 4	The Bureaucratic Style
Chapter 5	Person and Gender
Chapter 6	Multiple-Problem Examples and Exercises
Chapter 7	The Larger Picture
Chapter 8	How I Write
Appendix A	Possible Solutions to Multiple-Problem Exercises from Chapter Six
Appendix B	English Usage, Grammar, and Punctuation: A Primer
Appendix C	A Reservoir of Verbs

Good formal writing is built on clarity and precision, the subjects of Chapters 1 and 2. Chapter 3 is a treatment of three common writing problems: using too many words, expressing thoughts weakly, and writing clumsily. I devote all of Chapter 4 to an insidious stylistic indulgence likely to infect your writing without your realizing it: bureaucratese. In Chapter 5 I tackle the controversy over gender in writing—and to a lesser extent, person in writing. Chapter 6 amounts to a tool to help you reinforce and test skills you learned in the previous chapters. Chapters 7 and 8 offer a broader view of writing and a personal step-by-step view of the writing process.

Appendix A is a companion to Chapter 6. Appendix B offers concise information about parts of speech and parts of a sentence—basic information you may have tried to learn years ago when you were less receptive than you are now. Appendix B also shows a few common grammar errors and offers you help with punctuation. Appendix C is a short exposition on verb use, followed by lists of about 3,000 verbs that may help you invigorate your writing.

Throughout the chapters you will see comments enclosed in indented white boxes and titled "Bonus Tidbit." They are thoughts that come to me as I present examples. Some tidbits are elaborations; others are secondary points. I hope their unpredictability, like verbal asides in a classroom lecture, will add interest and heighten learning.

3. A Note About Revision

I cannot overstate the importance of revision to writing. ***Writing is revision. First drafts are tomorrow's trash; second and third drafts are momentum toward a good final copy.*** If you procrastinate when a paper is assigned and finally submit it without having taken time to revise thoroughly, you have not written a paper: you have careened recklessly through an obligation. To spend years careening through obligations in high school and college instead of writing papers is to risk more than your grade point average: you risk needing remedial work as a graduate student, particularly if you need to write a thesis or dissertation. Still more important, you risk becoming one of the professional world's inefficient communicators, which will threaten your reputation and your prospects for professional promotion and job tenure. I hope *The Readable Thesis* motivates you to revise—and helps you revise well—by providing you with two essential tools: a sensitivity to flawed writing and a set of specific approaches to repairing it.

4. A Note About Tolerance

Clear, precise language is more important to writing than to speaking, because writing is one-dimensional: the words on the page either do the job or they do not. In contrast, speakers can enhance their words with facial expression, body language, gestures, and even second tries. You will do well to work at speaking correctly yourself, but probably some amount of tolerance of spoken inaccuracies from others enhances communication: no one wants to risk speaking when the "Grammar Police" are listening.

Some written communication is also due a degree of tolerance, simply because a finely tuned product is less important in some circumstances than in others. I try to write well every time I put words on paper. Still, everyone writes memorandums and notes that have simple, short-term functions; extensive revision would take more time than it is worth. We need to exercise our standards and judgments within contexts.

A Closing Note

Read fine writing. Get the *sound* of it in your ear. One short, simple example that I enjoy is E. B. White's introduction to *The Elements of Style.* I think if you were to read it you would be fascinated and pleased with its easy flow, a virtue in all styles from short stories to doctoral dissertations. Sentences and paragraphs seem natural, easy, effortlessly crafted.

You may want to take the work of White, or any good author, as a model for the feel of your writing. If you do, be careful not to be lulled by the sense of effortlessness. Like a good third baseman's *effortless* throw to first, a good writer's *effortless* presentation of sentences and paragraphs requires, in fact, substantial effort and practice.

I hope you find success and satisfaction—even joy—in applying yourself to the task of improving your writing. Begin by reading Writing Principles Described, which starts on the next page. Think about those principles in relation to your own writing tendencies, then proceed with the book itself. Refer to some of your recent writing if you think that will be helpful. Whatever you do, be persistent and patient. The road to fine writing is neither quick nor easy, but the rewards at the other end are immense.

WRITING PRINCIPLES DESCRIBED

These few pages will help you understand my thinking relative to the 26 writing principles shown on the BOOKMARK. Keep the BOOKMARK out while you use *The Readable Thesis* so you can refer to it as needed when you see boldface writing-principle numbers enclosed in wavy brackets { }. If you lose the BOOKMARK, photocopy the duplicate from the last page of this section.

1. Write from knowledge; revise from ignorance.

Knowing your subject well gives you credibility as a writer, but it can also blind you to what others do not know. Guard against omitting important material by rereading your work from the mind-set of one who knows little, then revise it to fill in holes. An excellent way to double-check for omissions and confusing assumptions is to have another person read your work, particularly one who knows less than you about the subject.

2. Limit the reach of the project, and of each sentence and paragraph.

Define the specific function of your writing project, then resist material that takes you outside that function. As you write, keep in mind that well-written sentences and paragraphs also have definable functions; overstuffed sentences and paragraphs do not.

3. Arrange material logically.

Order of material in writing is critical to the reader's understanding. When your writing threatens to disorient readers—even for a second or two—for lack of information yet to come, present that information earlier (unless important considerations dictate otherwise). This principle applies to sentences as well as to paragraphs and complete documents.

Disorienting: *Student motivation is high and discipline problems are declining, according to Jefferson High School's principal.*

Orienting: *According to Jefferson High School's principal, student motivation is high and discipline problems are declining.*

4. Link material with smooth transitions.

Read your writing with an ear to cohesiveness. Where one sentence does not lead smoothly to the next, pave the way with a transitional word or phrase. Where one paragraph does not lead smoothly to the next, pave the way with a transitional word, phrase, or sentence—or in unusual cases, even a transitional paragraph. Transitions take bumps out of the reader's road. Below, one word of transition smooths the reader's way by stating the specific relationship of the second sentence to the first.

Bumpy: *First-grade students consumed the books by Schaffer and ignored the books by Levine. Third-grade students consumed the books by Levine and ignored the books by Schaffer.*

Smooth: *First-grade students consumed the books by Schaffer and ignored the books by Levine. Conversely, third-grade students consumed the books by Levine and ignored the books by Schaffer.*

5. Keep terms and format consistent.

You risk losing readers when you refer to a single entity with multiple terms, e.g., *subjects, children, students, pupils.* Construct a logical system of terms and apply it consistently throughout a given document. Also, be consistent in matters of format: do not vary, for example, the capitalization pattern or type size of section headings, the underlining of a particular kind of term, or the sizes of margins and indentations.

6. Attribute thoughts, actions, and characteristics clearly to someone or something.

Do not make readers guess who is responsible for what. One key to clear attribution is careful use of pronouns.

Unclear: *When the superintendent introduced the researchers to the teachers, they were surprised.*

Clear: *The researchers were surprised when the superintendent introduced them to the teachers.*

Clear: *The teachers were surprised when the superintendent introduced the researchers to them.*

7. Say what you mean to say.

To write unintended meaning into a sentence or paragraph is alarmingly easy.

Written: *He agreed with the woman who had argued with him grudgingly.*

Intended: *He agreed, grudgingly, with the woman who had argued with him.*

8. Emphasize what you mean to emphasize.

Speakers can emphasize points by volume, inflection, or gesture; writers must rely on word placement. Strunk and White (1979) cite the end of a sentence as the placement of greatest emphasis and the beginning as the placement of second greatest emphasis. Notice the differences in emphasis among these three statements:

There was a murder, and the doctor has been charged.
A murder charge has been brought against the doctor.
The doctor has been charged with murder.

The question is not "which is better," but "which delivers the intended message and the intended effect with greatest strength and precision."

9. Write concisely.

In general, skillful writers use fewer words than unskillful writers. You will do well to think of *fewer words* as a beacon that lights your way through every sentence and paragraph. The primary tools of concision are a rich vocabulary and a commitment to revision.

10. Avoid slow-start phrases.

Slow-start phrases (there was; it is) lengthen sentences and rob them of strong subject-verb combinations; the effect on the reader is one of slow-motion reading.

No *It was about noon before there were signs of life in the camp.*

Yes *The camp finally came to life about noon.*

11. Avoid overstatement.

When you write dogma *(There is no discipline in the public schools),* or when you overuse qualifiers *(very; extremely),* you endanger your credibility with the reader.

12. Describe action with verbs, not nouns-as-verbs or nominalizations.

Some words are equally strong as a noun or as a verb (light; shovel); others are strong only as a noun, but are commonly pressed into service as a verb (impact; dialogue). While widespread use of nouns as verbs over time forces legitimate language shifts, your writing will be strongest in the here and now if you choose not to lead the way. Also, avoid nominalizing the action of a sentence.

Nominalization: *He has an understanding of how to proceed.*

Stronger: *He understands how to proceed.*

(See Appendix C: A Reservoir of Verbs)

13. Use parallel structures.

Parallel structure speeds comprehension between paragraphs, between sentences, between parts of sentences, and between words. For example, readers will assimilate the second statement below more quickly than the first:

Nonparallel: *The Anderson party chose to travel by day, but night travel was chosen by the Carson party.*

Parallel: *The Anderson party chose to travel by day, and the Carson party by night.*

14. Choose active voice over passive.

Use passive voice sparingly and purposefully. Circumstances sometimes make passive voice preferable, but generally *X tested Y* is stronger than *Y was tested by X.*

15. Choose positive form over negative.

Negatively written statements are like inside-out socks: they become useful only after someone has turned them. Do not give that job to your readers.

No *He was not so unproductive when he worked with people who were not strangers.*

Yes *He was more productive when he worked with people he knew.*

16. Choose specific terms over general.

General terms hint at information: *He participated on a regular basis.* Specific terms convey information: *He attended every meeting and chaired the research committee.*

17. Choose simple terms over complex.

Resist temptations to create intellectual effects with unnecessarily complex terms. Complex terms dazzle a few readers: *His pedagogy was fraught with insipidness.* Simple terms communicate with many: *As a teacher, he was a bore.*

18. Choose the most precise (effective) term.

Assuming that the writer of these statements intends to honor the *established boundary,* the second statement is more precise than the first.

I choose not to ignore such a clearly established boundary.
I choose not to violate such a clearly established boundary.

This third version is still more precise, but it will be effective only if readers can give full meaning to the word *transgress.*

I choose not to transgress such a clearly established boundary.

Expand your vocabulary constantly, be sensitive to fine shadings of meaning, and know your audience; then search diligently for the most effective words as you write and revise.

19. Write rhythmically graceful and phonetically pleasing sentences and paragraphs.

Read your writing aloud to monitor its rhythm and sound.

Awkward:	*The boys were on the boat without the girls, who were ashore, so the parents felt relaxed.*
Rhythmically graceful:	*The boys were aboard and the girls ashore, so the parents felt relaxed.*
Awkward:	*The function of diction correction is the improvement of oral delivery.*
Phonetically pleasing:	*The purpose of studying diction is to improve oral delivery.*

Sound-related flaws in writing impede comprehension by distracting readers.

20. Use punctuation to the reader's advantage.

To force a comma or period to do the job of a semicolon or colon is awkward and inefficient—like forcing a table knife to do the job of a screwdriver. Study the uses of punctuation marks until you can take full advantage of them in your writing. (Section 3 of Appendix B is one source of information.)

21. Organize details within a numbering system, a list, or a table.

When long, involved phrases or large numbers of details complicate a narrative description, consider sorting the factors visually for the reader by using numbers within a sentence or by creating a list or a table.

22. Present insertions (lists, figures, tables) clearly.

Prior to inserting a list, figure, or table into your document, prepare the reader for exactly what is coming. Then present the insertion in a form that is easy to read and consistent with other insertions in the document.

Important: figures and tables need numbers and titles. A number makes a figure or table easy to cite; a title describes its function.

23. Explain and define terms that might be misunderstood.

Define for the reader—before you use them—coined terms, uncommon terms, and common terms that you use in uncommon ways.

24. Cite all material that comes from an external source.

Give sources of all information not attributable to you, including material you paraphrase and material you have received verbally, as by interview. You may use one of several techniques—footnotes, endnotes, bibliographic references within the text—but be consistent. (Refer to a manual of style for details about options.)

25. Avoid informal expressions.

Informal expressions—jargon, abbreviations, and contractions acceptable in informal writing—are not acceptable in research reports and other documents designed to transmit information.

26. Avoid using gender-specific pronouns in gender-neutral circumstances.

For centuries, writers have applied generic-masculine pronouns *(he, him, his)* to circumstances that apply to both male and female. Some modern writers react to that practice by applying generic-feminine pronouns *(she, her, hers)* in the same way. Do neither: let the advice in Chapter 5 help you avoid the gender tug-of-war.

BOOKMARK

WRITING PRINCIPLES

		Described on page
1.	**Write from knowledge; revise from ignorance.**	6
2.	**Limit the reach of the project, and of each sentence and paragraph.**	6
3.	**Arrange material logically.**	6
4.	**Link material with smooth transitions.**	7
5.	**Keep terms and format consistent.**	7
6.	**Attribute thoughts, actions, and characteristics clearly to someone or something.**	7
7.	**Say what you mean to say.**	7
8.	**Emphasize what you mean to emphasize.**	8
9.	**Write concisely.**	8
10.	**Avoid slow-start phrases.**	8
11.	**Avoid overstatement.**	8
12.	**Describe action with verbs, not nouns-as-verbs or nominalizations.**	8
13.	**Use parallel structures.**	9
14.	**Choose active voice over passive.**	9
15.	**Choose positive form over negative.**	9
16.	**Choose specific terms over general.**	9
17.	**Choose simple terms over complex.**	9
18.	**Choose the most precise (effective) term.**	9
19.	**Write rhythmically graceful and phonetically pleasing sentences and paragraphs.**	10
20.	**Use punctuation to the reader's advantage.**	10
21.	**Organize details within a numbering system, a list, or a table.**	10
22.	**Present insertions (lists, figures, tables) clearly.**	10
23.	**Explain and define terms that might be misunderstood.**	10
24.	**Cite all material that comes from an external source.**	11
25.	**Avoid informal expressions.**	11
26.	**Avoid using gender-specific pronouns in gender-neutral circumstances.**	11

For elaboration on these principles, turn to p.6, Writing Principles Described.

References to these principles in the text are bold numbers enclosed between bold wavy brackets **{ }**.

CLARITY AND PRECISION IN CONSTRUCTION

To be sure we are thinking similarly, I should offer my definitions of clarity and precision as they pertain to formal, nonfiction writing—the domain of this book:

> Clear writing lets readers read through without doubling back or asking questions about content.
>
> Precise writing gives readers information, descriptions, and definitions that are accurate and exact.

Clarity and precision together form the foundation for good formal writing. ***Nothing is more important.*** They so permeate any discussion about writing that every chapter in this book—whatever the principal issue—has clarity and precision lurking in the background as secondary issues.

In these first two chapters, clarity and precision take center stage. Suppose you were to write a page that is pristine in its clarity and precision. That page would give the reader's mind a straight, uninterrupted path to follow from beginning to end, as represented by the drawing in Figure 1.

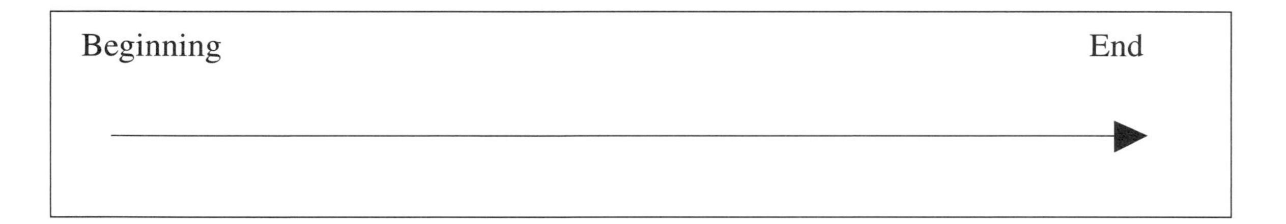

Figure 1. Representation of a Straight, Uninterrupted Reading Path

On the other hand, suppose you were to write a page quite deficient in clarity and precision. That reading path is represented by the drawing in Figure 2.

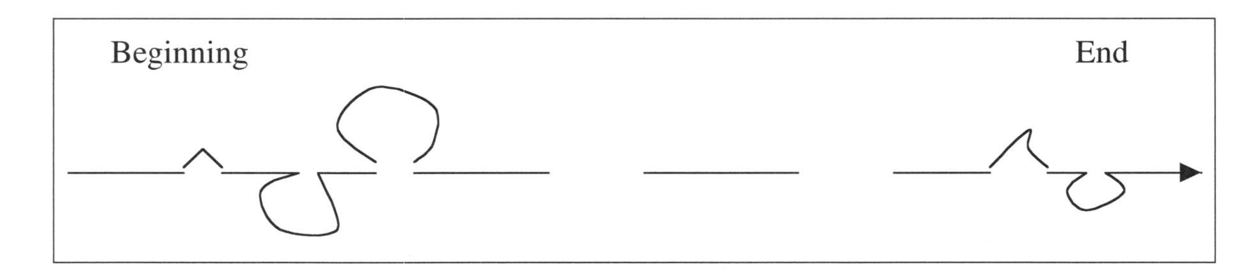

Figure 2. Representation of a Reading Path Fraught with Side Trips and Backtracking

The detours in Figure 2 indicate imprecise words, tangled sentences, prematurely placed material, backtracking to the prematurely placed material, and other writing glitches that interrupt the reader's progress. Some readers will fight their way through such obstacles; others will just walk away. "Why try to read this," they think, "when I can spend my time reading something well-written?" That may sound brutal, but think of the hard choices all of us make in a world filled with more good writing than we can ever read. Never lose track of this important thought: ***When you write, you are a seller in a buyer's market.***

How clearly and precisely do you write? The answer to that question depends partly on how well you choose your words (Chapter 2: Clarity and Precision in Word Choice). It depends also on the way you construct sentences and paragraphs; that is the subject of this chapter. Some examples of faulty construction shown here are less flawed than others, but all are worth correcting: as a writer, you will want to spare readers even small amounts of unnecessary work. I have organized the examples around eight foibles of construction that keep writing from being as clear and precise as it might be. The terms I use come more from commonsense observations of student work than from standard writing pedagogy:

1. Overstuffed Sentences
2. Overstuffed Paragraphs
3. Shortcuts
4. Disjointedness
5. Nonparallel Construction
6. Vague or Tangled Construction
7. Misleading Construction
8. Personification

1. Overstuffed Sentences

Do you ever "get on a roll" while writing, and think only of content for a long period of time? That is when you are most likely to write what I call overstuffed sentences: sentences that contain more information than the reader can digest in that form. In parentheses above each revision in this section you will see an account of the solution applied to an overstuffed sentence: division into multiple sentences **(Division);** use of numbers **(Numbers);** use of dashes or parentheses **(Dashes; Parentheses)**; or use of a table (**Table**) **{2}**.

{2} indicates that the issue under discussion is related to writing principle number 2, as shown on the BOOKMARK. For an explanation of this and other information vital to your making good use of this book, read the Introduction.

Example 1: Overstuffed Sentences

Original	**Revision**
1a. (Overstuffed Sentence)	(Division)
While critics claim that music teachers fail to teach basic musicality and aesthetic sensitivity, music teachers respond that with limited time in rehearsal and pressure from the community to perform at athletic events, outside programs, competition, and recruitment programs there is little time to develop a true music education program.	Critics claim that music teachers fail to teach basic musicality and aesthetic sensitivity. Music teachers counter that rehearsal time is limited and that the community presses for performances at athletic events, nonschool functions, and competitions. Add the need for recruitment activities, and little time is left to develop a comprehensive music education program.

The length of sentence **1a** and the number of phrases it contains hint at overstuffed construction, and reading confirms it. In the revision, I used an opening sentence for the claim the writer is presenting, a second sentence for the rebuttal, and a third sentence for a statement of the consequence. One anomaly is that I let recruitment ride along as an introductory clause to the third sentence to separate it from the topics of the second, all of which are unrelated to recruitment. These are the kinds of logic-based decisions you have to make to keep from coupling divergent pieces of material within a sentence, a practice that confuses and irritates readers and makes reading less efficient **{2}**.

1a Bonus Tidbit

Notice also that I replaced true with comprehensive in the last phrase to make the language more precise **{18}**. For more about precise word choice, see Chapter 2.

Original

1b. (Overstuffed Sentence)

She found that verbal scores for Korean students were higher than tactile scores, there was not a significant difference in the ATS mean scores between Korean students and American students, and the relationship between ATS scores and IQ scores for Korean students were similar to the same relationship for American students.

Revision

(Numbers)

She reported three results: 1) ATS score differences between Korean students and American students were not significant; 2) Korean students were similar to American students in the relationship of their ATS scores to their IQ scores; and 3) Korean students scored higher on the verbal subtest than on the tactile subtest.

The **1b** revision makes material easier to digest in four ways: 1) the numbers help readers shift gears between topics **{21}**; 2) topics are ordered from general to specific **{3}**; 3) each new topic is introduced directly (not with a slow-start phrase: there was not) **{10}**; and 4) parallel construction helps the reader organize material mentally while reading it **{13}** (more about parallel construction in Part 5 of this chapter).

1b Bonus Tidbit

Overstuffed sentences distract the writer as well as the reader, making grammatical errors more likely. Notice the disagreement in number between subject and verb in the last clause of the original: relationship . . . were.

Two writing characteristics that make reading difficult are sentences having great numbers of words and words having great numbers of syllables. Read **1c** and its revision.

Original

1c. (Overstuffed Sentence)

To measure personal tempo and heart rate, Buchanan used a phonoelectrocardiogram machine, which simultaneously monitors and graphs the stimulus at a given tempo, the subject's heart rate, and the subject's rhythmic activity, in this case, bilateral patting on a table.

Revision

(Division, Numbers, Dash)

To measure personal tempo and heart rate, Buchanan used a phonoelectrocardiogram machine. The machine simultaneously monitors and graphs 1) the stimulus at a given tempo, 2) the subject's heart rate, and 3) the subject's rhythmic activity—in this case, bilateral patting on a table.

A nine-syllable word in **1c** (phonoelectrocardiogram) calls for a short sentence as compensation. Then, because three elements were measured, and the third element (rhythmic activity) called for interpretation, I chose numbers and a dash to help present everything clearly for the reader. The use of numbers (or letters: a, b, c) within a complicated sentence is an outstanding organizing device that seems to be underused **{21}**. (Be careful. It can also be overused.)

Original	Revision
1d. (Overstuffed Sentence)	(Dashes)
Most of the ideas, once extracted from the writing, being relevant to education, would seem obvious to the moderately observant and experienced educator.	Once extracted from the writing, most of the ideas—being relevant to education—would seem obvious to the moderately observant and experienced educator.

The confusing string of phrases in **1d** seems to call for dividing the sentence into two or more, but dashes used skillfully can be an outstanding clarifying agent **{20}** (See Appendix B, Part 3, Example B-19). The revision depends also on choosing the most logical order for the material. Once extracted from the writing makes an ideal first phrase because it qualifies the rest **{3}**.

Original	Revision
1e. (Overstuffed Sentence)	(Parentheses)
Laban labeled four basic elements of human movement in reaction to the mechanical fact that the weight of the body, or any of its parts, can be lifted and carried into a certain direction of space, and that this process takes a certain amount of time, depending on the ratio of speed, or flow.	Laban labeled four basic elements of human movement on the premise that the body moves its parts (weight) in specific directions (space), and that duration (time) depends upon rate of speed (flow).

Example **1e** shows an ideal circumstance for use of parentheses. With their help I contained the message in one clear sentence, cut the number of prepositional phrases in half, and presented the four important Laban elements explicitly rather than leaving them hidden like spotted owls in a forest **{8, 9}**. ***Be careful not to overuse parentheses; use them only when they clearly outperform more conventional construction.***

1e Bonus Tidbit

Ratio is misused in the last phrase: the ratio of speed. A ratio is a relationship between factors, as in " the ratio of X to Y" **{18}**.

Original

R

1f. (Overstuffed Sentence)

The third year predictive validity of SVT with mechanical achievement test scores (MAB) is .78 spatial, .74 depth, .68 perspective, and .81 composite; the validity with classroom teachers' judgments is .33 spatial, .31 depth, .28 perspective, and .35 composite; the validity with judges' evaluations of drawings is .58 spatial, .66 depth, .61 perspective, and .68 composite.

Revision

(Table)

Three-year predictive validity coefficients for the SVT subtests and composite are shown in Table 1.

TABLE 1. Three-year Predictive Validity Coefficients for SVT, with Three Criteria: Mechanical Achievement Scores (MAB), Classroom Teacher Judgments, and Drawing Assessments.

SVT Battery	MAB	Teacher	Drawings
Spatial	.78	.33	.58
Depth	.74	.31	.66
Perspective	.68	.28	.61
Composite	.81	.35	.68

The overstuffed feeling in **1f** stems from a visual entanglement of coefficients and factors, making interpretation and comparison nearly impossible. Whenever you report details that strain the capacity of a sentence format, organize those details in some other format. In this case—and frequently in the case of research writing—a table gives the reader the visual help needed to interpret the coefficients and compare them easily to each other **{21}**.

Notice that the overstuffing of sentences does not equate one-to-one with sentence length. Example **1b** is more than 40 words long both before and after revision. I rescued the reader from that overstuffed feeling by opening with a short orienting statement followed by a colon, then by using numbers and parallel construction to give the reader benchmarks along the way. Moral: longer does not always mean less readable. Still, two important words in that moral are <u>not always</u>. Short sentences generally are more readable than long sentences. I improved the readability of **1a** by reducing it from a 51-word sentence to three sentences that average 18 words. I reduced **1e** from 54 words to 32. That is still a long sentence, but the terms in parentheses function as benchmarks to help counterbalance length.

So how long should sentences be? First, they should vary in length; that alone helps readability (See Chapter 3, Example 13e, and Appendix B, A Closing Note). Beyond that, the most explicit guide to sentence length I know comes from Rudolph Flesch, a long-time advocate of "plain English." Flesch (1972) tells us to average no more than 20 words per sentence—and he feels more comfortable with an average of 16 or 17.[2] Can we justify longer average sentence lengths for academic writing? After all, academic content is more complicated than general content and academic readers are more schooled than general readers. The argument is valid to a point, but be careful not to lean on it too heavily. My sense is that differences in optimal sentence length among adult readers is not as great as we tend to think. I use this rule of thumb: ***As average sentence length rises from 20 words, readability falls correspondingly for all readers.*** You will find more thoughts about length in Chapter 3, in the context of general wordiness **{9}** rather than overstuffed sentences.

---

[2] Do not rely on a word processing program to count average sentence length accurately for a full document that contains columns, tables, lists, etc. Instead, select several paragraphs or pages of straight prose, then ask for the average word count.

2. Overstuffed Paragraphs

How long should a paragraph be? Paragraphs are the writing units in which you organize, develop, and present your specific thoughts. To develop anything requires at least two sentences, and most paragraphs will contain three or more. Single sentences sometimes stand alone for special effect, but by definition a single sentence is not a paragraph. Write freestanding sentences only rarely, and then with a specific function in mind, e.g., a transition of some kind **{4}**.

At issue here, though, are paragraphs having too much rather than too little. Overstuffing a paragraph—and this is an extremely important point—is more than a matter of sheer length. A paragraph can be well-crafted with 200 words or overstuffed with 50. You overstuff your paragraphs when you combine thoughts so diverse that the reader cannot assimilate and digest them efficiently. Sometimes diverse thoughts are simply run together (**2a**); other times they are badly entangled (**2b**).

Example 2: Overstuffed Paragraph

Original

2a. (Overstuffed Paragraph)

Athletes and musicians, as different as their pursuits seem from one another, have much in common. Both rely on practice, self-discipline, physical control, and mental and physical quickness. They differ from one another only in specific application. Recognizing that athletes and musicians might profit from studying the other's domain, two professors at Framingham State College have collaborated. George Amsden and Neil Campbell, professors of music and physical education respectively, are working with each other's students. After one full year of cross-curricular exploration, the two agree that students have benefited significantly. Readers interested in the work of Amsden and Campbell may write to them care of this publication. Send name, address, and SASE. Expect a response within 30 days.

Revision

Athletes and musicians, as different as their pursuits seem from one another, have much in common. Both rely on practice, self-discipline, physical control, and mental and physical quickness. They differ from one another only in specific application.

Recognizing that athletes and musicians might profit from studying the other's domain, two professors at Framingham State College have collaborated. George Amsden and Neil Campbell, professors of music and physical education respectively, are working with each other's students. After one full year of cross-curricular exploration, the two agree that students have benefited significantly.

Readers interested in the work of Amsden and Campbell may write to them care of this publication. Send name, address, and SASE. Expect a response within 30 days.

To revise **2a** I simply located points at which to begin new paragraphs. That gives the reader a pattern of visual organization for easier reading and quicker comprehension. Now read **2b** and its revision; it will take longer to read than any other example outside Chapter Seven, but reading it is important to your seeing clearly the damage done by a truly muddled paragraph.

Original

2b. (Overstuffed Paragraph)

Hobbies are important diversions for people of all ages. I was about 12 when I became a numismat. As I recall, the important-sounding name itself had some appeal. Still, what hooked me for good was the excitement of the hunt. "Numismatic" means "of or pertaining to currency," and "numismatics" has become the official name for hobbiests who collect coins. I remember striking up a friendship with an older man who introduced me to his hobby when I was young. A young person who has not yet reached the frenetic activity of the teen years needs a hobby around which to begin organizing life; a retired person who has just left the frenetic activity of a profession needs a hobby around which to continue organizing life. Looking for just that right coin becomes a joyful obsession. A numismat becomes facile at sorting through a handful of change, looking for that 1950D Jefferson nickel or that 1955S Lincoln penny. The letters after the dates are mint marks: lack of any mark signifies Philadelphia, D signifies Denver, and S signifies San Francisco. (The San Francisco mint closed in 1955.) Some old coins have an O mint mark for New Orleans, where there was a mint until early in this century. Location of the mint mark varies from coin to coin, marks on the face being referred to as "obverse" and marks on the back as "reverse." In time, Mr. Nielson and I came to have much in common.

Revision

Hobbies are important diversions for people of all ages. A young person who has not yet reached the frenetic activity of the teen years needs a hobby around which to begin organizing life; a retired person who has just left the frenetic activity of a profession needs a hobby around which to continue organizing life. I remember striking up a friendship with an older man who introduced me to his hobby when I was young. In time, Mr. Nielson and I came to have much in common.

I was about 12 when I became a numismat. "Numismatic" means "of or pertaining to currency," and "numismatics" has become the official name for hobbyists who collect coins. As I recall, the important-sounding name itself had some appeal. Still, what hooked me for good was the excitement of the hunt. Looking for just that right coin becomes a joyful obsession. A numismat becomes facile at sorting through a handful of change, looking for that 1950D Jefferson nickel or that 1955S Lincoln penny.

The letters after the dates are mint marks: lack of any mark signifies Philadelphia, D signifies Denver, and S signifies San Francisco. (The San Francisco mint closed in 1955.) Some old coins have an O mint mark for New Orleans, where there was a mint until early in this century. Location of the mint mark varies from coin to coin, marks on the face being referred to as "obverse" and marks on the back as "reverse."

Diverse thoughts are interwoven within **2b.** When you find you have written such a paragraph, you need to identify major components and organize them into several shorter paragraphs of their own **{2}**.

> **2 Bonus Tidbit**
>
> Paragraphs serve a function beyond combining thoughts into logical units: they let the reader up for air. No matter how strong your case that page after page of text develops one thought, you will do well to find a logical place for a paragraph break at least once each page. In double-spaced material you may make an occasional exception; in single-spaced material, multiple breaks per page will be the norm.

3. Shortcuts

I saw this title in a research journal: "The Effectiveness of Three Listening Packets on the Musical Achievement of Fifth-Grade Students." Contrary to the literal message of that title, the subjects of the study did not listen to packets. The writer had simply used a writing shortcut, oblivious to the reader's unfamiliarity with the meaning of packets **{1}** within that study. I have identified four shortcuts writers take at the expense of readers:

Example 3	Missing Information	Example 5	Reckless Back-Reference
Example 4	Vague Collective Noun	Example 6	Jargon

Example 3: Missing Information

Be careful not to write a simplified version of your message that leaves the reader grappling for information you have omitted.

Original	Revision
3a. (Shortcut: Missing Information) In his early work, Piaget observed pairs of children as they interacted with their environment. He focused on the development of language and forms of thinking in the child. Then he extended his method to include children of all ages, giving older children learning tasks and varying the circumstances to validate a given interpretation.	(No revision can be written without first having the missing facts.)

Nowhere in the paper from which the **3a** excerpt was taken did the writer tell readers the ages of Piaget's subjects. Were the initial pairs of children 2 years old, or were they 5, 7, or 10? Does children of all ages mean children as old as age 18? Age 16? When information about a subject becomes second-nature to a writer, that writer is in danger of overlooking the reader's need to be told **{1}**.

Original	**Revision**
3b. (Shortcut: Missing Information)	
Art historians disagree about whether Gilbert Stuart or Charles Willson Peale was the finest artist of the late Colonial period.	Art historians disagree about whether Gilbert Stuart or Charles Willson Peale was the finest American painter of the late Colonial period.
 **3c.** (Shortcut: Missing Information)	
The student's singing of each melody was preceded by the preparatory sequence.	Prior to singing each melody, students listened to a recording of the preparatory sequence, sung by the researcher.

Missing qualifiers in **3b** could cause readers to think of Stuart or Peale as the finest artist of the time, regardless of country or medium. When the aim of writing is straightforward delivery of information, as in this case, the reader should not have to make any kind of interpretation to receive the writer's message. In the research study behind excerpt **3c**, was the preparatory sequence sung or played? By whom? Live or on tape? The revision answers these questions. Notice also the conversion from passive to active structure **{14}.** (For more about active versus passive structure, see Chapter 3, Part 2, Example 11.)

3c Bonus Tidbit

When writing a research report, think in terms of other researchers who may want to replicate your study. That will encourage you to include the kind of detail you see in the revision.

Original

R

3d. (Shortcut: Missing Information)

Thirty minutes of rehearsal time will be allotted to each composition during each of twelve rehearsals over a four-week period.

COMPOSITION/COMPOSER	APPENDIX	DATES OF STUDY
1. Variation On a Psalm Tune (Williams)	C	Nov. 15 to Dec. 17
2. Dance of Joy (Balconie)	D	Jan. 12 to Feb. 14
3. Scenic Splendor (Furgeson)	E	Feb. 17 to March 16

Revision

Thirty minutes of rehearsal time will be allotted to each composition during each of twelve rehearsals over a four-week period. Shown in Figure 7 are titles and composers, Appendix locations within this document, and designated rehearsal dates.

COMPOSITION/COMPOSER	APPENDIX	DATES OF STUDY
1. Variation On a Psalm Tune (Williams)	C	Nov. 15 to Dec. 17
2. Dance of Joy (Balconie)	D	Jan. 12 to Feb. 14
3. Scenic Splendor (Furgeson)	E	Feb. 17 to March 16

Figure 7. Compositions to be Studied

The figure in **3d** simply appears, leaving readers to connect it to the text and appendices by inference. Before you present a figure or table, give the reader all the information needed to interpret it immediately and easily. Also, give each table or figure a number for easy reference, and give it a title to draw attention to its specific function **{22}**.

Example 4: Vague Collective Noun

Citing a collective entity as actor leaves the true actor's identity a mystery.

Original	Revision
4a. (Shortcut: Vague Collective Noun)	
To collect data in the hospital, you will need permission from the administration.	To collect data in the hospital, you will need permission from the vice president of Personnel Services.
4b. (Shortcut: Vague Collective Noun)	(One Possible Meaning)
Schools do less than they should to prepare students for careers.	School curriculums are not designed to prepare students for careers.
	(A Second Possible Meaning)
	Teachers tend to emphasize the theoretical over the practical, leaving students unprepared for careers.
	(A Third Possible Meaning)
	Career counseling services in our schools are inadequate.

Do not identify groups of people (board, administration) and institutions (business, school, government) as subjects responsible for thoughts or actions that can be laid to a specific source. That leaves the reader guessing who did what or who thought what. The three revisions of **4b** show the kinds of multiple interpretations a reader needs to consider when faced with a vague collective noun, in this case schools **{6}**.

Example 5: Reckless Back-Reference

Original	Revision
5a. (Shortcut: Reckless Back-Reference)	
Two other schools will be selected randomly by use of the already mentioned method.	Two other schools will be selected by use of a table of random numbers.

Original	**Revision**
5b. (Shortcut: Reckless Back-Reference) In addition to the above mentioned characteristics of the culture, children experience music formally by learning to play an instrument.	In addition to being surrounded daily by the music described in Table 1, children experience music formally by learning to play an instrument.

The phrases already-mentioned and above-mentioned, as used in **5a** and **5b**, usually signal a writer's shortcut: the reader is sent on a search. Never ask readers to do a job that you can do more easily as writer **{16}**. Sometimes previous material is too substantial to restate in total, as was the Table 1 material referred to in the revision of **5b**. In that circumstance, do two things: 1) Provide enough specific information to give substance to the sentence (being surrounded daily by the music as compared to the above mentioned characteristics of the culture). 2) Refer to previous material by specific location for the convenience of the reader (in Table 1).

5a and b Bonus Tidbit

Write terms like above-mentioned, hard-fought, and well-worn with hyphens to help readers recognize them immediately as compound adjectives.

Original	(Revision Note)
5c. (Shortcut: Reckless Back-Reference) As health and physical education teachers, we should use this aspect of the child's growth by teaching at this level.	(Revision is not possible. Information about this aspect can be found in the original work by a diligent reader, but the exact meaning of this level is a mystery.)

The writing shortcut exemplified in **5c**, sometimes referred to as an "unattended this," is common. Unless you are sure the reader can instantly and unmistakably identify the material to which this or these refers, incorporate the material itself into the sentence. After you have written a paper, article, or chapter, you may want to read each sentence that contains this or these to be sure you have not sent the reader on a hunting expedition **{16}** (see also Chapter 2, Part 3; this, these).

Example 6: Jargon

If you write jargon—offhanded daily language that some readers may not understand—it will have come from one of two basic sources: your personal environment (colloquialisms) or your professional environment (shop talk).

Original	Revision
6a. (Shortcut: Jargon [Colloquialisms]) Second graders were the easiest kids to test and kindergarteners were the hardest.	Second-grade children were the easiest to test, and kindergarten children the most difficult.
6b. (Shortcut: Jargon [Colloquialisms]) The union rep said clerks wouldn't work past five unless they were given comp time.	The union representative said clerks would work past five only if they were given compensation time.
6c. (Shortcut: Jargon [Shop Talk]) To do that, the ED needs an OK from legal.	To do that, the Emergency Department needs approval from Legal Services.

Colloquialisms that pass unnoticed in everyday speech look childish in writing. Notice four such words in **6a**: grader (someone who grades?), kid, kindergartener, and hardest. The abbreviations and the contraction in **6b** (rep; comp; wouldn't) are commonly spoken; so are the three informal terms in **6c**—the colloquial OK and the job-related jargon ED and legal. None are acceptable in good formal writing **{25}**.

Why is colloquial and job-related jargon unacceptable? The reason is more important than wanting to sound formal, or even wanting to be more precise. First, jargon is provincial: readers outside your sphere, and especially readers for whom English is a second language, suffer when you use jargon. Second, jargon is fleeting: standard English will give library users a better chance of understanding what you have written after a century passes. Perhaps you find that thought daunting, but if you write well enough, someone may be reading your writing a hundred years from now.

6c Bonus Tidbit

The collective nouns (Emergency Department; Legal Services) might be replaceable with specific information, but not if approval is granted and received between departments by any number of persons. When you write about true group functions, you need collective nouns.

4. Disjointedness

Disjointed writing is like a jigsaw puzzle—scattered pieces waiting to be assembled. How unfair of a writer, the only person who knows the intended picture, to leave assembly to the reader! First drafts are disjointed by nature, so the main line of defense against disjointedness is revision: a writer who produces a terribly disjointed final copy, more likely than not, has failed to take a fresh look at the page and make adjustments. I have identified five specific transgressions that cause writing to be disjointed:

Example 7	Within-Sentence Disjointedness
Example 8	Separation of Related Words
Example 9	Between-Sentence Disjointedness
Example 10	Disjointed Insert
Example 11	Misused Preposition or Conjunction

<u>Example 7</u>: Within-Sentence Disjointedness

Be careful not to disrupt reading flow by putting material into a sentence in less than the best order. Readers probably will understand what you have to say, but your poor sequence will delay their understanding.

Original	Revision
7a. (Disjointedness: Within-Sentence)	
That statement tends to confuse teachers, because they neither recognize the difference between the two nor understand the terms.	That statement tends to confuse teachers, because they neither understand the two terms nor recognize the difference between them.
7b. (Disjointedness: Within-Sentence)	
Body actions should reveal features of inner life, according to Laban, with time and weight factors of movement playing a part.	According to Laban, body actions should reveal features of inner life, with time and weight factors of movement playing a part.
7c. (Disjointedness: Within-Sentence) **R**	
The IMMA composite and the IMMA subtest reliability estimates are shown in Table 2.	Reliability estimates for each IMMA subtest and for the composite are shown in Table 2.

In **7a**, the reader should know the object of the sentence (terms) early enough to make use of it. Also, *understanding* naturally precedes *recognizing differences*. If, as in **7b**, you attribute a statement to another person, reveal the source at the beginning. Why should readers have to read the first half of a statement out of context, discover the context, then reread the first half and mentally paste it to the second? The shortcoming in **7c** is similar: why make readers wait to discover that reliability is the specific information you are giving relative to subtest scores and composite scores **{3}** ?

7c Bonus Tidbit

Notice a subtle change from original to revision: I reversed the order of presentation for subtest scores and composite scores. Researchers obtain scores by subtest, then combine subtest scores to form composite scores. The virtue of the change is its logical sequence **{3}**.

Example 8: Separation of Related Words

I could have presented this flaw as a subset of within-sentence disjointedness, but I think it deserves a category of its own. When you separate words that complement each other you create a specific effect: readers are left in a holding pattern, waiting for the related word to appear. In severe cases, the reader is in doubt about exactly how to put the puzzle back together **{3}**. In examples **8a–d**, words that belong together are underlined.

Original	**Revision**
8a. (Disjointedness: Sep. of Related Words)	
Temperament may be as important a factor to researchers attempting to understand the nature of academic achievement as intelligence.	To researchers attempting to understand the nature of academic achievement, temperament may be as important a factor as intelligence.

By moving the first five words of **8a** down rather than moving the last two up, I put orienting material at the beginning **{3}** and information needing emphasis at the end **{8}**. Removal of the words a factor would streamline the revision a bit, but might lead some readers to think in terms of the temperament and intelligence of the researchers.

Original	**Revision**
8b. (Disjointedness: Sep. of Related Words)	
Each student heard the rhythm section play one complete chorus of the tune before improvising.	Before improvising, each student heard the rhythm section play one complete chorus of the tune.
8c. (Disjointedness: Sep. of Related Words)	
Some children even find instructions difficult to follow in individual administrations of tests.	Some children find instructions difficult to follow even in individual administrations of tests.
8d. (Disjointedness: Sep. of Related Words)	
Children can only develop normally if left free to exert their powers.	Children can develop normally only if left free to exert their powers.

Notice that **8b, c,** and **d** are open to misinterpretation. For example, reverse the clauses of the **8d** original to give yourself a clear view of its literal message: "Left free to exert their powers, children can only develop normally." A guarantee of normal development in exchange for freedom was not the writer's intended meaning. Having a modifier next to that which it modifies is indispensable to clarity **{3, 7}**.

> **8d Bonus Tidbit**
>
> Only is so commonly misplaced that readers have become generally adept at understanding the intended meaning. In less severe cases than this (and perhaps in this case), the effect is simply a weakening of the sentence's impact. For examples, see Chapter 3, Part 2, Examples 6a–c.

Example 9: Between-Sentence Disjointedness

Between-sentence disjointedness leaves inexplicit relationships dangling between sentences for the reader to interpret through inference. A church secretary once posted Sunday's sermon title on the marquee, failing to notice its effect in combination with the weekly message posted at the bottom.

WHAT IS HELL LIKE?
Come in and Hear our Choir Sing.

Like the church secretary, your only defense against unfortunate interpretation is to close loopholes in your writing. Think about how your sentences link to each other. The church secretary might have seen the interaction between the two statements, then made the most of it by linking them purposefully with a few additional words:

WHAT IS HELL LIKE?
For a Piece of Heaven, Come in and Hear our Choir Sing.

You can forge links between sentences by use of a phrase (for a piece of heaven), a single word qualifier (similarly, conversely, first, second), punctuation (colon or semi-colon) **{20}**, or logical sequencing **{3}**. Devices applied to **9a, b,** and **c** are identified in parentheses above the revisions.

Original	**Revision**
9a. (Disjointedness: Between-Sentences)	(Single-Word Qualifier)
Gordon recommends that learners progress from aural/oral learning through symbolic learning (including verbal) before approaching theoretical learning. Piaget has cautioned us to leave theoretical learning until the formal operations stage.	Gordon recommends that learners progress from aural/oral learning through symbolic learning (including verbal) before approaching theoretical learning. Similarly, Piaget has cautioned us to leave theoretical learning until the formal operations stage.
9b. (Disjointedness: Between-Sentences)	(Colon)
A basic aesthetic principle of art is its independence of representational riders. Art is not the servant or end of any other entity.	A basic aesthetic principle of art is its independence of representational riders: art is neither the servant nor the end of any other entity.

Readers of **9a** are left to infer a relationship between two sentences that could be either congruent or contrasting; one added word (underlined) clarifies the relationship **{4}**. In **9b**, the second sentence amplifies the first. By use of a colon, the writer can make that relationship explicit for the reader. A semicolon would also show a closer relationship than the original, but the colon's function of amplification/interpretation makes it strongest and most appropriate (see Appendix B, Part 3, Examples **B-12** and **B-16) {20}**.

9b Bonus Tidbit

Use of the neither/nor construction in the revision converts the last clause to positive form (what music is rather than what music is not) **{15}**. Also, nor as compared with or leaves no doubt about the complete independence of servant and end **{18}**.

Original

9c. (Disjointedness: Between-Sentences)

According to Gordon, a valid standardized music aptitude test helps music teachers "diagnose students' individual musical differences, comparing each student to himself as well as to other students" (Gordon, 1988, p. 5). A valid standardized music aptitude test for purposes of measuring developmental music aptitude (birth to age nine) is a test of music audiation. One example is Gordon's Intermediate Measures of Music Audiation (IMMA), described in detail in Chapter Three. Gordon states that "audiation is the basis of music aptitude" (Gordon, 1988, p. 3). "Audiation takes place when one hears and comprehends music for which the sound is not physically present" (Gordon, 1988, p. 3).

Revision

(Logical Sequence)

According to Gordon, a valid standardized music aptitude test helps music teachers "diagnose students' individual musical differences, comparing each student to himself as well as to other students" (1988, p. 5). Music aptitude is dependent on a psychological construct that Gordon has labeled *audiation.* "Audiation takes place when one hears and comprehends music for which the sound is not physically present," and "audiation is the basis of music aptitude" (Gordon, 1988, p. 3). Therefore, a valid test of developmental music aptitude (birth to age nine) is a test of music audiation. One such test is Gordon's Intermediate Measures of Music Audiation (IMMA), described fully in Chapter Three.

In **9c**, the definition of audiation is held until the last sentence, leaving uninitiated readers to interpret references to audiation and to audiation tests without knowing what the term means. After the topic sentence, the sequence needed in this paragraph to keep from confusing the reader is 1) introduce audiation as a coined term for a psychological construct important to music aptitude, 2) define audiation **{23}**, 3) equate a test of music aptitude to a test of music audiation, and 4) refer to the test of audiation relevant to the study **{1}**.

9c Bonus Tidbits

1. An author's name can be given either within the sentence, as in sentence one of the revision, or within the citation parentheses, as in sentence three of the revision. It should not appear in both places, as in sentence one of the original paragraph.
2. Use of the generic pronoun "himself," as in the first sentence, has become a questionable practice (see Chapter 5) **{26}**.

Example 10: Disjointed Insert

You may choose to use lists, figures, and tables in your writing to give the reader information in an efficient, easily understood form. Be careful not to diminish the advantage of your inserted material by presenting it clumsily. The writer of example **10**, by following the dangling verb were with complete sentences, created an awkward bump for the reader. The bump can be removed by changing either the stem (first revision) or the list (second revision) **{19, 22}**.

Original

10. (Disjointedness: Insert)

The problems of the Moore study were

1. Do a child's pitch and rhythm responses correlate with his home environment?
2. What kinds of experiences in the home relate to his pitch ability?
3. What kinds of experiences in the home relate to his rhythm ability?

Revision

(First Revision)

The problems of the Moore study were these:

1. Do a child's pitch and rhythm responses correlate with home environment?
2. What kinds of experiences in the home relate to a child's pitch ability?
3. What kinds of experiences in the home relate to a child's rhythm ability?

10 Bonus Tidbit

Notice that in writing the revisions I removed generic masculine pronouns, sometimes by omission and sometimes by using that child's **{26}**. For more on the subject, see Chapter 5.

Revision

(Second Revision)

Moore studied

1. correlation between a child's pitch and rhythm responses and that child's home environment,
2. the kinds of home experiences that relate to pitch ability, and
3. the kinds of home experiences that relate to rhythm ability.

Notice carefully the fine points of the revisions shown in Example **10**. When you introduce a list of complete sentences with a complete-sentence stem, as in the first revision, follow the stem with either a period or a colon. When you write the stem and the list as one continuous sentence, as in the second revision, use no punctuation after the stem. Then use a lower case letter at the beginning of each item (they are phrases within a sentence), a comma after each item except the last, a conjunction after the last comma, and a period at the end. An alternative to the commas—if you want a stronger break between entries—is semicolons, but be consistent from one list to another within a document **{5}**.

You will see inserts in two other parts of this chapter. In Part 3 (Shortcuts: Missing Information) you saw an example that would have fit here, because another way to disjoin an insert from the text is to omit important information. In Part 5 (Nonparallel List Construction), you will see other ways in which writers sometimes handle lists poorly.

Example 11: Misused Conjunction or Preposition

Choose conjunctions and prepositions carefully to avoid a feeling of disjointedness. To use in for on, or to use of for for, or to use and for or or but is to alter logical relationships between the groups of words they join. In the following examples, misused conjunctions and prepositions in the originals are underlined, as are their replacements in the revisions.

Original	Revision
11a. (Disjointedness: Misused Conjunction)	
The problem was to compare spatial perception scores of Ugandan Children and spatial perception scores of American children.	The problem was to compare spatial perception scores of Ugandan children to spatial perception scores of American children.
11b. (Disjointedness: Misused Conjunction)	
The technician forgot to set the temperature control for the laboratory, and the plants survived.	The technician forgot to set the temperature control for the laboratory, but the plants survived.
11c. (Disjointedness: Misused Conjunction)	
The body can move forward, backward, upward, downward, and side to side.	The body can move forward, backward, upward, downward, or side to side.

In each case—**11a**, **b**, and **c**—the better choice of conjunction brings precision and cohesiveness to the sentence **{18}**. The **11b** original might be usable for special emphasis, with an exclamation point at the end, but the revision is more conventional. The **11c** revision, on the other hand, is essential in any case: a person trying to demonstrate literally the claim of the original could become seriously injured **{7}**.

11a, b, and c Bonus Tidbits

1. Writers sometimes use a double conjunction rather than take time to decide which is most appropriate. Use and/or and similar couplings only when no other construction will do the job you want done. If you adopt that policy, coupled conjunctions will become extremely rare in your writing.
2. For more thoughts about misuse of and, see Chapter 2, Part 3, A Collection of Troublesome Words.

Original	**Revision**
R	
11d. (Disjointedness: Misused Preposition)	
The researcher decided to administer a test for verbal skill before teaching.	The researcher decided to administer a test of verbal skill before teaching.
11e. (Disjointedness: Misused Preposition)	
He revolutionized the disciplines of music, astronomy, mathematics, and religion in his time and in years to come.	He revolutionized the disciplines of music, astronomy, mathematics, and religion in his time and for years to come.

A test for verbal skill, as stated in **11d**, implies that the researcher was testing for the presence or absence of skill. A test of verbal skill assumes the presence of some skill—which would certainly have been the case—with the objective being to identify the level. The person cited in **11e** never resided in years to come, unless as an apparition. The effect of the work he did in his time lingered after death, but his activity obviously stopped **{18}**.

5. Nonparallel Construction

Parallel form in writing helps readers see information clearly and absorb it quickly. Imagine looking at a symmetrical building, then a building with a sprawling addition on one side. Details of the symmetrical building will be easier to absorb and hold in visualization over time because characteristics of one half reinforce characteristics of the other. Just as we perceive symmetrical images more efficiently, so do we perceive symmetrical writing more efficiently. (Here is a nonparallel version of the last sentence: Just as we perceive symmetrical images more efficiently, so do we perceive writing more efficiently when it is symmetrical.)

I have identified four types of nonparallel construction:

Example 12	Nonparallel Sentence Construction
Example 13	Nonparallel Terms
Example 14	Nonparallel List Construction
Example 15	Nonparallel Paragraph Construction

Example 12: Nonparallel Sentence Construction

Original	Revision
12a. (Nonparallel Sentence Construction) To understand music one must understand musical sounds and their combinations, just as one's understanding of literature comes from an understanding of words and their combinations.	(First Revision) To understand music one must understand musical sounds and their combinations, just as to understand literature one must understand words and their combinations. (Second Revision) Just as one understands literature by understanding words and their combinations, one understands music by understanding sounds and their combinations.
12b. (Nonparallel Sentence Construction) Just as every student is required to study English, mathematics, and history, so art should be accorded the same weight in the overall education of the child.	Just as every student is required to study English, mathematics, and history, so every student should be required to study art.

When you use just as, or a similar connective phrase, you announce your intention to place two thoughts side by side. Then you must write the comparison in parallel form to keep the second thought from taking on a plodding, awkward feeling—like shoes on the wrong feet. Notice the symmetry of the revisions to **12a** and **b** and the ease with which they are read. Even where you have not used introductory language that suggests comparison, you will find many circumstances in which parallel form from one part of a sentence to another makes reading more efficient **{13}**.

12a Bonus Tidbit

In the second revision I improved on the first by reordering material: most familiar to least familiar. No hard-and-fast rule dictates such an order. It is simply a matter of putting oneself in the reader's place and asking "what order of material will make comprehension easiest?" **{3}**.

12b Bonus Tidbit

A writer interested in stating directly that art should be accorded the same weight should avoid just as: "Every student is required to study English, mathematics, and history; art should be accorded the same weight in the overall education of the child."

Example 13: Nonparallel Terms

Original	Revision
13a. (Nonparallel Terms)	(First Revision)
People from more than one hundred world cultures now reside in the United States, millions from Asia and another 40% from Mexico, Central and South America, and the Caribbean.	People from more than one hundred world cultures now reside in the United States, millions from Asia and tens of millions from Mexico, Central and South America, and the Caribbean.
	(Second Revision)
	People from more than one hundred world cultures now reside in the United States, 28% of them from Asia and 40% from Mexico, Central and South America, and the Caribbean.
13b. (Nonparallel Terms)	
She found important personality traits to be excitability, aggression, independence, anxiety, self-confidence, curiosity, and imagination.	She found important personality traits to be excitability, aggressiveness, independence, anxiety, self-confidence, curiosity, and imagination.

Nonparallel terms in **13a** keep readers from comparing the populations directly. To compare millions to 40% is—to lean on a cliché—like comparing apples to oranges **{5}**. (Numbers and percentages in the revisions are fictitious.) The problem in **13b** is subtle: aggression is an act, not a trait. The parallel term needed is aggressiveness **{18, 13}**.

Original	Revision
13c. (Nonparallel Terms)	
Vibration that stimulates hearing becomes audible, or in other words, sound; vibration that stimulates sight becomes light, color, and therefore visible.	Vibration that stimulates hearing becomes audible, or in other words, sound; vibration that stimulates sight becomes visible, or in other words, image.

Having used the terms hearing, audible, and sound in the first half of **13c**, the writer should use sight, visible, and image in the second. Why? Because the two sequences are parallel, and parallel sequences make reading more efficient **{13}**.

13c Bonus Tidbit

Light and color represent a level of terms different from those used in the first half of the sentence; the writer might use them well in a subsequent sentence about the nature of images.

Example 14: Nonparallel List Construction

Original	Revision
14a. (Nonparallel List)	
. . . the following temperament traits.	. . . the following temperament traits.
1. Persistence/attention span 2. Adaptability 3. Predictability 4. Distractibility	1. Persistence 2. Adaptability 3. Predictability 4. Distractibility

In **14a**, attention span is a disruptive appendage to trait number 1; it keeps the reader from making a quick, clear comparison with traits 2 through 4. A better approach would be to simply incorporate information about attention span into a description of persistence.

Original	Revision
14b. (Nonparallel List)	
Bennett Reimer states that music educators have fallen short of musical goals for four reasons.	Bennett Reimer states that music educators have fallen short of musical goals for four reasons.
1. Performance has not become a natural outgrowth of preparation.	1. Performance has become an end rather than a natural outgrowth of preparation.
2. There are excessive performance commitments.	2. Performance commitments are excessive.
3. Music performed is not of good quality.	3. Music performed is of questionable quality.
4. Different aspects of the program are out of balance.	4. Extramusical activities siphon time from the teaching of musicianship.

Points one and three of **14b**, each beginning with a subject and a verb, are well written but in negative form. In contrast, point two hides its real subject and verb behind a weak there are **{10}** and point four is a vague generality **{7, 16}**. I used points one and three (converted to positive form **{15}**) as models for rewriting the others. That makes the list easy to read, due not only to its directness and specificity, but to its parallel construction **{13}**.

> **14b Bonus Tidbit**
>
> Many writers use the term different (point 4) recklessly. See different in Chapter 2, Part 3, A Collection of Troublesome Words.

Example 15: Nonparallel Paragraph Construction

Original	Revision
15. (Nonparallel Paragraph)	
Laban compares body movements to an orchestra. Sometimes the orchestra performs as a whole, sometimes an instrument solos while the rest wait patiently, but still ready, and sometimes only a few instruments work together as the others sit quietly, always prepared.	Laban compares the human body and its performing parts to an orchestra and its performing musicians. The parts perform sometimes as a whole, sometimes in small groups, and sometimes in solo. All the while, inactive parts stay ready to be called upon.

The first sentence of **15**, comparing body movements to an orchestra, is incongruous. Logic tells us that Laban compared the body to an orchestra and body parts to orchestra members. Parallel construction is indispensable to drawing those comparisons **{13}**. Notice also the illogical progression in the original from full orchestra to solo to small groups, converted in the revision to full orchestra, small groups, then solo. Like parallel construction, logical sequence helps readers comprehend more efficiently what is on the page **{3}**. Both eliminate the job of unscrambling and reconstructing, a task that too often falls to the reader.

6. Vague or Tangled Construction

Some writers force readers to guess or untangle sentences to find the meaning. I use arbitrary terms here to label those conditions:

Example 16	Vague Language
Example 17	Unsorted Factors
Example 18	Confusion/Contradiction

<u>Example 16</u>: Vague Language

Original	Revision
16a. (Vague Language)	
During the five years I taught elementary school, I did a variety of things in my classes.	During the five years I taught elementary school, I vacillated from one approach to another for lack of direction.
16b. (Vague Language)	(First Revision)
The young biology teacher hoped earnestly that his last-hour honors class would be better next week.	The young biology teacher hoped earnestly that he would do a better job of teaching his last-hour honors class next week.
	(Second Revision)
	The young biology teacher hoped earnestly that his last-hour honors class would behave better next week; he was losing confidence in his ability to maintain discipline.
	(Third Revision)
	The young biology teacher hoped earnestly that his last-hour students would score higher on next week's test: he was embarrassed at such low scores from honors students whom he had taught.

Only by talking to the writer of **16a** did I learn the intended meaning, a meaning far afield from my initial interpretation. Having not talked to the writer of **16b**, I can only guess about the meaning of the vague phrase <u>would be better</u> **{16}**.

Original	**Revision**
16c. (Vague Language) As a result, the more complex ideas will have a foundation on which to build.	(First Revision) As a result, the more complex ideas will have a foundation on which to be built. (Second Revision) As a result, the student will have a foundation on which to build more complex ideas. (Third Revision) As a result, the teacher will have established a foundation on which to build more complex ideas.

The form of vagueness seen in **16c** leaves a key agent of action (the builder) unknown. The first revision is free of the silly implication that ideas might build themselves. The second and third revisions are still stronger, because active voice removes the effect of dangling half a message and letting the reader guess at the other half **{6, 14}**.

Example 17: Unsorted Factors

What I refer to as unsorted factors in a sentence are not necessarily densely packed, as in overstuffed sentences (Example **1**), nor are they necessarily presented in a badly arranged sequence, as in disjointed sentences (Example **7**). Instead, parts of these sentences simply run together in a way that disorients readers.

Original	**Revision**
17a. (Unsorted Factors) The need is great for more high quality musicianship achievement instrumental music programs.	The need is great for more high-quality instrumental music programs based on music achievement.

A string of adjectives as seen in **17a** can deceive the reader into thinking that one adjective after another is the noun, in this case beginning with musicianship, then moving to achievement, and so forth. Limit the number of adjectives you string together, avoid adjectives easily mistaken for nouns in the context of your sentence (achievement), and help the reader by hyphenating compound adjectives (high-quality) **{3}**.

17a Bonus Tidbit

The construction dilemma you often face is this: eliminating prepositional phrases generates a series of adjectives, and eliminating a series of adjectives generates prepositional phrases. You need to find balance. The best guide is your ear, so read the alternatives aloud to help yourself make good choices **{19}**. For more about reading aloud and constructing sentences that are rhythmically graceful, see Chapter 3, Part 3, Ungainly Writing.

Original

R

17b. (Unsorted Factors)

In teacher-report temperament scales, correlations between distractibility and higher academic achievement and IQ scores were found.

Revision

Using teacher-report temperament scales, researchers have found that distractibility correlates positively with academic achievement and with IQ scores.

The writer of **17b** strung factors together without identifying which were paired and correlated. There is hardly a worse place to leave readers guessing about details than in the writing of research procedures **{1}**.

17b Bonus Tidbit

Notice how much stronger the revision is for having been converted from passive to active voice **{14}**. Reading a sentence that ends with *were found* is a bit like kicking a football that has half its air missing: thud!

Original	**Revision**
R **17c.** (Unsorted Factors) The researcher will calculate Pearson correlation coefficients between personal tempo score, the temperament trait scores for distractibility, persistence, rhythmicity, adaptability, and with a composite temperament trait score. [I underlined the three primary factors to make them easier to find while reading the analysis below.]	The researcher will calculate Pearson correlation coefficients between personal tempo score and the temperament trait scores of distractibility, persistence, rhythmicity, and adaptability—and between personal tempo score and a composite temperament trait score.

Again in **17c**, the writer has strung factors together without telling which scores have been paired and correlated. This example is particularly perplexing, so the analysis to follow is more complex than for any other example in the book. You will have to read the next paragraph more than once and refer back and forth from it to the example.

Between should lead to and, i.e., between X and Y. Assuming that personal tempo scores are factor X and temperament trait scores are factor Y, will correlations be calculated among the four subfactors of Y, as it appears from the writing? (In reality, no.) When and does arrive on the scene, it is followed immediately by a with that launches the reader into factor Z (composite temperament trait score). That third factor should not be tacked onto the pile to be untangled by the reader; it should be presented clearly, in a form parallel to the first part of the sentence **{13}.** The form of the revised sentence becomes this: *between X and Y (Y consisting of Y1, Y2, Y3, and Y4) and between X and Z* **{3, 7}.**

Example 18: Confusion/Contradition

Writers of the next three sentences twisted them either by not bothering to know what they wanted to say or by withholding their insight from the reader **{1}**.

Original	**Revision**
18a. (Confusion/Contradiction) Few modern aestheticians direct students to the nature of the beautiful in poetry, but rather accede to the subjective reality of the students.	Few modern aestheticians direct students to the nature of beauty in poetry; most accede to the subjective views of the students.

The writer of **18a** needed to recognize two dichotomous populations of modern aestheticians: the few who do as the writer prescribes and the many who do something else. Only then can the two populations be separated clearly for the reader.

18a Bonus Tidbit

In the revision I used beauty, a noun, in place of the original beautiful, an adjective pressed into service as a noun **{18}**.

Original	Revision
18b. (Confusion/Contradiction)	
Not that learning words is unnecessary, but teach that the child should understand concepts before trying to teach terminology.	The lesson for educators is that concepts must be taught ahead of terminology if children are to learn efficiently.
18c. (Confusion/Contradiction)	
The determination of the body strength used is in proportion to the weight carried or the resistance given to it.	Body strength needed is in proportion to weight carried and resistance encountered.

In the first clause of **18b**, who is learning? In the second, who is teaching and who is being taught **{6}**? At the end of the original sentence, absurd as it would be, the child seems to have become the teacher of terminology. The revision is necessarily built on a little guesswork.

Several complexities make **18c** a chore to read: 1) Early use of the ambiguous term determination, which can mean either *decision making* or *firmness of purpose,* leaves the reader adrift **{18}**. 2) Used leads the reader to believe that the statement is one of practice, when in fact it is a statement of theory **{7, 18}**. 3) An overload of prepositional phrases creates wordiness and entanglements **{9, 19}**. In reading the revision, notice that clear expression tends to be clean and simple. Notice also the role played by the three parallel word pairs: strength needed, weight carried, resistance encountered **{13}**.

7. Misleading Construction

While scanning a book in the library recently, I saw an interesting chapter title: "What Happens to Children When They Act Aggressively in Six Cultures?" The subjects of the study must have been wealthy little globetrotters; few children I know spend enough time in six cultures to have had their behavior observed and reported in each!

Writers mislead readers, or at least confuse readers temporarily, when they write one message while meaning another. The person least likely to recognize unintentional meaning in a sentence is the person who wrote it, one more reason to have others read your writing before you make a final copy. You may find the twisted sentences in this section entertaining, but be wary: we are all capable of contributing to the collection.

Example 19: Misleading Construction

Original	**Revision**
19a. (Misleading Construction) The child's mind unfolds just like his body as a result of developmental processes. **R**	(First Revision) Just as a child's body grows and develops over time, so does a child's mind. (Second Revision) Just as children's bodies grow and develop over time, so do their minds.
19b. (Misleading Construction) Most researchers rely on subnormal intelligence as the key definitional feature of mental retardation.	Most researchers define mental retardation in terms of subnormal intelligence.
19c. (Misleading Construction) Strauss does not use a final climax. He closes the piece by dying away in rhythmic motion and dynamic intensity. **R**	Rather than write a climactic ending, Strauss closes the piece by letting the rhythmic motion and dynamic intensity die away.
19d. (Misleading Construction) Eighteen phrases, equally divided among the three compositions, will be copied onto an evaluation tape.	Eighteen phrases, taken in equal number from each of the three compositions, will be copied onto an evaluation tape.

Taken literally, the phrases the child's mind unfolds just like his body **(19a)**, researchers rely on subnormal intelligence **(19b)**, and he closes the piece by dying away **(19c)** elicit bizarre imagery **{7}**. In **19d**, equally divided among implies that, from an original pool of eighteen phrases, six were assigned a place in each of three compositions. That was not the case: the researcher began with three compositions and extracted six phrases from each **{7}**.

19a Bonus Tidbit

Conversion to plural (Revision Two) allows the use of a pronoun (their) in place of a second use of *child's,* yet avoids both the generic *his* and a potential disagreement in number between antecedent and pronoun: child's body . . . their mind (see Chapter 5: Person and Gender).

Original	**Revision**
19e. (Misleading Construction)	
Deviant children were studied longitudinally within two groups. In one group, studied from birth to age five, all were born prematurely. The second deviant group, studied from age five to age eleven, was mildly retarded.	Deviant children were studied longitudinally within two groups. Children in the first group, studied from birth to age five, had been born prematurely. Children in the second group, studied from age five to age eleven, were mildly retarded.

Children in the first group cited in **19e** were not born in that group at the time of the study, but rather had been born prematurely. Children in the second group were mildly retarded as individuals; that is different from saying that the group was retarded **{7}**. Time problems presented by this passage—birth having been in the past and mild retardation in the present at the time of the study—put demands on the writer's knowledge of verb tense (present, present perfect, past, past perfect, future, future perfect). Learn them, and use them to give the reader proper time perspectives (see Appendix B, Part 1, Parts of Speech: A More Detailed View).

19e Bonus Tidbit

Once I began to clarify the meaning of the paragraph, I felt compelled to cast the second and third sentences—the group comparisons—in parallel form **{13}**. As principles of good writing become ingrained in your thought processes, you will begin to feel an internal force channeling your writing toward one construction over another.

Original	Revision
19f. (Misleading Construction)	
In reviewing art and thoughts about art in society over the past sixty years, I began to see . . .	In reviewing art of the last sixty years, along with thoughts written about it, I began to see . . .
19g. (Misleading Construction)	
Arrangements of popular tunes and classical excerpts were forced to squeeze into this format.	Arrangements of popular tunes and classical excerpts longer than five minutes could not be recorded on one disk.

The writer of **19f**, far short of sixty years old, seems to have begun reviewing art in a previous life **{7}**. The writer of **19g**, whose topic was early recording technology, used a form so misleading as to obscure content. The implication of the original is that pieces of music, against their wills, squeezed into small spaces **{7}**.

19g Bonus Tidbit

Compare the wording squeeze into this format—so general as to appear almost evasive—with the specific wording be recorded on one disk. Why leave the reader guessing at meaning when you can provide it easily **{16}**?

8. Personification

Personification—ascribing human attributes to inanimate objects—adds spice to children's books (The little house felt lonely) and to adult storytelling (Having spread itself across both lanes, the tree stubbornly refused to budge). When your task is formal writing, however, you will sacrifice precision and reading efficiency if you introduce any more than a hint of personification. For example, if you were to write *this graph shows* or *the evidence tells us,* you might communicate efficiently without disturbing the reader; a reader can conceive of something on a sheet of paper, in a sense, *showing*. On the other hand, you should not write that inanimate objects (studies, theories, literature) dispute, examine, strive, find, seek, concern themselves, or in some other way engage behavior that requires human will. Such indirect, imprecise language is at least distracting, and sometimes it is misleading **{18}**.

Example 20: Personification

Original	Revision
20a. (Personification)	
Objectivist aesthetics disputes Crocker's notion; it rarely focuses on a specific medium.	Proponents of objectivist aesthetics dispute Crocker's notion; rarely do they focus on a specific medium.
20b. (Personification)	
Physical education programs find themselves being examined closely.	Teachers of physical education find their programs being examined closely.
20c. (Personification)	
The literature also suggests that specific, comprehensive leadership training is important.	Many school administrators have written about the importance of specific, comprehensive leadership training.
20d. (Personification)	(First Revision)
This paper will concern itself with the subject of educating a child to become a consumer.	The subject of this paper is consumer education for children. (Second Revision) My purpose in writing this paper is to promote consumer education for children.
20e. (Personification)	
A study by Richard Reese (1985) involving first-grade children examined methods of instruction that affect motor development.	Richard Reese (1985) examined methods of instruction that affect motor development in first-grade children.

You will find the revisions of **20a–e** direct, orderly, and reality-oriented: who did what relative to whom or what **{6}.** Keep that approach well in mind while you write. If you do, you will help readers assimilate your message quickly and accurately.

A Closing Note

Just as doctors think in terms of *good cholesterol* and *bad cholesterol* when they evaluate the health of their patients, you will do well to think in terms of *good inferences* and *bad inferences* when you evaluate the health of your sentences and paragraphs. Good formal writing prompts readers to think beyond what is on the page; that is, it encourages readers to draw inferences that exercise their minds (good inferences). Unclear, imprecise writing forces readers to untangle sentences and fill gaps; that is, it forces readers to draw inferences that exercise their patience (bad inferences). I call the second type *nuisance inferences* to describe the effect they have on readers.

Be good to your readers. Purge your writing of nuisance inferences.

CHAPTER 2

CLARITY AND PRECISION IN WORD CHOICE

The pair of observations I made at the beginning of Chapter 1 apply to this chapter as well: clear writing lets readers read through; precise writing gives readers exact information. Beyond the issues of construction presented in the preceding chapter, thoughtful and perceptive word choices contribute heavily to clarity and precision in writing. The first two sections of this chapter show problems created by unclear and imprecise words; the third is an alphabetical list of troublesome words and phrases—with examples of advisable and inadvisable use; the fourth is a short perspective on language growth.

1. Clarity Lost to Poor Word Choice
2. Precision Lost to Poor Word Choice
3. A Collection of Troublesome Words
4. New Words, New Uses

Underlined words in Sections 1 and 2 will help you read the examples efficiently; periodic reference to writing principles shown on the BOOKMARK will help you generalize the comments to your writing. Section 3 is unique: probably you will read it in small pieces rather than straight through, and you will want to make notes in the margins. After you have read it all once, you are likely to return periodically for reference. Section 4 offers food for thought.

1. Clarity Lost to Poor Word Choice

I have identified three types of clarity problems created by mischosen words:

Example 1 Double Meaning
Example 2 Misleading Term
Example 3 Inconsistent Terms

Specific cases of unclear terms are infinite in number, making these few examples too narrow a view to constitute any kind of model: they are no more than illustrations. The only reliable defenses against writing the kinds of sentences you see here are vigilance and a rich vocabulary.

Example 1: Double Meaning

Original	Revision
1a. (Double Meaning) David Moritz Michael contributed a large amount of instrumental music to the Moravians.	David Moritz Michael composed a great number of instrumental works for the Moravians.
1b. (Double Meaning) Finally, in correlation to the stages of learning, he has left theoretical understanding until the end of the sequence.	Finally, in relation to the stages of learning, he has left theoretical understanding until the end of the sequence.
1c. (Double Meaning) **R** Subjects for this study were 101 five-year-old children.	Subjects for the Moore study were 101 five-year-old children.

Readers of **1a** unfamiliar with Michael as a composer might think he donated a collection to the Moravian library. The term correlation in **1b** has a specific statistical meaning; using it to describe a nonstatistical relationship in research writing may confuse readers **{18}**.

> **1b Bonus Tidbit**
>
> Another such word is significance. Because the terms statistical significance and practical significance carry such specific meaning in the writing of research, you should avoid using the term significance in general contexts within a research article. Other words, like substantial, will serve your purpose without raising questions in the mind of the reader.

The writer of **1c** was reviewing another researcher's work, but the words this study might cause the reader to believe the writer means the study being read at the time (the writer's study). To avoid confusing readers, use the term this study only to refer to the study you are writing; cite all other studies by author.

> **1c Bonus Tidbit**
>
> Some writers describe studies of other researchers in the possessive (Moore's Study), but the adjectival form (the Moore Study) offers a better perspective. Your purpose is not to tell readers about something owned by Moore; your purpose is to cite a study. Moore is simply an adjective by which you identify the study.

Example 2: Misleading Term

Original	Revision
2a. (Misleading Term)	(First Revision)
Structure encompasses readiness for learning.	Structure is important to readiness for learning.
	(Second Revision)
	Students learn best within some kind of structure.
2b. (Misleading Term)	
The school's fifth-grade students were divided into athletic groups.	The school's fifth-grade students were categorized by athletic interest.

Does structure encompass readiness (**2a**)? Considering the dimensions of readiness, the reverse is more likely true (first revision) **{7}.** The second revision is still more clear, thanks to a subject-verb combination that identifies actor and action specifically **{6}**. Example **2b** depicts children from a single large group being divided, perhaps arbitrarily, to form subgroups. That was not the case at all. Children from naturally existing subgroups (differences in athletic interest) had been combined into one large group (fifth grade), and now they were simply having their interests identified: they were being categorized, not divided **{18}**.

Example 3: Inconsistent Terms

You can make life easier for readers by ascribing the same name to a given entity each time you refer to it. Reject the notion that an interesting variety of terms is a higher virtue than consistency: any reader lost in a research report will tell you otherwise.

Original	Revision
3a. (Inconsistent Terms)	
The House of Care, a shelter for homeless persons, was the first in the city. The agency was founded by Esther Waller in 1926.	The House of Care, a shelter for homeless persons, was the first in the city. The shelter was founded by Esther Waller in 1926.

Original	Revision
3b. (Inconsistent Terms) R	
Each class met for instruction twice weekly. One level met on Mondays and Wednesdays and the other on Tuesdays and Thursdays. The two groups were taught by the same teacher.	Each of the two instruction groups met twice weekly, the E1 group on Mondays and Wednesdays and the E2 group on Tuesdays and Thursdays. The two groups were taught by the same teacher.

In **3a,** is agency synonymous to shelter, which is synonymous to House of Care? Yes it is; why burden the reader to infer what can be written easily? The writer of **3b** should either choose one label and hold to it or provide the reader with a legend (class = level = group)! If you write something like this in reporting an experimental study, some readers will reread your design to see if you divided classes into groups that worked at a variety of levels **{5}**.

3b Bonus Tidbit

Pairs of adjacent letters (A and B, X and Y) are used commonly in research reports to label groups. Before taking that common approach, search for letters/numbers relevant to unique characteristics of the groups. For example, label experimental and control groups E and C, or multiple experimental groups E1, E2, E3, and so forth. If treatment is aural and tactile, label the groups A and T. This practice will help readers attach meaning to the labels instantly throughout the reading of the study.

Original	Revision
3c. (Inconsistent Terms)	
1. African-American pupils comprised 63% . . .	1. African-American pupils accounted for 63% . . .
2. Hispanic pupils represented 9.4 % . . .	2. Hispanic pupils accounted for 9.4 % . . .
3. Asian pupils accounted for 4.2% . . .	3. Asian pupils accounted for 4.2% . . .
4. White pupils represented 23.3 percent . . .	4. White pupils accounted for 23.3 % . . .

In a span of four statements in **3c**, three verbs (comprised, represented, accounted for) serve the same function. Do not vary language simply to avoid repetition. More than one label applied to factors identical in function can be confusing, and confusion is a greater sin than repetition **{5}**. If you find yourself bothered by repetition as shown in the revision, you might consider avoiding the verb altogether by constructing a table **{21}**.

> **3c Bonus Tidbit**
>
> The writer's use of percent for the last entry, after having used % for the first three, is also a bothersome inconsistency. That error, however, is more likely to be an oversight—like a typographical error—than an error in judgment.

In bringing consistency to the list in **3c**, I chose accounted for over comprised or represented because it is most precise. Comprised means embraced: the whole embraces the parts, as in "The school population comprised 732 African Americans, 41 Asians," etc. Represented, which has specific meaning beyond simply existing, sounds backward in this context: it seems that a percentage of the population represents Hispanic pupils more than Hispanic pupils represent a percentage of the population **{18}**. ***This kind of diligent thought about precise meaning is the subject of the next section***. Problems of clarity and problems of precision have been enmeshed in some of the preceding examples, but for each example in Part 2, the meaning is clear. The writer in each case has simply chosen words that are less precise than they might have been.

2. Precision Lost to Poor Word Choice

In one of his comic routines, Jack Benny claimed titillatingly that he was about to demonstrate fine differences in word meaning. The words he chose to compare were *irritate* (bring to an abnormally sensitive condition) and *aggravate* (worsen; add to a problem). Benny chose a phantom telephone number at random, dialed it, and asked for Harry. He was ostensibly told by the party answering that no one by the name of Harry lived there. After a moment he called the same number, used a different voice, and pushed a bit harder to talk to Harry. Then he called a third time, using yet another voice, and insisted Harry had given that number to him to call. After completing that third call, he told the audience he had just demonstrated *irritation*. "Now this," he announced, "is *aggravation*": he called the same number a fourth time, using a fourth voice, and said, "Hello, this is Harry. Are there any messages for me?"

Because of fine differences in meaning among words, ***word choice nearly always moves the message toward or away from greater precision***. When you write, as compared with when you speak, you have ample time to be precise. Do not settle for the first word that comes to mind.

That is like painting a window frame with a blunt 6-inch brush just because you happen to have it in your hand, rather than bothering to look through your painting supplies for a beveled 2-inch sash brush. The underlying question is simple: Are you going to bother yourself to do the job well, or are you willing to accept whatever you can produce quickly and easily **{18}**?

Example 4: Precision Lost to Poor Word Choice

	Original	Revision
4a.	Next I will discuss the setting in which the observations were made.	Next I will describe the setting in which the observations were made.
4b.	The child answers each test question by making a circle around the appropriate picture.	The child answers each test question by drawing a circle around the appropriate picture.
4c.	My new position in public relations will allow me to improve my speaking skills.	My new position in public relations will challenge me to improve my speaking skills.
4d.	The concerned citizens of Walnut Street set fire to the drug-dealer's home, then, wielding baseball bats and two-by-fours, chased him from the neighborhood.	The irate citizens of Walnut Street set fire to the drug-dealer's home, then, wielding baseball bats and two-by-fours, chased him from the neighborhood.
4e.	One of the biggest contributions of standardized tests to education is . . .	One of the most important contributions of standardized tests to education is . . .

We are surrounded daily by examples of imprecise word choices. The grocery store sign that says pet needs should say pet products; my pet needs are at home. The truck trailer sign that says safety is my goal is a nice sentiment, but we know the trucker's goal is to deliver cargo. As a writer, your expectations for word precision need to be higher than those of the general public. To meet those expectations you need to develop a rich vocabulary: study useful words that you cannot define; make a personal dictionary and study it systematically. Then you will have not only the will but also the ability to choose precise words.

3. A Collection of Troublesome Words

This section amounts to an alphabetical list of words and short phrases commonly misused or poorly used. Though I based the list on a compilation of student errors over many years, I am sure to have overlooked words that belong. If your appetite for misused words remains unsatisfied, you may want to consult lists in other sources: Strunk and White (1979) and Bernstein (1965) come to mind. Some advice from older lists is of questionable value now, because language is dynamic (see Part 4 of this chapter). Some words from those older lists are also on this list, with slightly different treatment.

You may want to limit time spent studying this kind of material: it is too information-rich to be digested, applied, and remembered in great quantity. Also, I recommend highly that you keep track of your progress with some system of marks. For example, if you were to place the following symbols in the margin of your book as you study, you would always know where you stand with each term.

—	Big Problem:	I use this word incorrectly.
+–	Some Problem:	I waver on correct use.
++	No Problem:	I use this word correctly.
?	Needs Discussion:	I either disagree or do not understand.

To save space, I have not used the headings original and revision in these entries. Know that in each case the left column is an example of inadvisable use and the corresponding right column is a suggested revision.

Consider using the alphabetical list below to enhance the value of the rest of this chapter. For example, you might try to predict what I have to say about each word before reading the corresponding entry. You might also try to incorporate each word into written sentences that you believe show proper and improper use. (Some entries, like the first, do not lend themselves well to this exercise.) Whatever your treatment of the words, such prereading work will almost surely make learning more vivid and enduring. You may find ways to improve on or add to what I have offered here, in which case I would welcome hearing from you. My source of definitions is Webster (1997), as cited in the References at the end of this book.

A List of Words and Phrases Contained in the Remainder of This Chapter

above, below, over, under
about, approximately
access
address
affect ≠ effect
all ready ≠ already
all together ≠ altogether
allusion ≠ illusion
amount ≠ number
and
another
anxious ≠ eager
any and all
any way ≠ anyway
area
as well as
a total of
below (see "above")
both ≠ each, two
by means of
center around ≠ center on, center in
check into
circumstance (see "situation")
(coined titles)
comprise
concern
confront
continual ≠ continuous
correlation
currently ≠ presently
deal with
determine ≠ identify
diagnose
different, separate
dilemma ≠ problem
discover
discussed
disinterested ≠ uninterested
divided
done
enormity
equally
exists
experience
farther ≠ further
feel ≠ believe
finalize
focus around ≠ focus on (see "center around")
how
however
if and when
impact
implement
imply ≠ infer
importantly
in ≠ into
include
individual
in order to
input
involve
it's ≠ its
joined together
latter ≠ last
lay ≠ lie
less ≠ fewer
like ≠ as
literally
look at
nor
often
one and the same
only
ongoing
onset ≠ outset
over (see "above")
persons ≠ people
personal
pinch hit
plus
point
proximity
reason, because
reason why
relatively
result
revisit
separate (see "different")
share in common
significance, significant
since ≠ because
site
situation, circumstance
some time ≠ sometime
that
that, which
the
the ≠ a/an
this, these
torturous ≠ tortuous
true facts
under (see "above")
unknown
up (see "down")
upcoming
update
utilize
veritable
where ≠ in which, for which, to which
whether or not
which (see "that, which")
would

above, below, over, under

Literally, these words signify location. When used figuratively they usually displace stronger, more precise terms.

Profits are above what was expected.	Profits are greater than expected.
Volume is below what was expected	Volume is lower than expected.
All means were over 24.5.	All means exceeded 24.5.
The rise in temperature was under 5 degrees.	The temperature rose less than 5 degrees.

about, approximately

These terms tend to be used redundantly, either to another term (first example: *estimated*), or to a given range (second example: *5 to 7 years*). In the second case, if the range given is too constricting, enlarge it rather than duplicate its function with a redundant term.

University enrollment is estimated to be approximately 28,000 next fall. The building project will take about 5 to 7 years.	University enrollment is estimated to be 28,000 next fall. The building project will take • 5 to 7 years. • about 6 years.

When you use about and approximately legitimately, note that they are not precisely synonymous. About is a rough estimate: *Will you be free about 4 o'clock?* Approximate means "nearly exact": *We have approximately two and one-half inches clearance.*

access (see Chapter 4, Part 4 for other nouns pressed into service as verbs)

As a verb, this term sounds pretentious, and generally displaces more precise language. It works much better as a noun: *A door in the back will give access from the larger parking lot.* Even though this particular noun-turned-verb seems to be making inroads toward an accepted language shift (probably due primarily to computer language), your writing will be stronger if you decide against leading the parade.

How do I access my file?	How do I • open my file? • enter my file? • retrieve my file?
He accessed the voting machine with help from the precinct captain.	He opened the voting machine with help from the precinct captain.

address (see Chapter 4, Part 4, for other nouns pressed into service as verbs)

As a verb, this term frequently creates a weak generalization.

We need to address the problem of poor attendance.	We need to solve the problem of poor attendance. We need to know why people are choosing not to attend.

affect ≠ effect

Generally, affect is a verb and effect is a noun.

The rain did not effect our plans. The rain had no affect on our plans.	The rain did not affect our plans. The rain had no effect on our plans.

When the reverse is true, affect as a noun means "feeling" or "emotion," and is pronounced with an accent on the first syllable: *Children need art and music for the affect it offers.* Effect as a verb means "make happen": *I did effect a change.*

all ready ≠ already

The first means "prepared"; the second means "previously."

That class is already to be tested. We all ready tested that class.	That class is all ready to be tested. We already tested that class.

all together ≠ altogether

The first means "simultaneously or collectively"; the second means "wholly or completely."

Now I want to hear you sing altogether. She taught 12 sections of drawing and painting all together.	Now I want to hear you sing all together. She taught 12 sections of drawing and painting altogether.

allusion ≠ illusion

An allusion is a passing reference, made directly or by implication (something alluded to). An illusion is an impression that seems real but is not.

His illusion that I was dishonest left me shaken.	His allusion that I was dishonest left me shaken.
The feeling of motion when a car next to you moves is an allusion.	The feeling of motion when a car next to you moves is an illusion.

amount ≠ number

Amount should not be used to describe quantities that can be counted.

The amount of students registered does not justify hiring a teacher.	The number of students registered does not justify hiring a teacher.
I cannot handle the amount of problems I am facing.	I cannot handle the • number of problems I am facing. • amount of trouble I am facing.

and (see also Chapter 1, Part 4)

Be careful not to let and weaken what could otherwise have been a strong cause/effect observation (first example), or make two thoughts coordinate when by nature they are not (second example).

Jim was the best student in his high school class and earned a full-tuition college scholarship.	As the best student in his high school class, Jim earned a full-tuition college scholarship.
Betty Bix earned a Ph.D. at Columbia and came here to practice law.	Betty Bix, a Ph.D. graduate from Columbia, came here to practice law.

another

Two things joined by another should be the same: X and another X, not X and another Y.

Sixteen computers were delivered yesterday, and another 10 today.	Sixteen computers were delivered yesterday, • and 10 more today. • and another 16 today.

anxious ≠ eager

Both terms imply anticipation, but do not use <u>anxious</u> where you mean <u>eager</u>. Anxiety is uneasy apprehension; eagerness is impatient longing.

As the time for the birthday party approached, Timmy was anxious for the guests to arrive so he could open his gifts.	As the time for the birthday party approached, Timmy was eager for the guests to arrive so he could open his gifts. As the time for the birthday party approached, Timmy was anxious about not receiving the gift he had wanted for more than a year.

any and all

This is a cliché. Choose one term or the other.

any way ≠ anyway

Most usage calls for <u>any way</u>; use <u>anyway</u> only to mean "in any case": *The battle is lost anyway.*

Data collection was difficult anyway we tried.	Data collection was difficult any way we tried.

area (see also Chapter 4, Part 1)

Evaluate carefully any use of this term to describe other than physical parameters. It is used commonly in place of more specific terms that would bring precision and strength to the sentence (first example). Other times it is simply extra baggage (second example).

In what area does this belong? I need to know more about his area of expertise to make a judgment.	In what category does this belong? I need to know more about his expertise to make a judgment.

as well as

This cliché sometimes replaces a simple term unnecessarily (first example), sometimes distorts the truth by implying equality of importance (second example), and sometimes duplicates the function of both or also (third example).

They came with pencils as well as paper.	They came with pencils and paper.
Medical quackery threatens the pocketbooks as well as the lives of patients.	Medical quackery threatens the pocketbooks of patients, but more important, it threatens their lives.
Higher rates will create a hardship for both the manufacturer of the product as well as the customer.	Higher rates will create a hardship for both the manufacturer of the product and the customer.

a total of

This is a common piece of word baggage.

She met with a total of 21 clients last week.	She met with 21 clients last week.

below (see **"above"**)

both ≠ each, two

Use both only when you mean "the two together" in contrast to "the two separately" or "only one": *Both men attended the dinner party last night.* The first example below implies that the two clients met jointly with the subject (He). The second implies nonsensically that in a different circumstance, one plane alone might come within a mile of each other.

He saw both clients for one hour.	He saw each client for one hour.
Both planes came within a mile of each other.	The two planes came within a mile of each other.

by means of

Usually the last two words of this hackneyed three-word phrase are baggage.

The flute vibrato is produced by means of an undulating motion of the airstream.	The flute vibrato is produced by an undulating motion of the airstream.

center around ≠ center on, center in

A center is a fixed point; to revolve around or gather around is possible, but not to center around.

He will probably center his political campaign around negativism toward his opponent. Problems of music performance tend to be centered around aural deficiencies.	He will probably center his political campaign on negativism toward his opponent. Problems of music performance tend to be centered in aural deficiencies.

Note: the term focus is used erroneously in exactly the same way as the term center.

check into

This is a colloquialism. One checks into a motel, but for most other checking, into is baggage. (Check on is sometimes warranted.)

The researcher spent the first day checking into schedule problems that had plagued the study.	The researcher spent the first day • checking schedule problems that had plagued the study. • investigating schedule problems that had plagued the study.

circumstance (see **"situation"**)

(coined titles)

Do not convert descriptive phrases into titles.

Renowned Jazz Musician Billy Taylor performed at the Main Street Station last night.

Billy Taylor, a renowned jazz musician, performed at the Main Street Station last night.

A renowned jazz musician, Billy Taylor, performed at the Main Street Station last night.

comprise

The whole comprises (embraces) the parts, not the other way around. This word has become so tainted with misuse that I use it only where no other word or construction works as well.

Two Democrats and three Republicans comprise the Board of Education.

Two Democrats and three Republicans constitute the Board of Education.

The Board of Education

- comprises two Democrats and three Republicans.
- consists of two Democrats and three Republicans.

Note: constitutes and consists of are two helpful terms if you want to skirt the dangers of comprise altogether.

concern (see also Chapter 4, Part 1)

Concern is a double-meaning word used in a variety of confusing ways. Sometimes the reader is left wondering whether it means "involve" or "worry" (first example), sometimes it is used to say not much of anything (second example), and sometimes it becomes a purveyor of vagueness by taking on the quality of a possession (third example). The word in all its forms (concerns; concerning; concerned) is fraught with possibilities for poor use.

Does this concern him?	Does this involve him? Does this worry him?
Let us reopen discussion of the issues concerning our last meeting.	Let us reopen discussion of the issues from our last meeting.
It is unfortunate that some persons have some concerns.	I regret the ambivalence of some members of the Board.

confront

This term can cause unintentional overstatement when used as a synonym for "face" or "meet." Confront implies assertiveness, aggressiveness, or even combativeness: *With truth as his only weapon, he confronted his accuser.*

When the preliminary work I just described is complete, I will confront the subjects of my study for the first time.	When the preliminary work I just described is complete, I will meet the subjects of my study for the first time.

continual ≠ continuous

These words have distinct meanings. <u>Continual</u> means repeatedly; <u>continuous</u> means without ceasing.

His continuous disruption of instruction scuttled the six-month experiment.	His continual disruption of instruction scuttled the six-month experiment.
She has been a member of the Philadelphia Orchestra continually since 1972.	She has been a member of the Philadelphia Orchestra continuously since 1982.

correlation (see also Chapter 2, Part 1)

This term has specific meaning in statistical reporting; avert confusion within non-statistical statements by using other terms.

I see no correlation between my leniency and the unruliness of the class.	I see no evidence that my leniency has led to the unruliness of the class. I found a low correlation (.18) between teacher leniency ratings and class scores on the Charles Hanson Anarchy/ Organization Scale (CHAOS).

currently ≠ presently

Currently means "now"; presently can mean either "now" or "soon." Tense usually makes meaning clear, but by reserving presently for the latter meaning you will avoid all chances of ambiguity.

You should think of me presently as the leader of the group.	You should think of me currently as the leader of the group.

deal with (see also Chapter 4, Part 1)

Too often this term is used interchangeably among sentences and left to mean whatever the reader chooses for it to mean.

The social worker was unable to deal with him yesterday.	The social worker was too stressed to see another client yesterday. The social worker handled his case poorly yesterday. His effect on the social worker has been cumulative; yesterday she gave up.

determine ≠ identify

Determine implies involvement—if not by taking action, at least by reasoning or calculating. Where the writer's role is passive, identify is more precise.

Last, we have to determine which children have had some experience.	Last, we have to identify children who have had some experience.

diagnose

Conditions are diagnosed; afflicted persons are not.

The doctor diagnosed him as suffering from carpal tunnel syndrome.	The doctor diagnosed carpal tunnel syndrome as the cause of his suffering.

different, separate

These words are commonly inserted unnecessarily into sentences. Omitting <u>different</u> from the first example will not prompt readers to believe the three meanings are the same, nor will omitting <u>separate</u> from the second example prompt readers to believe the meetings were simultaneous.

The word has three different meanings. The board held three separate meetings in an attempt to resolve the problem.	The word has three meanings. The board held three meetings in an attempt to resolve the problem.

Also, when you use <u>different</u> you are obligated to give the reader a clear answer to the question "different from what?" If different means "different from each other," probably another word would be more efficient and precise, e.g., diverse or various.

The company's motivational technique was different. We observed different styles of play among the children.	The company's motivational technique was different from anything I had known. We observed various (or diverse) styles of play among the children.

dilemma ≠ problem

A dilemma leaves nothing but unacceptable alternatives. If I can see a solution, I am facing a problem—not a dilemma.

The truancy dilemma has forced big-city schools to hire what amounts to an in-house police force.

(Here is a true dilemma.)------------->

The truancy problem has forced big-city schools to hire what amounts to an in-house police force.

Her dilemma was whether to keep the job and fail college or quit the job and learn the true meaning of hunger.

discover

To be discovered, a thing must be extant but previously unknown: *Hanson and Schmidt discovered a new species of butterfly in the Amazon rainforest.*

Montessori discovered a new approach to teaching young children.

Montessori developed a new approach to teaching young children.

discussed (see also Chapter 2, Part 2)

A discussion is a conversation between at least two persons. The term has been stretched to describe written text in which the author presents more than one point of view for the reader to consider, as at the end of articles in research journals. You will lose precision if you stretch it far enough to describe written information of all kinds.

The method by which the interviews were conducted will be discussed in the next chapter.

The method by which the interviews were conducted will be described (or presented) in the next chapter.

disinterested ≠ uninterested

Though a secondary meaning of disinterested is not interested, its primary and almost exclusive use is to describe a detached or unbiased party: *Before you and I begin negotiating, we should ask the opinion of a disinterested party.*

Perhaps too proud of his status as an Olympic athlete, he was disinterested in coaching high school track.

Perhaps too proud of his status as an Olympic athlete, he was

- uninterested in coaching high school track.
- not interested in coaching high school track.

divided

To divide is to break a whole into parts. A group of persons can be divided, but individual persons—despite the language of some research studies—are usually left whole.

Subjects were divided into three treatment groups.	Subjects were assigned to one of three treatment groups. The group of subjects was divided into three treatment groups.
Subjects were divided into high, moderate, and low IQ.	Subjects were categorized by IQ score as high, moderate, or low.

done

Done, as commonly used, is a colloquialism. Pot roasts are done; tasks are finished or completed.

Once I was done with data collection and analysis, I began to write in earnest.	Once I finished data collection and analysis, I began to write in earnest.

enormity

This word does not mean simply "of enormous size," but rather monstrous or heinous in nature: *The enormity of the mass murderer's deed shown immediately with the opening of the front door.*

The enormity of the bulk mailing task overwhelmed our staff; we had to call part-time helpers.	The magnitude of the bulk mailing task overwhelmed our staff; we had to call part-time helpers.

equally

Sometimes this word is used redundantly.

The weekend staff is equally as competent as the weekday staff.	The weekend staff is as competent as the weekday staff.

exists

The least that can be said about anyone or anything is that it exists; why use words to say so little?

The technology exists.	The technology is available now. The technology will be on the market within six months.
Unfortunately, that approach exists within the profession.	Unfortunately, some members of our profession practice that approach.

experience (see Chapter 4, Part 4 for other nouns pressed into service as verbs)

As a verb, experience is general, bland, vague, and impotent.

I want to experience the Native American culture.	I want to live among Native Americans, learn their history, and perhaps share some of their emotions.
I have not experienced music in any depth.	I listen to music only when driving my car, and have never learned to play an instrument or sing.

farther ≠ further

Use farther for physical references and further for non-physical.

We traveled further the second day than we had the first.	We traveled farther the second day than we had the first.
We should explore the possibilities farther.	We should explore the possibilities further.

feel ≠ believe

Frequently, the first is used erroneously in place of the second (I have not seen the reverse); ask yourself whether you are referring to an emotion or to an opinion.

I feel that Piaget has been woefully misunderstood. To become a social worker, one must feel that rewards will outweigh sacrifices.	I believe that Piaget has been woefully misunderstood. To become a social worker, one must believe that rewards will outweigh sacrifices.

finalize (see also Chapter 3)

This amounts to a pretentious version of some perfectly fine words.

I will finalize my research by the end of the month. The committee finalized its day's business with a vote on the Perkins proposal.	I will complete my research by the end of the month. The committee concluded its day's business with a vote on the Perkins proposal.

focus around ≠ focus on (see **"center around"**)

how

Avoid the common tendency to use <u>how</u> where it is superfluous.

He should learn how to type.	He should learn to type.

however (see also Appendix B, Part 3, Punctuation: Semicolons)

A run-on sentence is guaranteed and confusion is likely when <u>however</u>, enclosed between commas with an independent clause on each side, modifies the second of the two independent clauses.

<table>
<tr>
<td>He has misgivings, however, she helps him as much as she can.

Note: A run-on sentence is not created, however, when however modifies the first clause (as in this sentence).</td>
<td>He has misgivings, but she helps him as much as she can.

She helps him all she can, despite his misgivings.</td>
</tr>
</table>

When however is desirable as a conjunctive adverb to connect two independent clauses (probably of no advantage in the simple sentence above), place a semicolon before however to keep from disorienting the reader.

<table>
<tr>
<td>The researcher was ready, the subjects eager, and the equipment in place, however, a power failure ruined the first day of data collection.</td>
<td>The researcher was ready, the subjects eager, and the equipment in place; however, a power failure ruined the first day of data collection.</td>
</tr>
</table>

if and when

A writer who uses these words in tandem is hedging at the reader's expense. Decide what message you want to send, then send it by using one word or the other.

<table>
<tr>
<td>I will use that approach if and when I am hired.</td>
<td>I will use that approach if I am hired.

I will use that approach when I am hired.</td>
</tr>
</table>

impact (see Chapter 4, Part 4, for other nouns pressed into service as verbs)

As a verb, this term sounds pretentious and generally displaces more precise language. It works much better as a noun: *The impact of this decision will be felt for generations.*

<table>
<tr>
<td>How will this policy impact your agency?

We are trying to impact the legislature in our favor with this petition.</td>
<td>How will this policy affect your agency?

We are trying to influence the legislature in our favor with this petition.</td>
</tr>
</table>

implement (see also Chapter 4, Part 4)

Writers of bureaucratese give the impression that people no longer do, use, apply, or install anything; everything is implemented. As you can see from these examples and the examples in Chapter 4, a great amount of specific, meaningful communication is lost.

Teachers tried to implement the Board's policy, but it was unworkable.	Teachers tried to apply the Board's policy to their teaching, but it was unworkable.
Administrators need to implement the discipline code firmly.	Administrators need to enforce the discipline code firmly.
The researcher implemented the interview process as designed.	The researcher conducted the interview process as designed.

imply ≠ infer

Both words have to do with an indirect message, but the sender implies and the receiver infers. Infer is used commonly where imply is needed.

By saying that, are you inferring that I let you down?	By saying that, are you implying that I let you down?

importantly (see also Chapter 4, Part 4)

This awkward adverb, along with its cousins firstly, secondly, and so forth, is both pretentious and inaccurate. Think about whether you are trying to tell the reader what (important) or how (importantly).

Most importantly, establish a firm schedule before you begin to collect data.	Most important, establish a firm schedule before you begin to collect data.

in ≠ into

Go jump in the lake. That old colloquialism, taken literally, conjures a picture of someone standing in the lake and jumping. The real message is *go jump into the lake;* that is, transport yourself from out of the lake to in the lake. For the example below to be correct in its first version would require either a very small student or a very large microphone.

Students were asked to sing in the microphone.	Students were asked to sing into the microphone.

include

To describe items as included is to imply that other items are excluded, i.e., that the list is partial. Introduce complete lists with consists of and similar all-encompassing terms.

The triathlon includes swimming, bicycling, and running.	The triathlon consists of swimming, bicycling, and running. The events of the triathlon are swimming, bicycling, and running. OR, IF THE LIST IS PARTIAL . . . The triathlon includes swimming and bicycling.

individual

Individual is a cold, impersonal description for a human being; any object can be individual as compared to grouped. Also, the term breeds wordiness and pretension in bureaucratic writing.

He is an individual I admire.	He is a person I admire. OR BETTER . . . I admire him.

in order to

The first two of these three words are usually baggage.

I tested subjects early in the morning in order to ensure freshness of mind.	I tested subjects early in the morning to ensure freshness of mind.

input (see also Chapter 4, Part 2)

This bureaucratic vocabulary eater supplants a great number of more precise words.

Give us your input.	Give us your • view. • opinion. • reaction. • advice. • impression. • assessment.

involve

This word is weak when used in place of specific information.

The researcher will involve classroom teachers in the study. Building principals were heavily involved in the decision.	The researcher will use classroom teachers as test monitors for the study. Building principals cast the deciding vote.

it's ≠ its

Use the apostrophe only for contractions: *It's a dreary day*.

The bird broke it's wing.	The bird broke its wing.

joined together

The adverb is redundant; nothing is ever joined apart.

The computer billing system and the main office computer will be joined together.	The computer billing system and the main office computer will be joined.

latter ≠ last

<u>Latter</u> refers only to the second of two; for reference to the final entry in a series of three or more, use <u>last</u>. Be careful not to overuse either term; back-reference writing is inconvenient for the reader as compared with use of specific terms.

Writers should own a dictionary, a thesaurus, and a handbook of usage. The latter may be the most difficult to select.	Writers should own a dictionary, a thesaurus, and a handbook of usage. The last may be the most difficult to select.

lay ≠ lie

When you place yourself down, you lie down; when you place something other than yourself down, you lay it down. I see lay used mistakenly in place of lie, but not the reverse.

May I lay on the couch? He spent the day laying around the house.	May I lie on the couch? He spent the day lying around the house.

The various tenses of these words can be troublesome.

tense	***(lie; lay; lain)***	***(lay; laid; laid)***
present	May I ***lie*** on the couch?	May I ***lay*** it here?
future	I will ***lie*** on the couch tomorrow.	I will ***lay*** it down soon.
past	I ***lay*** on the couch for an hour.	I ***laid*** it down an hour ago.
present, past, & future perfect	I have ***lain*** (had ***lain;*** will have ***lain***) on the couch all day.	I have ***laid*** (had ***laid;*** will have ***laid***) it here every day.

less ≠ fewer

Do not use less to describe a reduction in something that can be counted; use fewer. Less is the counterpart to amount; fewer is the counterpart to number (see amount).

We have less customers than last week.	We have fewer customers than last week. We have less business than last week.

like ≠ as

Like modifies nouns and pronouns *(I am dirty, like him. She smells like a rose);* as modifies phrases and other parts of speech *(He was on time, as he should have been. She was late, as usual.).*

Data collection was time consuming, like I had predicted it would be.	Data collection was time consuming, as I had predicted it would be.

In the speech of today, like takes a beating that defies explanation: *I was like going to go, but like I changed my mind and like stayed home.* To describe that practice as banal is almost complimentary.

literally

Oddly, literally is most often used when its opposite is meant: figuratively. Even used correctly, the word is usually superfluous. That is, in most cases all but the dullest of readers can discriminate between the literal and the figurative by context.

The appointment as clinical psychologist was literally handed to him on a silver platter.	The appointment as clinical psychologist was handed to him on a silver platter.

look at (see also Chapter 4, Part 1)

This term has become a fashionable understatement among bureaucratic writers. Avoid using it to mean anything other than to simply look: *Look at the moon.*

We will look at that issue next time. We need to look at the problems between departments.	We will discuss that issue next time. We need to identify the problems between departments and solve them.

nor

Do not let a negative expression lure you into using nor where or belongs.

The interrogation was not long nor difficult.	The interrogation was • not long or difficult • neither long nor difficult. • not long, nor was it difficult.

often

Use often only where frequency is the issue: *He often found himself short of cash.*

To improve cash flow, retailers often reduce inventory and rely on daily deliveries.	To improve cash flow, many retailers reduce inventory and rely on daily deliveries. A common practice among retailers is to improve cash flow by reducing inventory and relying on daily deliveries.

one and the same

The first two words of this hackneyed phrase are not needed.

The high school principal and the head of the English Department are one and the same person.	The high school principal and the head of the English Department are the same person. The high school principal is also head of the English Department.

only (see also Chapter 1, Part 4 and Chapter 3, Part 2)

This may be the most frequently misplaced word in the language, sometimes creating confusion (first example), other times creating only weakness (second example).

Motorists can only use the south road for the next five days.	Motorists can use the south road for only the next five days. OR Motorists can use only the south road for the next five days.
Students here will only succeed if they try.	Students here will succeed only if they try.

ongoing (see also Chapter 4, Part 2)

This bureaucratic vocabulary eater supplants a great number of more precise words.

The noise pollution has been ongoing.	The noise pollution has been continuous.
This is an ongoing project.	This is a long-term project.
We have an ongoing agreement.	We have an open-ended agreement.
Students were reprimanded on an ongoing basis.	Students were reprimanded continually.

onset ≠ outset

Onset carries ominous overtones: if not the onset of disease, at least the onset of winter. Avoid using it where the more benign term, outset (meaning simply beginning), is more appropriate. Probably the best advice is to jettison outset, use beginning when you mean beginning, and save onset to describe wars and plagues.

The researcher was careless about subject selection at the onset of his study.	The researcher was careless about subject selection • at the outset of his study. • at the beginning of his study.

over (see **"above"**)

persons ≠ people

Ten people, after nine had left, would be reduced to one people; therefore, the original should read "ten persons." Use persons where the number is known or conceivably could be known; use people where the number is irrevocably indefinite, as in a classification of people: *the Chinese people*.

Michigan stadium seats 110,000 people.	Michigan stadium seats 110,000 persons.
This part of the country has an abundance of annoying persons.	This part of the country has an abundance of annoying people.

A much more strict interpretation is that people applies only to an ethnic classification *(the Chinese people)*. According to that view, the original version of the second example above would be correct. I favor the revision, because the size of the annoying-person population can hardly be estimated, much less counted; that makes *annoying* a classification.

personal

Be careful not to create redundancy by using this word to modify something commonly acknowledged to be personal.

She is a personal friend of mine. My personal opinion is that the research data was collected carelessly.	She is a friend of mine. My opinion is that the research data was collected carelessly. I believe the research data was collected carelessly.

pinch hit

This term is generally inappropriate for formal writing. If you do use it, however, be sure the substitute performance is expected to exceed the original. To pinch hit, as borrowed from the game of baseball, is to bring to bear talent superior to that of the person replaced: *John will pinch hit for me at next week's meeting; he is more familiar with the case than I.*

John will pinch hit for me while I am out of town.	John will take care of my business while I am out of town.

plus

Use this term only within the context of a mathematical description, not as a bridge between two parts of a loosely-crafted sentence.

The DSS caseworker was frustrated by a heavy caseload and an immovable bureaucratic structure, plus the emotional drain of helpless, demanding clients.	The DSS caseworker was frustrated by a heavy caseload and an immovable bureaucratic structure—and by the emotional drain of helpless, demanding clients.

point

Be sure this word has a function when you use it; it tends to be baggage.

He stressed the point that schedules had to be adhered to strictly.

He stressed that schedules had to be adhered to strictly.

proximity

Proximity means "nearness"; avoid the common practice of preceding proximity with close, thus producing the oddly redundant message "close nearness."

The researchers chose the testing room for its close proximity to the classrooms.

The researchers chose the testing room for its proximity to the classrooms.

reason, because

Use these words separately; their similarity in connotation creates awkwardness when they are used together.

One reason he found no significant differences between groups is because the treatment ended after only twelve weekly sessions.

One reason he found no significant differences between groups is that the treatment ended after only twelve weekly sessions.

He found no significant differences between groups, in part, because the treatment ended after only twelve weekly sessions.

reason why

Avoid inserting why as baggage following reason.

That is the reason why he resigned.

I have no interest in when he did it or how he did it; I want to know the reason why.

That is the reason he resigned.

I have no interest in when he did it or how he did it; I want to know the reason.

relatively

Use relatively only when the relationship is evident (what is relative to what).

The writing of my dissertation is progressing relatively well.	The writing of my dissertation • is progressing well. • is progressing relatively well, considering how I struggled with my master's thesis.

result (see also Chapter 4, Example 11f, and corresponding Bonus Tidbit)

To use result as a verb is to couch action in terms of the receiving end rather than the sending end. Be sure you want to do that before using the word in that way. If not, write the type of construction shown in the right column below—construction that begins with the sending end and carries through without changing direction midstream.

The use of young subjects resulted in testing problems. Too little control will result in internal invalidity; too much control will result in external invalidity.	The use of young subjects led to testing problems. Too little control will damage internal validity; too much control will damage external validity.

revisit (see also Chapter 4, Part 4)

If my father is not well when I stop for a visit, I may decide to revisit him soon thereafter. To write about revisiting issues, on the other hand, is simply to jump on the bandwagon with the latest little bureaucratic cute-talk word, sometimes at the expense of a specific message that might have been delivered.

I would like to revisit the issue of subject confidentiality at our next research seminar. When data collection flagged, the researcher and her associates revisited the plans they had made two weeks earlier.	I would like to talk about the issue of subject confidentiality in greater detail at our next research seminar. When data collection flagged, the researcher and her associates revised the plans they had made two weeks earlier.

separate (see **"different"**)

share in common

These words used together create redundancy.

Length of class session is all that the treatment groups shared in common.

Length of class session is all that the treatment groups had in common.

The groups were treated differently in every way except length of class session.

significance, significant

Like correlation, significance has specific meaning in statistical reporting; avert confusion within nonstatistical statements by using other terms.

None of the actions I observed today seemed to have significance compared with what I observed yesterday.

None of the actions I observed today seemed as fundamentally important as the actions I observed yesterday.

Differences were statistically significant ($p < .05$).

since ≠ because

Since is strongest when used in relation to a time frame: *She had not seen him since his wife died.* Since means because only in a distant sense; for clarity and strength, use because when you mean because.

Since the graduate assistants administered the tests, they were asked also to score them and interpret them.

Because the graduate assistants administered the tests, they were asked also to score them and interpret them.

site

A site, a piece of land at a particular location, has nothing to do with structures.

The third-floor laboratories at the Jefferson site are inadequate.	The third-floor laboratories in the Jefferson building are inadequate.

situation, circumstance

Situation sometimes serves as a life raft for writers struggling to keep description afloat. If you find your description difficult to put into words, how much more difficult a time will the reader have trying to interpret a bail-out word (first example). Also avoid adding situation as baggage after giving specific information (second example).

The science teacher was frustrated continually, and finally resigned because of his situation.	The science teacher was frustrated continually. Finally he resigned rather than teach large classes of diverse students in a small, ill-equipped room.
He will soon be facing an unemployment situation.	He will soon be facing unemployment.

An oddity of the first practice is that situation, even if its use was desirable, is probably less precise than circumstance. Situations arise suddenly, then change (a rainstorm or a mugging); circumstances are more likely to be in place for a period of time (poor teaching conditions, a disability, or an unhappy marriage).

some time ≠ sometime

Use some time only when you mean "a quantity of time": *I will need some time to think about it*. When you mean "at some yet undetermined time," use sometime.

Some time he will have to face the truth.	Sometime he will have to face the truth.
We need to meet some time soon.	We need to meet sometime soon.

The plural, sometimes, means "on some occasions": *Sometimes he faces the truth; sometimes he does not.*

that

That is used frequently where it is not needed. Overexuberant purging, on the other hand, can create awkwardness; note my decision to leave one that in the sentence below. You need to acquire a sense for when that functions to the betterment of the sentence and when it is simply an irritating bump in the road.

John teaches in the same way that Charles teaches, except that Charles knows that tact is important.	John teaches in the same way Charles teaches, except that Charles knows tact is important.

that, which (see also Appendix B, Part 3, Examples B-8c and d)

You can eliminate ambiguity by introducing restrictive clauses with that, followed by no comma (or with no relative pronoun at all), and by introducing nonrestrictive clauses with which (followed by a comma).

This is the coordination test which I told you to use.	This is the coordination test that I told you to use. This is the coordination test I told you to use. This is the coordination test, which I told you to use.

The question behind the example above is this: are you restricting meaning to a particular coordination test from among two or more tests (first two revisions; restrictive), or are you identifying a single test, then adding information (third revision; nonrestrictive)? Which without a comma, as in the original, may cause the reader to wonder whether you intended a restrictive clause or simply omitted the comma by mistake.

the

The can become baggage in the same way that becomes baggage. Hunt through your writing and purge it of the baggage.

The books he read and the ideas he exchanged with others helped fulfill the dreams of a lifetime for this boy from the blue-collar neighborhoods of Chicago.	Books he read and ideas he exchanged with others helped fulfill dreams of a lifetime for this boy from a blue-collar neighborhood of Chicago.

the ≠ a/an

Used in place of a or an, the can restrict meaning by implying "the one and only" (a common practice in conjunction with result used as a verb).

Original	Revision
Unreliable test scores were the result of his careless approach to data collection.	Unreliable test scores were a result of his careless approach to data collection. His careless approach to data collection caused test scores to be unreliable. Note: The second revision is better because it progresses logically from cause to effect.
The superintendent was abrasive, and the result was a revolt from building principals.	One result of the superintendent's abrasiveness was a revolt from building principals.

this, these

Each time you use one of these words, ask yourself this question: "Can I make reading easier for the reader by giving the specific information to which this or these refers?" If the answer is "yes," even if you save the reader no more than a slight hesitation, give the specific information. In the first sentence of this paragraph, for example, these refers clearly and instantly to the boldface words immediately above, and this refers clearly to information beyond the colon. In contrast, the meaning of this in the original sentence below is unclear.

Original	Revision
He graduated from a highly-rated school, but with marginal grades, and one of his letters of recommendation was strong. The personnel director took this into consideration.	He graduated from a highly-rated school, but with marginal grades, and one of his letters of recommendation was strong. The personnel director • took the inconsistency of his portfolio into consideration. • took the reputation of the school and the strong letter into consideration.

torturous ≠ tortuous

Torturous means painful; tortuous means indirect or winding.

We spent a full day traveling one mile along the torturous path of the river. Three of the seven hostages were hospitalized after their tortuous ordeal.	We spent a full day traveling one mile along the tortuous path of the river. Three of the seven hostages were hospitalized after their torturous ordeal.

true facts

Use this phrase and consider it not redundant only if you can name a false fact with which to contrast your true facts.

Only her therapist knows the true facts behind her condition.	Only her therapist knows the facts behind her condition.

under (see **"above"**)

unknown

What is unknown to you is not necessarily unknown altogether. The subjects in this sentence were probably quite aware of their addresses.

I could see that a follow-up study would be valuable, but the addresses of the subjects were unknown.	I could see that a follow-up study would be valuable, • but the addresses of the subjects were unavailable. • but I had no access to the subjects' addresses.

up (see **"down"**)

upcoming (see also Chapter 4, Part 2)

The primary function of this bureaucratic vocabulary eater is not to inform, but to titillate. Sometimes it replaces a more precise word (first example) and sometimes it just fills space (second example).

Students are encouraged to attend the upcoming game. The upcoming University Lecture Series will be held in Barronson Hall.	Students are encouraged to attend Saturday's game. The University Lecture Series will be held in Barronson Hall.

update (see also Chapter 4, Part 2)

This bureaucratic vocabulary eater supplants a great amount of more precise information.

The aide gave the teacher an update.	The aide • oriented the teacher to the new procedures. • reported the day's events to the teacher.

utilize (see also Chapter 4, Part 4)

Utilize is no more than a pretentious variation of use.

We try to utilize everything we receive to good advantage. Is he utilizing all of his talents in that job?	We try to use everything we receive to good advantage. Is he using all of his talents in that job?

veritable

This word almost always carries more decorative value than meaning.

Even as a graduate student, she was a veritable model of scientific thought.	Even as a graduate student, she was a model of scientific thought.

where ≠ in which, for which, to which

Where is a matter of location; inappropriate use creates odd statements.

The best photographs were those where everyone stood. Students can afford to take only those classes where they receive degree credit. The only statements to be published are those where we all agree.	The best photographs were those in which everyone stood. Students can afford to take only those classes for which they receive degree credit. The only statements to be published are those to which we all agree.

whether or not

This phrase is useful when an alternative needs to be given equal weight: *The test will be given whether students are prepared or not.* More often, though, or not is baggage.

Whether the students would be available for a sufficient time or not was still to be determined.	Whether the students would be available for a sufficient time was still to be determined.

which (see **"that, which"**)

would

Do not use would without an accompanying if, but, or except.

Students would be tested in room 324.	Students will be tested in room 324. Students would be tested in room 324 if it were not being painted.

NOTE

In writing "A Collection of Troublesome Words" I had to decide whether to include words described fully in other chapters. I decided I would, despite redundancy, to provide an alphabetical list for use as a freestanding reference. Therefore, expect to find words from this list—with brief commentary and additional examples—elsewhere in the book, particularly in Chapter 4: The Bureaucratic Style.

4. New Words, New Uses

The list of troublesome words in the preceding section varies somewhat from lists of a generation ago (Strunk and White, 1979) and two generations ago (Bernstein, 1965). That is because language problems change with shifts in culture—particularly shifts in schooling—and because language, to quote an old saw, "is dynamic." Be aware, though, that substantial changes in language occur gradually. We hardly miss a beat when we read century-old writing, and with a little work we can read and understand writing of four centuries ago. Few long-term language changes are likely to occur within your years of writing. For that reason, you may want to be cautious about jumping onto the next "dynamic language" bandwagon that comes along. You need to protect the power of your communication in the here and now by evaluating carefully the effect of new words and new word uses as they come to your attention.[3] I evaluate a new word or a new word use by asking myself two questions before adopting it: 1) Does it offer distinct meaning? 2) Is it applied to the benefit of the reader?

Distinctness of meaning is a matter of whether the new word or word use accomplishes something that an existing word or word use cannot. *Utilize* and *upcoming,* for example, are words written for effect rather than distinct meaning: *utilize* means *use* and *upcoming* means *coming*. *Utilize* has a pretentious, official sound, and *upcoming* has an upbeat, hyperactive sound. When your purpose in writing is to create one of those effects, you need those words; when your purpose is to convey meaning clearly and dispassionately, you do not. Similarly, a use of the word *revisit* that has appeared in recent years offers no distinct meaning: "When the committee reconvenes next month, it will *revisit* the issue of truancy." In writing such a sentence, one might choose from among several conventional terms, each of which yields specific information: *debate, reconsider, pursue further, continue discussion of.* Therefore, *revisit* seems useless in such a context, except perhaps to achieve intentional vagueness or to show that the writer has jumped onto the latest language bandwagon.

In contrast to the nondistinct words and word uses cited in the preceding paragraph, consider the words *update* and *input,* and consider the relatively new use of *parent* as a verb. All offer some distinct meaning. *Update* functions as a general term for informing a person of what has happened between the date of last information and the date of newest information. *Input* is a handy noun by which to describe, in general terms, any data put into a computer (more accurately, recorded on a hard drive or a disk; maybe *onput* would have been more precise). Fi-

[3] Because language development is gradual, a "new" word may predate you by decades.

nally, no word allows us to describe the act of being a parent as well as does *parent* used as a verb: Good *parenting* builds good societies!

So much for distinctness of meaning; now we need to think about how the reader does or does not benefit from particular applications of words and word uses. For example, we exceed parameters of usefulness when we use *update* mindlessly in place of specific terms *(inform, report, revise, tell),* or when we use *input* to describe any transfer of information *(opinions, ideas, advice),* or when we use *parent* as a verb where we might have said more with any of a number of terms *(nurture, comfort, protect, teach).* New words and new word uses become what I refer to as vocabulary eaters when we misapply them. We lose a great amount of communication power by allowing specific, information-rich words to wither for having been put into mothballs by *update, input,* and their kin.

You will read more extensively about such practices in Chapter 4: "The Bureaucratic Style." By the time you have finished reading *The Readable Thesis* you will be conscious of a great number of words and word uses that damage communication. Resist them, but recognize that all such words will not be purged from the language over time. Some new words and new word uses that lack distinctness now will hang on long enough to become dominant—will take on a new, widely understood meaning that renders previously used words impotent. When that happens, it is time to acquiesce. For example, I do not foresee *use* becoming impotent, but if that were to happen I would be obliged to acquiesce to *utilize.*

Meanwhile, I live and write by this dictum: ***While a new word or a new word use is marching toward possible usefulness, keep your writing strongest by letting others lead the way.*** Scientists ply their craft best by riding the front edge of change. Nonfiction writers do not. We ply our craft best by working skillfully with well-established, standard terms.

CHAPTER 3

LENGTH, STRENGTH, AND GRACE

The topics of this chapter are matters of style, which is no more than a particular way of doing something. To wear a sweater rather than a turtleneck or listen to jazz rather than rock are matters of style. To be offensive rather than congenial is also a matter of style. The difference is that sweaters and jazz generally do not breed rejection, while offensiveness does.

So it is with writing style. Move the tone of formality in your writing up or down a bit to establish the relationship you want with readers, use metaphor if you think it helps readers share your insight, or organize information into short paragraphs if you think that helps pull readers along. None of those style choices will set your audience scurrying for something else to read. Other style choices may. You will read here about three style-related issues analogous to offensive behavior: wordy writing, which steals readers' time; weak expression, which puts readers to sleep; and ungainly passages, which distract readers from content.

The inadvisable styles described in this chapter create background problems of clarity and precision. I will leave those problems in the background. Having read Chapters 1 and 2, you will identify many of the clarity and precision problems yourself as you read the examples. My primary purpose in this chapter is to encourage you to become disposed toward concise, strong, graceful writing. I want you to develop an appreciation for the differences those qualities make so you will be inclined to monitor more closely what you put on paper—a benefit to you and to your readers. The chapter is organized in three sections:

1. Wordy Writing
2. Weak Writing
3. Ungainly Writing

1. Wordy Writing

Writers for centuries have extolled the virtue of brevity, from Cicero's alleged postscript ("Had I had more time I'd have written you more briefly"), to Shakespeare's line in *Hamlet* ("Brevity is the soul of wit"), to William Strunk's lifelong battle cry ("Omit needless words")

{9}. Still, students frustrate teachers with bloated writing after asking the fateful question "how long should it be?" A good answer to "how long" is "not one word longer than needed to accomplish the objective." (A colleague's answer: "As long as necessary and as short as possible.") Given that perspective, *too short* comes to mean an undersized objective rather than too few words. Why burden readers with the writing shown in the left column below when the right-column version delivers the message efficiently?

Wordy	Concise
If researchers studying young children can record their subjects' play activities in a way that guards against the children's being distracted by the process, they should do so to keep the effect of those distractions from becoming a contaminating influence on the data.	Researchers should record young children at play unobtrusively to keep subject-distraction from contaminating data.

To trim writing wisely you will need 1) an eye for the extraneous (by the process contributes nothing), 2) a well-developed vocabulary (unobtrusively replaces 13 words), and 3) resourcefulness (subject-distraction[4] replaces 5 words) **{9}**. I have identified five specific writing transgressions that generate needless words:

Example 1	Immature Writing	Example 4	Redundancy
Example 2	Academically Inflated Writing	Example 5	Excessive Prepositional Phrases
Example 3	Filler Phrases		

Example 1: Immature Writing

Do not be put off by the term immature. Just as all of us exhibit immature behavior from time to time, all of us exhibit immature writing from time to time. If you write immaturely more than occasionally, you will probably want to recognize it and make corrections. Immature writing has a rarefied-air quality about it—fluffy sentences begging to be combined into fewer, more compact sentences. Immature sentences are the antithesis of overstuffed sentences, described early in Chapter 1.

---

[4] In Appendix B, Example B-18, you will find more information about using hyphens to invigorate language.

Original	Revision
1a. Choosing a program is not an easy job. There are many programs available, and not all are of good quality. Caution should be used in the selection process.	The many programs available vary in quality: choose cautiously.
1b. Montessori held a certain view of will and obedience. She said it is a commonly held thought that will and obedience are opposing concepts. Most people believe that we get children to obey by suppressing their wills and having them conform to the teacher's will. Montessori felt that this was a poor idea. She believed that a child will learn to obey only when his will is developed.	Montessori disagreed with the common view that children obey by conforming to a teacher's will. She believed, rather, that children learn to obey by developing their own wills.
1c. Robert Schumann's song cycle, *Frauenliebe und Lebe* (A Woman's Love and Life), is set to a cycle of poems by Adalbert von Chamisso (1731–1838). Chamisso's series of poems had the same title. Although Schumann's work contains eight songs, the original cycle, as written by Chamisso, included nine poems. Schumann omitted the final poem from his song cycle.	Robert Schumann wrote his song cycle *Frauenliebe und Lebe* (A Woman's Love and Life) as a setting of the first eight poems of Adalbert von Chamisso's (1731–1838) nine-poem cycle of the same title.

1c Bonus Tidbit

Lack of commas around the title of Schumann's song cycle in the revision signals a restrictive (defining) clause, telling the reader that Schumann wrote other song cycles. Had *Frauenliebe und Lebe* been Schumann's only song cycle, the clause would have been properly set off by commas as a nonrestrictive (nondefining) clause (See Appendix B, Part 1, English Usage Review [Parts of a Sentence: A More Detailed View], and Part 3, Example B-8).

Do not confuse mature writing with pretentious writing. Notice that I built revisions on relatively common words (vary and cautiously in **1a**; disagreed in **1b**), and on relatively simple word arrangements (the common view in **1b**; Chamiso's nine-poem cycle in **1c**). Fancy words and unusually applied words tend to create more problems than they solve **{17}**. In **1d** and **e**, for example, brevity—accomplished as it is by the use of unusual words in densely-packed phrases— becomes a kind of monster itself.

Original	Revision
1d. Test unreliability attenuates validity. R	A test must be reliable to be valid.
1e. A child's circumvention of authoritarian decree is intuitive.	Children naturally try to circumvent authority—to live by their own dictates rather than by adult decree.

So there are two sides to the coin: loose, immature writing wastes the reader's time, but overly tight writing (dense writing) puts a wall between the reader and the message. You will see the worst of all possibilities—writing that is both wordy and dense—in Example 2, Academically Inflated Writing, and more extensively in Chapter 4.

The question of how compact your writing should be cannot be answered in a vacuum. How intellectually mature is your typical reader? Any time you write you should have an audience in mind. *The Readable Thesis* is a text about formal writing; its intended audience is graduate and undergraduate students and professional persons who write. With that audience in mind, I judge the original versions of **1a–c** to be thinly written. That is, they contain less substance per sentence than befits the intellectual appetite of the average reader.

These last examples of immature writing (**1f–h**) are less wordy than **1a–c**, but still wordier than they need to be. For the audience of *The Readable Thesis,* I think the revisions constitute an efficient use of vocabulary, not the kind of oppressive density seen in **1d–e**.

Original	Revision
1f. There was some kind of breakdown in the electronic timer.	The electronic timer malfunctioned.
1g. They got together and made plans to kill the king.	They conspired to kill the king.
1h. He tried to show himself to be more highly educated than he is.	He masqueraded as an intellectual.

By comparing **1a–c** with **1f–h**, you can see that two kinds of maturity contribute to concise writing: maturity of construction and maturity of vocabulary. I revised **1a–c** primarily by more mature construction, and **1f–h** primarily by more mature vocabulary. To improve the maturity of your construction, begin by practicing straightforward word reduction—finding the shortest distance between two points. Take any paragraph you have written and try to reduce it to one-half the original number of words. (Wait until you have read all of this section about wordy writing). To improve the maturity of your vocabulary, notice how good writers achieve word efficiency. Be curious about their word use. Make lists of useful words you see and hear but cannot define; build a personal dictionary of them, and review them periodically. Do not memorize complex words and their meanings out of context, but pay particular attention to moderately difficult words at the fringe of your vocabulary, words common enough to help most readers without getting in their way. A rich vocabulary of verbs is particularly useful (see Appendix C). Also study Chapter 2 of this book extensively. ***To say much with few words you must know many*** **{9}**.

Example 2: Academically Inflated Writing

Even more damaging a form of wordiness than immature writing is academically inflated writing. Do not let an expanded vocabulary intoxicate you into overusing it.

Original	Revision
2a. As compared with school boards of three decades past, the school boards of today assume substantially greater responsibility for addressing social maladies to which their constituents may be vulnerable.	School boards take much more responsibility for social problems now than they did 30 years ago.
2b. The counselor's insightful advisement was indeed commensurate with the demands of Lydia's circumstances at the time.	The counselor advised Lydia well.

Resist particularly the misconception that instructors want you to write the kinds of sentences you see in **2a** and **b**. Generally they do not. A good antidote to academically inflated writing is an image of the readers you have in mind. Their "presence" should encourage you to reject high-sounding, circuitous sentences and paragraphs in favor of straight-line sentences and well-constructed paragraphs—sentences and paragraphs that you know they will read, understand, and appreciate **{2, 9, 17}**.

Example 3: Filler Phrases

Glib filler phrases—the fact that, a total of, and dozens of their relatives—lie in cranial repositories waiting to jump onto the page the second we become less than vigilant **(3a–c)**. Lack of vigilance also has us insert which is, who is, that were, and similar two-word phrases into sentences that define persons and objects **(3d–e)** **{9}**. Finally, the and that, essential words much of the time, at other times slip into writing as filler **(3f)**. Filler phrases and filler words are underlined throughout Example 3.

	Original	Revision
3a.	The researcher was unhappy about the fact that he was removed from the project.	The researcher was unhappy about his removal from the project.
3b.	A total of eighteen phrases was recorded for evaluation.	Eighteen phrases were recorded for evaluation.
3c.	In order to teach reading skills, the teacher must be well-versed in the teaching of patterns.	To teach reading skills, the teacher must be well-versed in the teaching of patterns.
3d.	The test that is given on Saturdays has low reliability.	The test given on Saturdays has low reliability.
3e.	The conference room, which was warmer than usual, caused discomfort.	The conference room, warmer than usual, caused discomfort.
3f.	Such vague style forces the reader to construct, without benefit of the facts, the message that the writer is supposed to have written. I only wish that I could report that this kind of writing is rare.	Such vague style forces readers to construct, without benefit of facts, the message the writer is supposed to have written. I only wish I could report that this kind of writing is rare.

Misuse and overuse of the and that are common; you may want to scan your writing for excesses as a matter of course when you revise. For more examples, see Chapter 2, Part 3, A Collection of Troublesome Words.

3a–e Bonus Tidbit

The number of filler phrases that clutter writing is indefinite. If you want to think more fully about them, you might write a few examples and revisions of your own. To get you started, here are some common filler phrases besides those shown in Example 2: who are; for the purpose of; by the process of; in the event that; in the best interest of.

Example 4: Redundancy

Free complimentary copies, past history, my own personal opinion, and similar redundancies bombard us daily. Make your writing more sensible at the same time you shorten it by avoiding redundancies **{9}**. The extra words in Example **4** are underlined.

Original	Revision
4a. The intervening years between the world wars were characterized by enormous growth.	The years between the world wars were characterized by enormous growth.
4b. The school curriculum has come under close scrutiny in recent years.	The school curriculum has come under scrutiny in recent years.
4c. By doing so, the teacher may enhance the necessary readiness for students.	By doing so, the teacher may enhance readiness for students.
4d. They represent several big companies from among the giants of corporate America.	They represent several companies from among the giants of corporate America.
4e. By comparison, the British faced more severe conditions than the French.	The British faced more severe conditions than the French.

Original

4f. R

Three hypotheses will be examined within this study.

1. There is some relationship between academic performance and personal tempo.
2. There is some relationship between personal tempo and temperament traits.
3. There is some relationship between temperament traits and academic performance.

Revision

Within this study I will examine hypotheses of relationships between

1. academic performance and personal tempo.
2. personal tempo and temperament traits.
3. temperament traits and academic performance.

The extra words underlined in **4a–e** duplicate information either written or implied elsewhere in the statement. The redundancy in **4f**, on the other hand, is a matter of word-for-word repetition. Whenever you introduce a list of items with a stem, be sure the stem includes whatever information is common to all the items in the list. You will irritate readers if you ask them to read the same words over and over. More important, reading those repeated words distracts readers from the unique information contained in each item **{9}**. (See Chapter 1, Example 10 for other forms of list writing) **{22}**.

4f Bonus Tidbit

Notice also the conversion from passive voice to active **{14}**.

Example 5: Excessive Prepositional Phrases

A sentence dominated by prepositions (in, on, of) is nearly always longer than it needs to be.

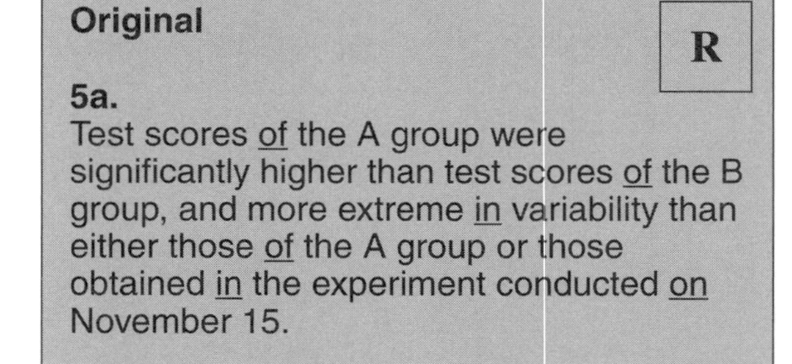
Original R

5a.

Test scores of the A group were significantly higher than test scores of the B group, and more extreme in variability than either those of the A group or those obtained in the experiment conducted on November 15.

Revision

A-group test scores were significantly higher than B-group test scores, and more variable than either B-group scores or scores obtained November 15.

Think of multiple prepositions as warning flags that say "write more compactly." The most common solution is to change prepositional phrases to adjectives, e.g., change test scores of the A group to A-group test scores.

In the final example of this section, **5b**, you will see that bloated writing is usually bloated for more than one reason. In a stage-by-stage revision, I eliminate excessive prepositional phrases first, then move to other issues. Key words are underlined in the original and in the first two stages of the revision; comments below the original, in the left column, reveal my thinking as I revise. If you find this helpful, be sure to make use of Chapter 6 after you have read the first five chapters: each example there involves multiple revisions, with explanations.

Original

5b.
The tones in the phrases in the tonal test are performed in beats of equal length, and the notes in the phrases in the rhythm test are performed on one pitch.

Comments: First-Stage Revision

Strings of prepositional phrases signal bloated writing; seven can be reduced to four by wise use of adjectives. Also, performed is extraneous—even distracting.

Comments: Second-Stage Revision

There are two unnecessary uses of the.

Comments: Third-Stage Revision

And can be eliminated by use of a semicolon, a good technique for streamlining a pair of independent clauses as closely related as these.

Revision

(First Stage)

The tones in the tonal test phrases are uniform in length, and the notes in the rhythm test phrases are uniform in pitch.

(Second Stage)

Tones in the tonal test phrases are uniform in length, and notes in the rhythm test phrases are uniform in pitch.

(Third Stage)

Tones in the tonal test phrases are uniform in length; notes in the rhythm test phrases are uniform in pitch.

Read the third-stage revision, then reread the original. That will give you a feeling for the refreshing brevity you can achieve by investing time and thought in revision.

A Final Thought About Wordy Writing

Never hesitate to jettison any amount of material—regardless of how much time you spent writing it or how attached you have become to it—if good judgment later tells you it is not needed. ***Words are to writers as strokes are to golfers: accomplished players use fewest***. Less is more. Each word removed wisely is a triumph. You will be amazed at how much you can improve your writing simply by reducing the number of words you use.

2. Weak Writing

Good writing is strong in two principal dimensions: content and construction. Strong construction will not rescue weak content: an old shoe beautifully packaged is still an old shoe. But assuming content is solid, you owe yourself and your readers a strong, vigorous presentation. The most worthy content in the world has no impact on a reader who has fallen asleep.

In Chapter 1, I presented basic characteristics of sentence construction and paragraph construction that damage clarity and precision. In contrast, the construction problems shown in this section have to do with siphoning energy from writing:

Example 6	Misplaced Modifiers	Example 9	Negative Form
Example 7	Misplaced Emphasis	Example 10	Empty Language
Example 8	Overstatement	Example 11	Passive Structure

Example 6: Misplaced Modifiers

"We can only accomplish all these things through God!" shouted the pastor at the end of his sermon. What he was trying to convey with volume he could have conveyed better with wise word placement. Did he mean only accomplish or only through God? He meant the latter, of course. The pastor lost strength of expression by failing to place only next to that which it rightly modified: "We can accomplish all these things only through God." Misplaced modifiers are common in writing, too, and the lack of an actual voice to compensate with inflection makes them even more damaging. Notice in Examples **6a–h** that every misplaced word (underlined) appears earlier than its optimal placement, seeming to indicate impatience and carelessness. Most readers will infer correct meaning, but the writers lose a chance for maximum impact **{6, 7}**.

Original	Revision
6a. The researcher could only test one class at a time.	The researcher could test only one class at a time.
6b. Students were only allowed to sit after they had recited accurately.	Students were allowed to sit only after they had recited accurately.
6c. That could only be accomplished in a recording studio.	That could be accomplished only in a recording studio.

Each statement carries an important qualification: only one class at a time; only after they had recited accurately; only in a recording studio. The writers removed these direct statements of qualification by pulling the trigger early on the modifier only. They risked misinterpretation and they guaranteed weakness. Look for intended qualifications in Examples **6d–f**, then read the revisions.

Original	Revision
6d. Teachers even face a great challenge if they like children.	Teachers face a great challenge even if they like children.
6e. Music aptitude bears similar characteristics to intelligence.	Music aptitude bears characteristics similar to intelligence.
6f. Arnold Bentley specifically designed a measure of abilities for use with children seven to fourteen years of age.	Arnold Bentley designed a measure of abilities specifically for use with children seven to fourteen years of age.

Example 7: Misplaced Emphasis

You may say precisely what you intend to say in writing, yet weaken your statement by failing to emphasize what you consider to be the point of emphasis. Relegate secondary material to subordinate positions within your sentences, and place primary material in a position of strength—the end, or perhaps the beginning.

Original	Revision
7a. Most important, you will need strong math skills to take on such a job as that.	Most important, to take on such a job as that you will need strong math skills.
7b. There are one hundred and eight movement forms in T'ai/Chi, but for this study the first seven forms will be used.	In this study I will use the first seven of the 108 T'ai/Chi movement forms.
7c. A descending scale begins in measure 154, signaling the close of the work.	Beginning in measure 154, a descending scale signals the close of the work.

In **7a**, strong math skills—being the point of the sentence—is a much stronger sentence-ender than such a job as that. Notice in **7b** and **c** how deceiving the opening statements are. The point of **7b** appears at first to be the number of movement forms in T'ai/Chi, and the point of **7c** to be that the descending scale is located in measure 154. In the revisions, those pieces of information are place in appropriately subordinate positions.

Example 8: Overstatement

Overstatement weakens writing by putting the credibility of the writer in doubt. A simple and common form of overstatement is the use of an adjective to elevate the word following it. Adults working with children, for example, sometimes overuse special until they feel the need to elevate the term to very special, and from there to very, very special. Eventually there is no place to turn for a superlative. I recommend using very and similar elevating qualifiers only when descriptions are clearly inadequate without them **{11}**.

Original	Revision
8a. He was a very warm, personable man.	He was a warm, personable man.
8b. For the next ten to fifteen years, Steiner really contributed little to the intellectual community.	For the next ten to fifteen years, Steiner contributed little to the intellectual community.

Original	Revision
8c. Voter turnout will be extremely crucial to the outcome of the election.	Voter turnout will be crucial to the outcome of the election.

When you are tempted to modify a word with an elevating adjective, let the nature of that word help you decide. In **8a**, warm and personable say enough to make very sound like overstatement, and in **8b** and **c**, what more could be needed beyond the words contributed and crucial? Very might legitimately modify such words as cold or difficult—but even then, only if circumstances absolutely warrant **{11}**.

Most damaging are elevating adjectives that modify dichotomous variables:

Original	Revision
8d. His findings are very compatible with Hanson's theory.	His findings are compatible with Hanson's theory.
8e. Sparta was a very typical settlement of Greece.	Sparta was a typical Greek settlement.
8f. The method is very unique.	The method is unique.

A thing is either compatible or incompatible; typical or atypical; unique or common. A writer who tries to impose degrees on such terms loses credibility with intelligent readers.

8e Bonus Tidbit

In addition to the issue of overstatement, this is a prime example of removing a prepositional phrase (of Greece) by replacing it with an adjective (Greek).

Still other types of overstatement are born of overenthusiasm mixed with poor judgment:

Original	Revision
8g. The other group believes that personal tempo has no physiological basis.	The other group believes that personal tempo is primarily nonphysiological.
8h. By omitting improvisation, music educators have weakened music programs.	By slighting improvisation, music educators have weakened music programs.
8i. The greatest contributors to objective thought and philosophy were René Descartes and Immanuel Kant.	Kaufman (1995) [fictitious] considers René Descartes and Immanuel Kant two of Western culture's greatest contributors to objective thought and philosophy.

Think of absolute statements like no basis (**8g**), omitting improvisation (**8h**), and the greatest (**8i**) as red flags that might signal an overstatement **{11}**.

8i Bonus Tidbit

When you find authorities to support claims you are unqualified to make (an academic obligation) **{24}**, you are likely to notice that persons who know most about a particular topic tend not to write dogma. Perhaps accomplishment breeds security and security breeds restraint.

In general, clear communication leans heavily on strong, direct language. Still, qualifiers like primarily, in part, generally, typically, and so forth have a legitimate place in writing: they allow a writer to avoid unsupportable overstatements. As an extreme example, the next statement sounds like a declaration of war.

Original	Revision
8j. Objectivist aesthetics is a trend rejected by art educators, who do not have the facility to approach art in an objective, accountable manner.	Objectivist aesthetics, a trend toward setting standards for art, is generally difficult for art educators to embrace.

Objectivist aesthetics—or any idea—can be promoted in a way that casts the writer as thoughtful and helpful rather than arrogant and condescending. Remember this as you write: ***Rational argument attracts intelligent readers; unsupported dogma repels them*** **{11}**.

Example 9: Negative Form

To imply what *is* by stating what is *not* is to burden readers with the job of turning inside-out phrases around. Your writing will be stronger in most cases if you give the reader direct access to your thinking **{15}**.

Original	Revision
9a. My approach as a teacher is to be open enough that parents and other teachers do not feel that I am inaccessible.	My approach as a teacher is to be open enough that parents and other teachers consider me accessible.
9b. The committee gave Ralston every chance to influence the proceedings, but he did not have very much to offer.	The committee gave Ralston every chance to influence the proceedings, but he had little to offer.
9c. Teachers were instructed not to use open questions frequently and to not have a slow pace.	Teachers were instructed to use open questions infrequently and to avoid a slow pace.

Negative statements are not always undesirable. As a writer, you will need to judge whether negative form weakens a statement, as in **9a**, **b**, and **c**, or whether it has some value in a particular circumstance.

Original	Revision
9d. Ignorance and indifference will not further the education and life experiences of our students.	Ignorance and indifference can only erode the education and life experiences of our students.
9e. In the end, the student will not be musical, will not be happy, and will not be inclined to continue studying.	In the end, the student will be unmusical, unhappy, and disinclined to continue studying.

Probably the revision of **9d** to positive form is an improvement, but the original might be preferred, depending on the writer's aim. In example **9e**, the negative form is likely to constitute a stronger statement than the revised, positive form. These kinds of demands on a writer's judgment make writing a fascinating art form rather than a simple, prescriptive, mundane task.

Example 10: Empty Language

A direct and common way to weaken writing is to write words that tell the reader little or nothing. This insightful headline preceded the running of the 1994 Kentucky Derby: "At Derby's end, only one shall stake claim to fame." Translation: at the end of the race, one horse will have finished ahead of the others. That is not exactly a news flash. Flowery language does not turn nothing into something **{7}**.

Original	Revision
10a. Changing demographics in rural communities result in different kinds of social realities.	Changes in rural demographics lead to changes in rural social structure.
10b. The keyboard and its literature were associated with the growth of the nation in a variety of ways.	Keyboard instruments and keyboard literature were important to the nation's social and cultural growth during the nineteenth century.
10c. Movement serves definite purposes according to Laban.	(Omit)

Some empty statements (**10c**) are purely banal: "Movement serves definite purposes according to Laban." And gravity serves definite purposes according to Newton! You and I and a few billion other persons know, without being told, that fundamental elements of life serve definite purposes. To state the obvious is to say nothing **{7}**!

Example 11: Passive Structure

Passive structure has a function. Depending on the writer's intended emphasis, "The best speech of the night was delivered by a newcomer" may be preferable to "A newcomer delivered the best speech of the night." Generally, though, active-structure writing feels strong because the subject acts, and passive-structure writing feels weak because the subject is acted upon **{14}**.

Passive	**Active**
The studying the students did was done after they had procrastinated, and then was not done effectively.	The students procrastinated, then studied ineffectively.

The terms "active voice" and "passive voice" reflect the reality that readers assimilate written language as covert sound, i.e., they "hear" through their eyes (more on the sound of writing in the next section). Writing dominated by active voice carries the reader along because it sounds alive and vibrant; writing dominated by passive voice becomes a kind of drone on paper.

Original	**Revision**
11a. Permission to enter the school was obtained by the researcher.	The researcher obtained permission to enter the school.
11b. Music educators generally agree that the skill to hear discriminately should be taught, but there is disagreement about how that skill is best developed in students.	Music educators generally agree that they should teach students to hear discriminately, but they disagree about how to accomplish it.
11c. The ability to focus attention on a single task should be emphasized in learning settings.	Teachers should emphasize to students that they need to focus attention on a single task.

Notice that passive voice generates prepositional phrases and nominalizations. A nominalization is a noun-form used in place of a verb-form, as in **11b**: there is disagreement in place of they disagree **{12}**.[5] Sometimes, as in **11c**, passivity leaves the reader the task of identifying the actor by inference. Readers resent, rightfully so, having to do the writer's job **{6}**.

In its most destructive form, passive writing leaves meaning in doubt; in a less destructive form, it forces readers to work for information the writer should have provided directly; in its least destructive form, it still robs the reader of what might have been a dynamic reading experience. You will read more examples of passive writing in the next chapter, because passivity is a byproduct of bureaucratic writing.

---

[5] For more about nominalizations, see Writing Principles Described, No. 12. See also, in Appendix B, Part 1, A Few Other Terms You Will Encounter in This Book.

3. Ungainly Writing

The perception of writing as sound extends beyond issues of active and passive voice. In writing about style, E. B. White praised F. Scott Fitzgerald for "the sound his words make on paper" (Strunk and White, 1979, p. 66). Good writing does make good sounds. It flows comfortably, gracefully. It engages readers and compels them to read. Each writer makes unique sounds— and needs to make unique sounds to establish an individual style—but still, there are two generic threats to the sound anyone's writing makes on paper.

Example 12	Disruptive Speech Sounds
Example 13	Ungraceful Rhythm

To appreciate fully the differences between originals and revisions for each example, ***read them aloud*** **{19}**.

<u>Example 12</u>: Disruptive Speech Sounds

Some word combinations draw attention to themselves, thereby stealing attention from content. In parentheses above the original statements in Example **12** you will see labels for the types of disruptive speech sounds exemplified: repetition of first sounds (Alliteration); repetition of syllables or words (Monotony); distracting proximity between words that rhyme (Rhyming).

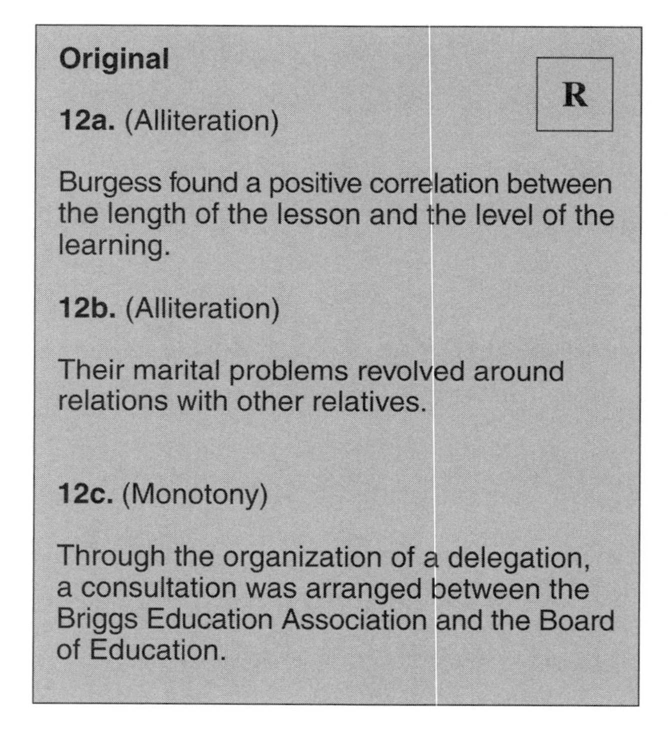

Original

R

12a. (Alliteration)

Burgess found a positive correlation between the length of the lesson and the level of the learning.

12b. (Alliteration)

Their marital problems revolved around relations with other relatives.

12c. (Monotony)

Through the organization of a delegation, a consultation was arranged between the Briggs Education Association and the Board of Education.

Revision

Burgess found a positive correlation between class length and achievement.

Their marital problems stemmed from relations with members of the extended family.

The Briggs Education Association sent delegates to consult with the Board of Education.

Original	**Revision**
12d. (Monotony)	
. . . The results are ostentatious, but the effort is impressive. I should not leave the impression that I think everyone is clamoring to impress.	. . . The results are ostentatious, but the effort is laudable. I should not leave the impression that I think everyone is clamoring to be noticed.

Monotony is usually a byproduct of other problems. In **12c**, the repeated tion sound is built on passive language and nominalizations. In **12d,** the writer unwittingly repeated complete words and their derivations (impress) **{19}**.

12d Bonus Tidbit

When you find yourself with a conflict between wanting to avoid word repetition and wanting to use consistent terms, as presented in Chapter 1, consistency is the greater value **{5}**.

Original	**Revision**
12e. (Rhyming)	
Teachers have a great amount to learn, for what they earn.	Teachers salaries are low, considering what they need to learn to do the job.
12f. (Rhyming)	
The official language of the school was Latin; a boy heard speaking French was punished with a day of dry bread or a day spent in bed.	The official language of the school was Latin; a boy heard speaking French was confined to bed for a day or given only dry bread to eat.

You may find yourself laughing, or at least smiling a bit, when you write unintentional rhymes. Just be sure you find them and change them so instructors, editors, and readers are not doing the laughing.

Example 13: Ungraceful Rhythm

In parentheses above the original statements in Example **13** you will see an account of the type of ungraceful rhythm exemplified: a rhythmic lilt or choppiness (Distracting Rhythm) or a droning sameness (Flat Rhythm).

Original	Revision
13a. (Distracting Rhythm: lilting)	
The poor fight to keep what they have, while the rich fight to get even more. The thieves steal all they can get, and care not one bit who they hurt.	While the rich struggle to become richer and the poor try to hold onto what they have, thieves steal indiscriminately from both.
13b. (Distracting Rhythm: lilting)	
Divorce is an event with a ripple effect. The couple is hurt, but they hurt others, too. Children feel rejected when parents are divorced.	The effect of a divorce is felt far beyond the divorcing couple. Their children, especially, are likely to feel rejected.

The lilting effect of **13a** would have an alluring quality if entertainment were the aim ("and the dish ran away with the spoon"), but such a lilt distracts readers when the aim is communication of information. In **13b**, three sentences of similar length and form establish a regular rhythm that can be distracting. Variation in sentence length and sentence construction are subtle but important contributors to readability **{19}**. (For more about the importance of variable sentence length, see Example **13e**, below, and Appendix B, A Closing Note.)

Original	Revision
13c. (Distracting Rhythm: choppy)	
The third session, even, if necessary, could be shortened by fifteen minutes—or at least ten.	If necessary, even the third session could be shortened by ten to fifteen minutes.
13d. (Distracting Rhythm: choppy)	
Testing should start next week, and the best room is in the west wing, but play practice will be in there Monday, Tuesday, and Wednesday, and part of Friday.	Testing should start next week, preferably in the west wing, but play practice will be there every day except Thursday.

Such rhythmically choppy sentences as **13c** and **d** usually come from writing without having thought ahead sufficiently. If you decide while writing a sentence to piece another thought or two into it, chances are good that it will not read smoothly; reread and revise that sentence immediately after writing it **{19}**.

I define rhythmically flat writing as sentences and paragraphs having little variation in emphasis: no highs or lows, no changes of pace. Sameness is the enemy—sameness in phrase and sentence length, sameness in punctuation, sometimes even sameness in type of word choice and number of syllables per word. Overabundant prepositional phrases contribute to flatness. So does passive language. To me, rhythmically flat writing is a lingual desert from which every drop of nourishment must be coaxed.

Original	**Revision**
13e. (Flat Rhythm)	
Lowell Mason was born in Medfield, Mass-chusetts in 1792. He received an education in the common schools there. He had a great love for music, which occupied his spare time. He was largely self taught. He spent years "playing on all manner of instruments that came within his reach."	Lowell Mason, born in Medfield, Mass-achusetts in 1792, was educated in the common schools there. He loved music. Principally self taught, Mason played "on all manner of instruments that came within his reach."
13f. (Flat Rhythm)	
It is generally financial hardship that is at the root of the problem in a case such as Wilson vs. Wilson.	Wilson vs. Wilson is a typical financial-hardship case.

The writer of **13e** amplified the flattening effect of similar-length sentences by beginning all but one sentence with the same word. Notice that the three-word sentence in the middle of the revision offers the reader two bits of help: relief from rhythmic tedium, and a simple, easily-digested thought with which to tie the two longer sentences together **{19}**. The rhythm of **13f** is flattened by wordiness that naturally follows weak noun-verb combinations (it is; that is), **{9, 10}**, and by a deadening pair of unnecessary prepositional phrases (at the root; of the problem) **{9}**.

Try to stay awake for one last example of flat, drab writing, and an extreme example at that:

Original	**Revision**
13g. (Flat Rhythm) We recommend that special attention be paid by the education profession to the theme of leisure that ran through many sessions of this conference. It is essential that education turn seriously to this development to make available to the public the fruits of its research for the formulation of a public and private philosophy for the significant use of time free from work.	We recommend that educators find ways to help the public fill leisure time with meaningful pursuits.

The bureaucratic paragraph in **13g** probably was generated by a committee. It contains all the enemies of rhythmic vitality: lack of variety in sentence length, lack of variety in phrase length, lack of variety in syllables-per-word, unbelievable strings of prepositional phrases, passive language, and wordiness that borders on criminal behavior **{19}**. Know that "formal" writing can be and should be rhythmically interesting. True, fiction writers and poets have greater license for rhythmic variety, but no writer—regardless of genre—is licensed to bore.

A Final Thought About Ungainly Writing

I want to encourage you again to ***read your writing aloud***. You need not make a performance of it: whispering, even mouthing the words, will do. What is important is that you slow your reading to the rate of speech, and that you sense fully the effect of the sound. Though others are unlikely to read your writing this way, you should do it for one simple reason: the gracefulness and the vigor of the sound you hear when you read your writing aloud bears on how efficiently readers will absorb it silently.

CHAPTER 4

THE BUREAUCRATIC STYLE

You saw in Chapter 3 that some styles of writing are less readable than others. The grandest form of unreadability yet devised may be a style known as the bureaucratic style, or *bureaucratese.* Bureaucratese takes its name from the paperwork of bureaucrats, officials who "work by fixed routine without exercising intelligent judgment" (Webster, 1997, p. 198). Bureaucrats have a reputation for using imprecise, contrived language to sound high-minded while avoiding specifics that might lead to accountability. Once associated with government agencies, bureaucratese is now a verbal smokescreen used by all manner of people wanting to appear to say more than they have. Before proceeding to details, let me show you briefly what I think bureaucratese is and is not.

The hallmark of any writing style is the effect it has on readers. A good formal writing style eases comprehension, and at the same time elevates thinking. Read this simple introductory phrase from a well-written document: The United States Declaration of Independence.

> We hold these truths to be self-evident:

The phrase is easy to read and understand, and it fires the mind to read on. Two centuries later, national leaders writing in the language of government might frame the thought like this:

> The self-evidence of the following has been deemed, through the input of all parties whose signatures are attached, to be viable, and therefore to warrant the pursuance of ongoing institutionalization of said values:

If the style sounds unfamiliar, you are apparently well insulated from memos, letters, minutes, articles, and most other writing generated by bureaucrats in government, social institutions, and even education. Bureaucratese has infiltrated professional written communication as crabgrass infiltrates dry lawns in summer. Its purveyors routinely use language that is outrageously passive **{14}**, vague **{6, 7, 16, 18}**, bloated **{9}**, bland **{10, 19}**, contrived **{3, 25}**, overwritten **{2}**, pretentious **{11, 17}**, and unclear **{1}**.

How have millions come to embrace a style that flies so blatantly in the face of sensible writing principles? Probably the roots of bureaucratic writing were planted by writers wanting to obfuscate the message (manipulators) and writers wanting to sound official (word-painters).[6] The style has been spread since by writers trying to follow what they consider fashionable (imitators) and by writers trying to avoid the burden of thinking (sloths).

While manipulators, word-painters, imitators, and sloths generate bureaucratese by the truckload every day, writers working from yet a fifth perspective help keep the candle of muddled communication burning: unintentional imitators. They write bureaucratese unconsciously from having been overexposed to the style. You are probably an unintentional imitator of the bureaucratic style—a style now so pervasive that even the most careful person dares not claim to be wholly free of it.[7]

Before proceeding, you need to understand a term I have coined—finding no suitable standard term—to describe what I think of as the primary element of bureaucratic writing: **bucket terms**. A bucket term is a word or group of words that brings multiple potential meanings to a sentence. The reader, metaphorically, has to reach into a bucket and select one of the meanings it carries. There was a time, for example, when people claimed to analyze, examine, adjust, solve, resolve, or arbitrate; now they address or look at. We are told to "deal with the problem," which could mean—to name a few possibilities—resolve the problem through negotiation, acclimate to it, enter into therapy, take tranquilizers, or assassinate an opponent.

Often writers of bucket terms have simply not thought specifically and thoroughly about what they mean to say and how to say it. Bucket terms then replace rigor. The writer's mind hums along on automatic pilot, pulling bucket terms out of storage and inserting them as interchangeable parts into sentences where words of specific meaning would have gone had more thought been applied. The cost is borne by the reader, who is left befogged.

---

[6] Richard Lanham (1991, p. 56) describes the syndrome as the "Official Style." Others use various profession-specific terms: legalese; educationese; academese.

[7] Exactly which terms deserve to be categorized as bureaucratic could be argued; many have become part of the general culture in recent decades. A more important distinction is which terms and uses of terms make written communication clear, precise, and efficient.

The most effective way to describe damage done by bucket terms is to examine effects of individual bucket terms in some detail. That is the function of the first three of this chapter's sections. The primary failing of all the examples within the bucket-term sections of this chapter is lack of specificity **{16}**, which of course keeps the writer from even approaching precision **{18}**. Throughout, I have underlined bucket terms and their specific counterparts to make comparison easier. The sections of the chapter are as follows:

1. Standard Terms Used as Bucket Terms
2. Mutated Terms Used as Bucket Terms
3. Additional Thoughts about Bucket Terms
4. Unusual Word Choice
5. Unusual Word Arrangement

1. Standard Terms Used as Bucket Terms

You have probably used the terms in this section legitimately hundreds of times. They are centuries old. Where you will damage your writing is in using them as general replacements for specific expression. Specific expression requires intense thought about fine differences in meaning among words. Your willingness to think through the options and make those choices creates genuine communication—a link between your thinking and the thinking of the reader—rather than just bathing the reader in words. I have written multiple interpretations into some of the revisions, symptomatic of the damage bucket terms inflict on clarity and precision.

Example 1: Deal with, Dealt with

"I can't deal with that right now." A person who says that is making an appropriate general statement. It tells others that the person is in no position even to think about the subject at hand. In contrast, deal with and dealt with as used in the following examples deprive the reader of insight into the writer's meaning—assuming the writer has arrived at a meaning before writing, which does not always happen. My revisions may or may not coincide with the writers' intended messages.

Original	**Revision**
1a. Classroom teachers need to deal with discipline.	Classroom teachers need to • establish order and control. • punish disruptive students.
1b. Some researchers deal well with statistics.	Some researchers • are facile with statistical manipulation. • present statistical data clearly.
1c. The aide dealt with group disagreements more efficiently than did the teacher.	The aide resolved group disagreements more efficiently than did the teacher.
1d. After adopting a more relaxed attitude, the manager of the computer laboratory found it easier to deal with outsiders.	After adopting a more relaxed attitude, the manager of the computer laboratory found it easier to • listen to outsiders. • tolerate outsiders. • take advice from outsiders. • ignore outsiders.

Writers sometimes try to imbue the bucket term deal with with an aura of specificity by inserting adverbs into the middle of it, as in **1b**. Sightings of more extreme versions have been reported: "He dealt quickly, confidently, and appropriately with the problem." Each intervening adverb gives the reader more information about *how* the person did whatever was done, but leaves what was done, in specific terms, shrouded in mystery.

Example 2: Concern, Concerned with

Concern, having taken on multiple connotations, has become a popular word (along with concerned and concerning) among writers who want to avoid specific meaning.

Original	Revision
2a. Look at the excerpts with a concern for the nature of the samples.	Look at the excerpts with attention to the nature of the samples.
2b. A one-way ANOVA permits the researcher to make a single inferential statement concerning the means of the population.	A one-way ANOVA permits the researcher to make a single inferential statement about the means of the population.
2c. I have been concerned with the teaching of French for ten years.	I have been associated with the teaching of French for ten years. I have sensed a decline in the teaching of French for ten years.
2d. When you come to the meeting, bring your concerns.	When you come to the meeting, bring your • suggestions. • complaints. • worries.
2e. During ages three to six, a child is concerned with manipulating the world through action.	During ages three to six, a child • is preoccupied with manipulating the world through action. • is interested most in manipulating the world through action. • is highly motivated to manipulate the world through action. • tries constantly to manipulate the world through action.

Bucket-term writing is clearly shallow-thought writing. A writer who had thought deeply and specifically enough to construct any of the options shown in the **2e** revision, for example, would not have settled for the mealy is concerned with.

Example 3: Address (as a verb)

I found this sentence in a recent newspaper article about problems of sexual abuse among priests:

> In its report, "Restoring Trust: A Pastoral Response to Sexual Abuse," the bishops' committee said most dioceses had addressed the issue.

Like so many other institutions, the church has bred its share of bureaucrats—masters at the art of *appearing* to say something. Persons needing to answer difficult questions that call for action, especially when working as committees, commonly dip into the bureaucratic bucket and pull out "address the issue." Any time you are tempted to lean on that vague phrase, think a little more deeply until you discover in specific terms what you mean to say.

Original	Revision
3a. Try to discover teaching strategies that address the issue of different learning styles.	Try to discover teaching strategies that accommodate differences in learning style among students.
3b. School boards need to address the issue of teacher strikes.	School boards need to • avoid teacher strikes through more effective negotiation. • lobby the legislature for protection against teacher strikes. • hold a tough line against striking teachers.

The chasm between the **3a** original and its revision is greater than a comparison of general with specific; it is more a comparison of noninformation with information. The writer of **3b** might be excused as having not yet thought specifically about the problem; on the other hand, should we not expect a person who puts words on paper to have thought first—to have brought to mind information, ideas, or questions? A statement that says little more than "do something" seems hardly worth taking time to write.

My claim is not that all your writing must be specific, but that you should write general statements sparingly—and only for preconceived general purposes, not for want of more thorough thinking. If a reader's reaction to "address the issue" in your writing is likely to be immediate curiosity about how, precisely, you think the issue should be addressed, you have probably used the term as a bucket term.

Example 4: Look at, Look to, Speak to

What does it mean to you to look at something? I think of looking at paintings, sunrises, children at play. Looking can be casual or it can be contemplative, but the verb look does not imply actions or solutions or descriptive analysis.

Political uses of looking at seem to stem from the same motivation as political uses of addressing: lack of commitment to investigating or working at a problem, much less solving it.

> The school board will look at the problem of student transportation at its next meeting.
>
> The first thing this administration needs to do is look at the welfare system.

Many uses of look at come from mindlessness. This newspaper headline gave me pause for thought:

> Twenty Years Later, a Book that Looks at Women as they Age.

After dismissing the problem of a book having no eyes, which means it can look at nothing, I began to think how long it would take to look at women as they age. The looker would be aging at the same rate! Nonsense breeds nonsense.

Why do I draw attention to all this? The kind of mindlessness that produced that headline might let you scatter bucket terms throughout your writing, not because you are dull but because the thousands of bucket terms you read and hear have conditioned you to be less than alert to their effect. Here are two other examples.

Original	**Revision**
4a. The procedures looked at in the previous chapter will be elaborated upon here.	The procedures described in the previous chapter will be elaborated upon here.
4b. When looking at circumstances that make a particular child productive in a classroom setting, one might look at that child's home life.	When investigating circumstances that make a particular child productive in a classroom setting, one might examine that child's home life.

Look at is simply too casual, too passive, and too limited in specific meaning to be used in place of describe, investigate, examine, analyze, study, or even observe.

> **4b Bonus Tidbit**
>
> Of course the specific terms in the revision do nothing for the bloated nature of the sentence. A writer conscious of writing concisely would be more likely to write this: "Home life may hold clues to a child's classroom productivity." **{9}**

Even more insidious than look at are the expressions look to and speak to. They seem to be perplexing and noncommittal by design.

Original	**Revision**
4c. The Plant A employees are looking to win next year's production award.	The Plant A employees are • hoping to win next year's production award. • planning to win next year's production award. • expecting to win next year's production award. • confident they can win next year's production award.
4d. The work I have seen speaks to his good will.	The work I have seen is evidence of his good will.

Example 5: Area

Having read the complete news article from which I took this quote, I am still unsure of the meaning of area.

> The thing that I like about Pennsylvania's program is that it made very good use of existing resources within the agencies of state government and focused those resources into particular areas.

If the term area had not been so tainted over time by use as a bucket term in place of subject, topic, issue, category, discipline, and a host of other words, I would know that area as used in the quote refers to Philadelphia, Pittsburgh, and Erie.

> **5 Bonus Tidbit**
>
> Notice two other classic bureaucratic phrases: existing resources and focused those resources. The sentence is typical of statements made daily by persons who have only the faintest working knowledge of specifics behind their bucket terms—persons more intent on giving an impression than on giving information.

In **5a–d** I have placed follow-up sentences in brackets after the bucket-term sentences. Each bracketed follow-up sentence demonstrates that its corresponding original might have been interpreted differently from the meaning shown in the right column.

Original	Revision
5a. That is an area I know little about. [I have never had a chance to go there.]	That is a subject I know little about.
5b. You should choose an area for discussion. [You may prefer the parlor to a classroom.]	You should choose a topic for discussion.
5c. That depends on what area you put it in. [Is it in the office or the storage room?]	That depends on how you categorize it.
5d. He knows his area well. [He has lived there all his life.]	He knows his discipline well.

The term <u>area</u> does have a legitimate secondary meaning, but if we were to limit its use to the primary meaning—description of a physical parameter—no one would again have to read a statement such as the following and then guess who respects Professor Swanson: child psychologists or residents of California.

> Professor Swanson, a child psychologist from the West Coast, is well respected in his area.

Context will often bail your readers out when you use such terms as <u>area</u> vaguely, but why put readers to the test? Why risk their misunderstanding, or even pausing, when you can nail meaning to the wall instantly by using a specific term **{16}**?

<u>Example 6</u>: Other Standard Terms Used as Buckets

<u>Deal with</u>, <u>concerned with</u>, <u>address</u>, <u>look at</u>, and <u>area</u> are only a few long-standing terms converted to bucket terms in recent decades by bureaucrats and their imitators. This chapter would become a book if I were to pursue the others in detail. Literature is rife with proclamations about <u>meeting needs</u> and <u>providing services</u>, with the specific needs and services left unknown to the reader (and sometimes, I am convinced, to the writer). You will read about children <u>at risk</u>, for example, but you may have to decide whether the problem is lack of vaccine, a learning disability, or danger of sexual molestation.

Original	Revision
6a. An easily distracted child may be <u>placed at risk</u> in the classroom.	An easily distracted child may be <u>at an academic disadvantage</u> in the classroom.

Before proceeding to a subcategory of bucket terms, I would like to present one more student-written example that shows the extent to which bucket terms have invaded student writing.

Original	**Revision**
6b. The problem of the study addressed the issues of the socioeconomic climate of successful, experienced band conductors, the elements of instrumental performance with which they are concerned, and the behaviors that band conductors employ in attempting to resolve these concerns.	The problem of the study was to analyze the work of successful, experienced band conductors working with students from impoverished communities, with specific interest in 1) the elements of performance they consider important, and 2) the methods they use to encourage students to achieve.

Any number of meanings might be hidden behind the clump of bureaucratic language in **6b**. Addressed the issues is classic. Socioeconomic climate is so general as to suggest that a range of such climates was studied. (It was not.) Sentence construction implies that the topic was the socioeconomic status of conductors—Do successful band conductors tend to be wealthy or poor? (That was not the topic.) Concerned could mean troubled, or simply involved; resolve these concerns implies that it meant troubled. (It did not.) Behaviors that band conductors employ sounds like the study entails teacher personality reconstruction more than teaching methods. (It does not.)

I might have labeled my revision of **6b** *translation,* because the original is written in a different language—a language of vagueness compounded by vagueness, forcing the reader to construct, without benefit of facts, the message the writer is supposed to have written. Sadly, this kind of writing is not rare.

6b Bonus Tidbit

Replacing The problem of the study addressed with The problem of the study was removes distracting personification, a problem described in Chapter 1, Part 8.

2. Mutated Terms Used as Bucket Terms

A family of word mutants has sprung forth recently like mushrooms after a rain, and found a cozy home in our reservoir of bucket terms. Language tamperers, with a gift for creativity if not aesthetics, have glued pairs of words together in reverse order to produce one-word mutations ugly to see, uglier to hear, and hazy in meaning. The new mutants have been embraced quickly. I think in most cases their appeal is not that they help us communicate, but that they help us skirt our responsibility to communicate—and hence our responsibility to acquire and use a rich vocabulary. Perhaps more to the point, they help us avoid our responsibility to think.

Many examples shown here are more common to speech than to writing, but written use is becoming uncomfortably common. By pointing out how overused these words have become and how much communication power we are losing to them, I hope to dissuade you from joining the trend.

Example 7: Input

A prime example of a mutant bucket term is "input." As a short term for data written onto a computer disk, the term is useful. (Computer development has spawned several useful compound words that would have sounded odd a generation ago: download, upload, undelete.) Unfortunately, unknown persons at some point decided that any act of "putting in" produces something called "input." Revisions of **7a–h** each present one of several possible meanings.

Original	Revision
7a. We want to hear your input.	We want to hear your opinion.
7b. We need your input.	We need your ideas.
7c. I am waiting for input from our lawyer.	I am waiting for information from our lawyer.
7d. Your input on the project will be appreciated.	Your assistance on the project will be appreciated.
7e. We value the input you have to offer.	We value the knowledge you have to offer.
7f. I sent the document, and I'm waiting for his input.	I sent the document, and I'm waiting for his reaction.
7g. I offered a lot of input to the meeting.	I contributed substantially to the meeting.
7h. We're asking for your input	We're asking for your advice.

The rule of the game seems simple: when the mind fails to produce instantly a word that describes some service given from one person to another, just insert input (or should I say input input?). Like other bucket terms, input encourages us to decrease our vocabularies. One who appreciates a rich vocabulary and precise word use shudders even at this partial list of terms used less often because of the all-purpose input: opinion, ideas, information, assistance, knowledge, reaction, contribution, and advice. These terms are not expendable where genuine communication is valued.

Even more curious than input used as a noun is input used as a verb. Only by ceasing entirely to think about relationships among words can a person replace "I put the information in," with "I input the information." I have even heard "I input the information in."

Example 8: Update

The world no longer has current information—only updates. Reports have also disappeared; persons who once issued reports now work exclusively with updates. We even have publications titled *Update*. Update has moments of usefulness as a colloquialism, and one might make a case for "updating" material that has just lost its timeliness to recent occurrences. In the transmission of specific information, however, update can be as imprecise as input.

Original	Revision
8a. George sent an update of last week's meeting.	George sent a report of last week's meeting.
8b. I updated Kathleen on yesterday's changes.	I told Kathleen of yesterday's changes.
8c. Update me on what you have been doing.	Tell me what you have been doing.
8d. Give me a quick update of your trip.	Give me a quick overview of your trip.

Language changes constantly. We need to promote changes that improve, tolerate changes that maintain, and resist changes that destroy. Changes destroy when they cause us to sacrifice clear, precise meaning.

Example 9: Ongoing

To say that a thing is "going on" rather than simply "going" or "occurring" is a colloquial convention akin to asking "where is it at?" rather than "where is it?" By attaching the superfluous, grammatically meaningless "on" to the front of "going," we create a curious word mutant applicable to whatever is not about to stop; that is, whatever is expected to keep going (on?).

Original	Revision
9a. Between Cleveland and Toledo, drivers will encounter ongoing road construction.	Between Cleveland and Toledo, drivers will encounter road construction.
9b. This will be an ongoing project.	This will be a long-term project.
9c. His behavior has been an ongoing problem.	His behavior has been a continual problem.
9d. The traffic noise is ongoing.	The traffic noise is continuous.
9e. This discussion will be ongoing through several meetings.	This discussion will continue through several meetings.
9f. The effects of our decision will be ongoing.	The effects of our decision will be far-reaching.
9g. I think we've gotten into an ongoing issue.	I think we've gotten into an open-ended issue.
9h. Schools are fighting an ongoing battle for funding.	Schools are fighting a constant battle for funding.
9i. I conduct business with him on an ongoing basis	I conduct business with him regularly.

Sometimes ongoing is meaningless filler (**9a**), but usually it replaces a specific term (**9b–i**). So in ongoing we have another vocabulary eater. Persons enamored with such vocabulary-eating words seem willing to sacrifice astounding quantities of meaning and clarity: one writer recently eliminated the word continuity by invoking ongoingness.

I have enough input left to ongo through several more sentences, but I will save them for an updated edition. It is time now to move to upcoming material.

Example 10: Upcoming

What a strange word, upcoming. The "up" appears to be a superfluous analog to "on" in "ongoing." Read the originals below and ask yourself what would be lost by removing "up."

Original	Revision
10a. The upcoming tests will be administered Monday at noon.	The tests will be administered Monday at noon.
10b. We are waiting for upcoming details.	We are waiting for details.
10c. Upcoming Events are listed on the back of the program.	University Recitals are listed on the back of the program.

In **10a** and **b**, removal of "up" exposes the nonsensical nature of the entire adjective: in each case, "coming" sounds extraneous. In **10c**, coming events or events to come would mean the same as upcoming events. Or maybe events alone would be adequate, because no one advertises past events, but that exposes events as a bland, vague noun. Might we consider replacing Upcoming Events with a specific term like University Recitals or Community Lectures? Horrors! To actually say what a thing is would sound downright old-fashioned!

For more insight into the nature of upcoming, imagine picking up a page on which a series of university recitals is listed. Whether the title was Upcoming Events or University Recitals, you would first scan the column of dates and times to distinguish recitals past from recitals yet to come. Those dates and times are your true source of information about whether a recital is "upcoming." The only function of the term upcoming is to create a feeling of expectation. The term has nothing to do with the transmission of information. The titillating quality of upcoming makes it useful to public relations personnel and advertising copywriters, whose principal goal is to affect rather than to inform, but that same quality disqualifies it as a legitimate word by which to transmit information in formal writing.

3. Additional Thoughts About Bucket Terms

Bucket terms are not to be avoided in all circumstances. Fiction writers use bucket terms to create suspense and to make dialogue realistic. Some politicians, bureaucrats, and advertisers use bucket terms intentionally to obfuscate. (Whether that practice should be considered unethical manipulation or business-as-usual will have to be debated elsewhere.) My point is that bucket terms damage research reports, or any formal writing intended to communicate ideas and information clearly.

You will need to be vigilant to avoid bucket terms. Just as "you are what you eat" in a physical sense, "you are what you read and hear" in an intellectual sense. Your memory stores bucket terms by the hundreds; some will jump from memory to page without your realizing it. To defend yourself against their deleterious effects, you need to do three things:

1. Improve your vocabulary continually so the reservoir of words from which you choose is large and varied (two sources within this book are Chapter 2 and Appendix C).
2. Compare key words in your sentences—for meaning, connotation, and sound—with other words you might have used.
3. Know that some bucket terms will slip past you in writing the first draft; find them and replace them with specific language when you revise.

Finally, I should make note of the big-picture effect of bucket terms on readers—besides blunting precision, sentence by sentence. Specific information, delivered by use of a rich vocabulary of words in unique combinations, captures and holds readers' attention. By contrast, the repetitive beeping of bucket terms makes a piece of writing seem less important to readers—less urgent because of its vaguely familiar sound. Bucket terms steal uniqueness from your writing, and with it, the full attention of the reader.

4. Unusual Word Choice

Bureaucratic language has a pretentious ring, seeming to have been written more for effect than for its message. I saw this fascinating sign at a motel desk:

We gladly provide
assistive devices
on request

I should give the writer credit for at least knowing the sign was unreadable; next to the sign was a picture of an ear, helping readers to equate "assistive device" with "hearing aid" **{17, 18}**. If the writer of that sign was reacting to demands, real or imagined, for political correctness, I think the effort was misguided. Neither political correctness nor any other agenda should impose, as a price of compliance, ambiguity and deception.

Verbs seem to be the principal instrument of pretension in the practice of bureaucratese:

Calvin and Hobbes **by Bill Watterson**

"Verbing" language, as in Calvin and Hobbes, has become fashionable. Never mind that the absence of verbs as verbs drains energy from writing: the object is not to invigorate, but to impress. As bureaucratese evolves and dictionary writers acquiesce, long-standing nouns are gradually being converted to verb functions. You have already read some examples while reading about bucket terms, e.g., address. Here are a few others.

Example 11: Nouns as Verbs

Original	Revision
11a. The cutbacks will not impact the curriculum adversely.	The cutbacks will not affect the curriculum adversely.
11b. We need to dialogue about our differences as soon as possible.	We need to talk about our differences as soon as possible.
11c. You may experience delays of 15 to 20 minutes.	You may be delayed 15 to 20 minutes.
11d. Last week's letter evidenced his willingness to cooperate.	With last week's letter, he showed his willingness to cooperate.
11e. We transitioned from an interview mode to a dialogue mode.	What had been an interview became a dialogue.
11f. The new teaching method is expected to result in higher test scores for students.	The new teaching method is expected to raise student test scores. We expect to raise student test scores by using the new teaching method.

11f Bonus Tidbit

A subtle effect of result as a verb is that it changes the reader's point of view. When X, the reader's starting point, is said to produce or lead to or raise Y, the reader sees X carrying the action to Y. In contrast, result used as a verb forces the reader to shift from an image of X moving toward Y to a new image of Y taking the action (result) from X.

The "value" of impact, dialogue, experience, evidence, transition, and result as verbs seems to be simply the "sound they make on the page." To show how detached language can become from reality, this is the public announcement from which I paraphrased **11c**: "Trains may experience delays of 15 to 20 minutes." Do you know of any trains—other than in children's picture books—that have "experiences"? If you do use experience as a verb (I recommend against it), do not apply it to something so mundane as a delay. Apply it to a genuine experience: "Through meditation, I experienced total relaxation for the first time in my adult life."

Another contrived-sounding noun-turned-verb, implement, doubles as a bucket term, but I present it in this section because its pretentious sound seems more attractive than its capacity for interchangeable use. Who would want to simply do or use something when instead they might implement it?

Original	**Revision**
11g. The teacher tried to implement what he had learned in the workshop.	The teacher tried to apply what he had learned in the workshop.
11h. The principal's next challenge would be to implement the curriculum changes adopted by the board.	The principal's next challenge would be to install the curriculum changes adopted by the board.
11i. The researcher was curious to see what would happen when she implemented the theory in the classroom.	The researcher was curious to see what would happen when she tested the theory in the classroom.
11j. The teacher found the techniques shown at the conference impressive, but difficult to implement.	The teacher found the techniques shown at the conference impressive, but 1. difficult to use without practice. 2. difficult to use with large numbers of students. 3. impractical.

Notice that implement bleeds life from sentences as compared with more verb-like verbs. Notice also that its interchangeability with other words makes it another vocabulary eater. These are common penalties to pay for "verbing" language

In Appendix C you will find two lists of active verbs. I have excluded obscure verbs (adumbrate; lucubrate; peregrinate) because they are generally not useful; I have excluded common verbs (go; see; make) because you will bring them to mind easily without help. The function of this appendix of mid-range verbs (abandon; enhance; sprawl) is to help you invigorate your writing by opening your mind to verbs that may not be on the tip of your tongue. Scan the lists periodically, maybe just a column or two at a time. The subliminal presence of those verbs in your mind may help you resist the lure of fashionably staid nouns-turned-verb.

Words fashionable for their sound are too great in number for me to do more than scratch the surface here. My purpose is not to spew forth a long collection of such words, but rather to encourage you to be vigilant about language—to have your eyes and ears open to the beating it takes. Do not simply follow the crowd. ***Think for yourself, and keep logic, word meaning, clarity, and precision as your guides.*** We are entangled in bureaucratic language today only because tens of thousands of persons have been willing—in many cases eager—to tailor their language more to making an impression than to communicating effectively.

Example 12: Fashionable Suffixes

Another observation I should make about pretentious sounds in writing is that writers sometimes gravitate to fashionable-sounding suffixes: ize and ly are two of the more popular forms. There is something official sounding, for example, about finalize and utilize as compared with finish and use. The ize sound has become a siren's song that led one student to write recently, "It acts as a concretized image of man." Of all the ize words, utilize may be the most seductive. Apparently having grown out of pretension, now the word is used widely as a substitute for "use."

Original	Revision
12a. Computers are now utilized in most human endeavors.	Computers are now used in most human endeavors.
12b. To utilize your strengths to your advantage is wise.	To use your strengths to your advantage is wise.
12c. I was thankful for the utilization of his knowledge.	I was thankful for the use of his knowledge. I was thankful to have his knowledge available to me.

Simply put, to utilize something is to use it. If predecessors in your profession have canonized utilize—given official meaning to its meaninglessness—you may be stuck with the term in that setting. Hospital administrators probably have to accept utilization review, and economists probably have to talk and write about capacity utilization: that is the price to be paid for efficient communication with colleagues after language has already run amok. In all other circumstances, do readers a favor: use use. If the twentieth-century American trend away from sensible word meanings continues full steam into the twenty-first century, it may be just a matter of time until someone replaces useful with utilizational **{17}**!

Another bureaucratic affectation is the use of ly words, e.g., firstly and importantly.

Original	**Revision**
12d. Most importantly, the evolution of class methods encouraged large numbers of persons to learn.	Most important, the evolution of class methods encouraged large numbers of persons to learn.

If firstly, secondly, and thirdly do not sound awkward to you, extend the sequence to eleventhly and twenty-eighthly, as rules of consistency would have us do. The awkwardness of the practice becomes apparent **{19}**. Aside from awkwardness, the adverbial form is less precise than the adjectival form. Secondly and thirdly answer the question "how?" By contrast, second and third answer the question "in what position?" With rare exception, your purpose in numbering points is to assign them identifiable positions relative to chronology or importance, or maybe as a simple matter of organization **{18}**.

A writer who chooses to use first, second, and third should then, as a matter of consistency, choose the term last over lastly. I would avoid the term lastly altogether. Even though its technical meaning is parallel to the meaning of finally, the term lastly has a contrived, pretentious sound to it. Similarly, I would chose important over importantly, not only to avoid pretension but to express myself more precisely. Does the writer mean that what is being said is important, or does the writer mean it is being said importantly? The former is almost always more accurate. Read Example **12d** again, just to confirm that important is more precise **{18}**.

Here is one final example of what a student writer can produce by aiming for impressive word sounds.

Example 13:

Original	Revision
Indications suggest the viability for movement instruction to have implications for children's rhythm skill.	Movement instruction appears effective as an approach to developing rhythm skill in children.

This is not writing; it is gobbledygook. Attraction to fancy words seems to have induced the writer to throw communication to the wind in favor of seeing indications, viability, and implications in the sentence **{17}**. ***Never use a word just for the sake of using it!*** Writers may be forgiven for complex writing born of complex thoughts, but not for complex writing born of mindlessness and affectation. Let me conclude this section with a simple and clear rule of thumb. ***If two words compete equally in every way but complexity, the simpler of the two is the better choice*** **{17}**. A writer who chooses otherwise apparently would rather impress a few readers than communicate with many.

5. Unusual Word Arrangement

Unusual word arrangement affects sentences in a more subtle way than unusual word choice. A classic rearrangement is to change from the standard subject-verb-adverb to the more pretentious sounding subject-adverb-verb, sometimes creating split infinitives as shown in **14c**. (For more about split infinitives, see Appendix B, Part 1, Parts of Speech: A More Detailed View.) These examples may be similar to sentences you have read.

Example 14:

Original	Revision
14a. Anderson further explains that appreciation of extrinsic factors is enhanced by familiarity with intrinsic factors.	Anderson explains further that appreciation of extrinsic factors is enhanced by familiarity with intrinsic factors.
14b. Components of comprehensive musicianship can be best understood when studied within the context of high-quality literature.	Components of comprehensive musicianship can be understood best when studied within the context of high-quality literature.

Original	Revision
14c. That allows the reader to more efficiently conceptualize them.	That allows the reader to conceptualize them more efficiently.

Each of the cute little perversions of logical word sequence, **14a**, **b**, and **c**, puts an unnecessary hitch in the reading. In **14a**, Anderson further explains implies an awkward question: "Who does how what?" In the revision, Anderson explains further implies a logical question: "Who does what how?" The only feature of the first not offered by the second is its pretentious ring.

Should adverb ever precede verb? Yes, if the reader needs the adverb in advance as a qualifier: "Jason apparently likes you best." How does a writer know which word order to use? A glib answer would be "by the feel and the sound of it." A more specific answer would be to judge by how natural the word order feels and by how easy the sentence is to understand. The writer of the next example became so entangled in word sequence that the sentence needs two or three readings for its meaning to become clear.

Example 15:

Original	Revision
Children more easily sing descending rather than ascending tonal patterns.	Children sing descending tonal patterns more easily than they sing ascending tonal patterns.

What kind of entanglement did the writer of Example **15** create? The adverb phrase more easily precedes the verb sing, and the adjective descending is hooked to another adjective (ascending) while the reader waits to learn that the object is tonal patterns. The superfluous word rather creates an additional puzzle for the reader to manipulate. Such word scrambles as this come to us courtesy of a poor writer's ear for bureaucratic indirectness. Avoid this kind of entanglement by keeping clarity and precision in full view all the time you are writing.

A Closing Note

Ambiguous writing forces readers to create meaning rather than receive it. At best, the writer of bureaucratese relinquishes what could have been a strong position as communicator; at worst, the writer of bureaucratese frustrates and annoys readers until they dismiss the work as a waste of time.

Some people write bureaucratese intentionally, wanting to obfuscate meaning. They need all the tools of the style. They are rascals, and bureaucratese helps rascals paint themselves as something other than rascals—helps them appear to say something while avoiding statements they might have to defend later. If that is your intention, study bureaucratese, use it as you will, and let readers beware. On the other hand, if you write in the bureaucratic style unintentionally, because it has seeped into your thinking as pollutants seep into the water table, you need to think about how much the style poisons your writing.

Let me finish with an unfortunate example of bureaucratese from a national education symposium, heralded in its time as a Herculean effort to assess the profession and make recommendations for reform. In this single recommendation, taken from a long list of recommendations written in similar style, bureaucratic bloat is obvious. No one will ever know whether clear language would have encouraged educators to realize those recommendations more fully.

Example 16:

Original	Revision
We recommend that there be established machinery within the education profession by means of which an ongoing communication is established with all other relevant disciplines and interests. Further, we recommend that such discussion should be built into the agenda of professional meetings, and increasingly, in journal articles.	We recommend that educators communicate regularly with persons from related professions, then share what they learn with colleagues through professional meetings and journal articles.

Notice the confluence of not only bucket terms and pretension, but also nominalizations, passive structures, excessive prepositional phrases, flatness, and wordiness. This style of writing—a style that has made unfortunate inroads in educational establishments, of all places—amounts to a showcase of poor writing practices.

CHAPTER 5

PERSON AND GENDER

As a writer you face two fundamental style decisions before writing anything: 1) Will you write in first person (I, me, my) or third person (the writer, the researcher, he, she, they)?[8] 2) How will you reconcile demands for clear expression with demands for gender inclusiveness when the two conflict?

1. Person in Writing

A convention among writers of theses, dissertations, and research articles has been to refer to oneself in third person:

> The researcher chose subjects from among college seniors attending seven small Northeastern liberal arts schools. After assigning subjects randomly to one of two groups, she assigned group treatments.

The rationale is that readers absorb content more easily without a writer's presence distracting them, as in first-person writing:

> I chose subjects from among college seniors attending seven small Northeastern liberal arts schools. After assigning subjects randomly to one of two groups, I assigned group treatments.

On the other hand, third-person writing can sound awkward, especially when applied to research implications. Notice how the first-person version of the following observation allows the writer to "talk" to the reader, as compared to the somewhat stodgy third-person version.

1st Person	Evidence generated by this study contradicts my observations of children in the classroom over time. I can only surmise that . . .
3rd Person	Evidence generated by this study contradicts this researcher's observations of children in the classroom over time. This researcher can only surmise that . . .

---

[8] Second-person writing (you, yours) is commonly coupled with first-person writing: "I find the test effective; you might try it."

Some researchers think third-person writing is appropriately detached; others think it is artificial, passive **{14}**, and wordy **{9}**. Those who recommend first-person research writing need to realize that it can grow tiresome and boorish when personal pronouns are overused. Notice how distracting the first version of the next passage is as compared with the more judiciously crafted second version, both written in first person.

> I had more subjects than I could test in a single room, so I reserved the all-purpose room. To eliminate cheating, I sat subjects at alternate seats on one side of the tables. Time constraints kept me from using my normal procedure of escorting students myself, so I enlisted assistants from the upper grades to help me.

> Because of the large number of subjects, I used an all-purpose room for testing, with subjects seated in alternate seats on one side of the tables to eliminate cheating. Students from the upper grades saved my time by escorting subjects to the testing room.

Some writers of theses, dissertations, and research articles will want to hold to the tradition of writing in third person. Others may want to experiment with a judicious use of first person. Still others may want to use third person for rationale, purpose, problems, design, and procedures, then shift to first person for the discussion/implications section. Regardless of the point of view you choose, use personal pronouns sparingly to avoid diverting the reader's attention from content.

When you write papers, articles, and books other than formal research reports, you may want to use first person as a matter of course. You would not want me to begin a sentence of this type, for example, with "The reader would not want this writer to begin a sentence of this type . . ." You will decide for each project whether to write in first person or third person, but in some circumstances an instructor, a thesis adviser, or an editor will temper your decision.

2. Gender in Writing

The issue of gender in writing is more complex than the issue of person. Centuries of convention are at odds with contemporary thought. The use of "he" as a pronoun where gender is indefinite (generic masculine pronoun) strikes many as an affront to women, regardless of the writer's intent **{26}**. On the other hand, most new approaches to gender-neutral language damage clarity and style. As writers, we need a system that avoids replacing injustice to women with injustice to readers.

Background

For centuries, feminine pronouns have had one function and masculine pronouns two:

Gender-Specific Feminine Pronoun

Sarah Williams has written extensively on the subject since she first taught the seminar.

Gender-Specific Masculine Pronoun

David Bratkowski is a researcher, but he is at his best as a teacher.

Generic Masculine Pronoun

If a reader skims a science text rather than reading thoroughly, he will miss technical detail needed to score well on exams.

The meaning in the generic example is clear. Why? Because we have been conditioned to the possibility of a generic he, and in this context see no reason to exclude female readers from the consequences of skimming a science text. If she were inserted in place of he, on the other hand, most readers would be disoriented by the apparent exclusion of men, and some might be affronted by what they perceive as innuendo toward women as students of science. Why? Because she does not have a dual connotation: it has no history of generic use.

Problem

If we are communicating clearly by means of a long-established system, why should we change? Unfortunately, the established system is not as innocent as the sentence about reading a science text implies. The dual role of masculine pronouns enables writers and readers to obscure the line between gender-specific use and generic use.

If you go to a doctor, I believe he will confirm my suspicions.

Technically, he is generic; but functionally, the masculine pronoun reinforces a widely-held conception of doctors as male. "But," you might say, "my responsibility is to inform readers about my topic, not to crusade against gender bias." True, but as a writer you control only half the communication process. Your writing is open to interpretation by readers, who are free to interpret a generic pronoun as gender specific.

For decades, writers have been trying to craft an alternative to generic pronouns. Look at these examples.

Generic Masculine

If a teacher treats his students with respect, he will increase his chance of being respected in return.

Avoidance of Generic Masculine

1. ***either/or approach:***

If a teacher treats his or her students with respect, he or she will increase his or her chance of being respected in return.

2. ***slash approach:***

If a teacher treats his/her students with respect, s/he will increase his/her chance of being respected in return.

3. ***noun/pronoun disagreement-in-number approach:***

If a teacher treats their students with respect, they will increase their chances of being respected in return.

These approaches to avoiding generic masculine pronouns—and the generic use of feminine pronouns—all cause problems. Generic feminine pronouns sound contrived to most readers, and contrivance steals attention from content. The either/or approach and the slash approach disrupt sentence flow and break the reader's concentration by crowding two pronouns into a space normally occupied by one. Noun/pronoun disagreement is a grammatical violation that grates on literate readers' ears much as "I seen" or "we was going" would grate, yet it seems to be gaining limited acceptance by default. That is, generic masculine pronouns have become so uncomfortable—and other approaches are so awkward—that speakers and writers flee to noun/pronoun disagreement in apparent hope that the grammatical violation will escape notice.

Solution

An important question to ask is this: How necessary are generic pronouns, i.e., pronouns whose antecedent nouns (teacher, doctor, pilot, artist) are of indefinite gender? Can sentences containing generic pronouns be rewritten to exclude them without sacrificing clarity or gracefulness? I would answer that question with a qualified "yes."

Generic Masculine Pronoun

If a teacher treats his students with respect, he will increase his chance of being respected in return.

If you go to a doctor, I believe he will confirm my suspicions.

Avoiding the Generic Pronoun

A teacher who treats students with respect will increase the chance of being respected in return.

I believe a doctor would confirm my suspicions.

Reconstructing a sentence to avoid generic pronouns may actually strengthen it. The sentence about the doctor is a case in point: the second version exceeds the first in brevity, directness, vigor, and clarity, and at the same time avoids use of the generic pronoun. What a payoff!

Can we avoid generic pronouns altogether and maintain a strong, clear, graceful writing style? This book has been a test case: I have avoided generic pronouns throughout. If you have read the preceding chapters, by now you should have a sense of any adverse effects. Of course this is only one book. I cannot claim confidently that generic pronouns are wholly dispensable, but I do believe a writer committed to avoiding them can do so almost completely, if not completely. Examples in the next section of this chapter will show you the kind of sentence construction needed to accomplish that.

What if you discover that you cannot eliminate generic pronouns altogether within the parameters of good writing? At that point you will have to decide which course to take. I believe the *least* intrusive option is he or she, but it must be used sparingly; frequent recurrence is distracting. I believe the most intrusive options are disagreement in number between subject and verb and the use of generic she alternating with generic he by chapter—or worse, by paragraph. Alternate generic pronouns create a campaign-for-equality subplot that runs beside and takes attention from the content. Whatever compromise form you choose, if your primary tactic is to avoid generic pronouns on every occasion possible, your compromises will be relatively innocuous because of their rare appearance.

This chapter should be interesting to read years from now, when writers are perhaps closer to consensus. My hope is that avoidance of the generic pronoun will win favor as the first solution. Where we find avoidance awkward, perhaps we will have agreed on he or she or some other standard solution. Or maybe we will have decided to change the rules of grammar; that is, maybe we will view the first sentence below as unacceptable and the second as acceptable, even though each contains exactly the same grammatical error: a plural pronoun referring to a singular antecedent.

1. If a ball is perfectly round, they will roll easily.
2. If a person is highly intelligent, they will learn easily.

I find both sentences discordant to the ear; to me, disagreement in number between a pronoun and its antecedent noun is the least acceptable of all possible solutions (Appendix B, Example B-2). Still, odd shifts occur over time. (In spoken English, the shift to disagreement in number seems to be in full swing now.) The axiom "a lie told often enough becomes the truth" may apply to grammar: "Grammatically incorrect language used often enough becomes accepted as correct."

The examples that complete this chapter will help you become skillful at avoiding generic pronouns in your writing. If you can avoid them altogether, so much the better. If not, you will have to decide how to handle the rare exceptions.

Examples

These examples show four techniques for avoiding generic pronouns:

Example 1	Omit the Pronoun	Example 3	Convert to Plural
Example 2	Monitor Introductory Clauses	Example 4	Reconstruct

All examples relate to **{26}**, shown on the BOOKMARK. In parentheses above each original statement is a notation of the specific problem solved by the revision.

Example 1: Omit the Pronoun

Simply omit a generic pronoun if the sentence can stand without it.

Original	Revision
1a. (Generic Masculine)	
How can a sensitive, committed teacher teach disruptive students without abandoning either his sensitivity or his productivity?	How can a sensitive, committed teacher teach disruptive students without abandoning either sensitivity or productivity?
1b. (Noun/Pronoun Disagreement)	
The classroom teacher may resent having a student miss their class for a music lesson.	The classroom teacher may resent having a student miss class for a music lesson.

Example 2: Monitor Introductory Clauses

Avoid an introductory clause having a singular noun of indefinite gender. Most such clauses are conditional, and most begin with a preposition; if and when are most common.

Original	Revision
2a. (Generic Masculine)	
If a teacher allows class to begin late the first week, he will fight tardiness the entire year.	A teacher who allows class to begin late the first week will fight tardiness the entire year.
2b. (Slash)	
When a student is absent, s/he must call me for the assignment.	After an absence, a student must call me for the assignment.
2c. (Either/or)	
If one teaches in a homogeneous community, he or she cannot disregard social influences already present.	One who teaches in a homogeneous community cannot disregard social influences already present.

Example 3: Convert to Plural

To circumvent generic pronouns, convert singular nouns and pronouns to plural.

Original	Revision
3a. (Generic Masculine)	
A sensitive social servant tends to become involved personally with clients, but if he does so excessively his effectiveness will be impaired.	Sensitive social servants tend to become involved personally with clients, but if they do so excessively their effectiveness will be impaired.

When you convert nouns and pronouns to plural, be sure to make surrounding writing plural as well. For example, the revision in **3a** should not be followed by "A wise social worker is ever aware of the dangers," but by "Wise social workers are ever aware of the dangers."

Original	**Revision**
3b. (Generic Masculine) I tell each student who enrolls that he will receive only the education to which he commits himself.	(First Revision) I tell students who enroll that they will receive only the education to which they commit themselves. (Second Revision, to note individual telling.) In individual meetings, I tell students who enroll that they will receive only the education to which they commit themselves.
3c. (Slash) The learner who has trouble adapting to a variety of teaching styles may become frustrated and easily distracted. In some cases, he/she may be unable to learn unless helped to make his/her learning style more flexible.	Learners who have trouble adapting to a variety of teaching styles may become frustrated and easily distracted. In some cases they may be unable to learn unless helped to make their learning styles more flexible.
3d. (Noun/Pronoun Disagreement) I would diagnose the latter as a hyperactive child, based solely on their classroom behavior.	I would diagnose students of the latter type as hyperactive children, based solely on their classroom behavior.

<u>Example 4</u>: Reconstruct

You may need to reconstruct a sentence creatively to retain good form while eliminating a generic pronoun. That can be as simple as changing one word (**4a**) or as complex as reworking an entire structure (**4b**, **c**, and **d**).

Original	**Revision**
4a. (Noun/Pronoun Disagreement) The nurse was instructed to inoculate each child in their buttocks.	The nurse was instructed to inoculate each child in the buttocks.

Original	**Revision**
4b. (Slash; Generic Feminine) While performing a task, does the child look up at any sudden noise? Is he/she out of her seat inappropriately? Is his/her attention easily captured by other things?	(First Revision) While performing a task, does the child look up at any sudden noise; walk about the room inappropriately; allow external distractions in general to pull attention from the task? (Second Revision) While performing a task, does the child look up at any sudden noise? Walk about the room inappropriately? Allow external distractions in general to pull attention from the task?

The **4b** original is both awkward and inconsistent, her being mixed with he/she and his/hers. The distraction may keep both writer and reader from noticing that the last of the three circumstances (attention easily captured by other things) encompasses the first and second. I inserted in general into the third question to acknowledge its relationship to the first two.

4b Bonus Tidbit

The second revision is creative and eye-catching, if unorthodox. The sentence fragments, each carrying does the child along by implication, help emphasize each thought, but such form is rare in formal writing. You are likely to violate with impunity such an important writing dictum as "write complete sentences" only if you are an accomplished writer and if circumstances are compelling.

Original	**Revision**
4c. (Generic Masculine) The writer needs to recognize that he is describing dichotomous populations—one that does as he prescribes and one that does something else—and then he must separate the two clearly for the reader.	The writer needs to recognize the dichotomous populations—one that does as the writer prescribes and one that does something else—and then needs to separate the two clearly for the reader.

Example **4c** is a difficult case that forces us to confront the problem squarely and make a difficult decision. Is the revision a clear-cut improvement? I did eliminate the generic pronoun he, but I lost clarity and stuck myself with repetition of the awkward expression the writer. Is that too great a price to pay? Are generic pronouns truly dispensable? Would I do well to retain the original for its clarity and let the political chips fall where they may? With diligence, might I have found a better solution? Writers can answer these questions only subjectively. Here is one last example.

4d. (Slash; Generic Feminine)

The ability of a child to organize the content of what she is learning into a sequence that makes learning efficient is critical to her academic success. Not only must she be able to organize content; she must be able to organize content at various rates, depending on the complexity of the learning task. What if a child is unable to organize information at more than one rate? What if he/she becomes easily distracted when he/she tries to diverge from her most comfortable learning rate?

A child's ability to organize content into an efficient learning sequence is critical to academic success. Beyond simply organizing content while learning, children must organize it at various rates, depending on the complexity of the learning task. What if a child is unable to organize information at more than one rate? What if divergence from the child's most comfortable learning rate creates distractions that impede learning?

You may find yourself frustrated, confused, and indecisive when caught between demands for gender equity on the one hand and clarity on the other, as the writer of **4d** apparently was. At first the writer seems to rebuff the use of generic masculine pronouns by saying "Two can play that game." Then, as if conscious that the generic feminine pronoun is likely to be disorienting, the writer switches to he/she in the last sentence before lapsing back to her. Even when you find yourself in such a cumbersome situation, if you work carefully and diligently at reconstruction you are likely to find that you can accommodate both gender-equity and clarity.

4d Bonus Tidbit

Notice that I made subtle changes beyond the gender issue to streamline the paragraph a bit. As an exercise, see if you can find those changes and understand what I accomplished by them.

Practice

Find a few written examples of generic masculine pronouns and their cumbersome alternatives—perhaps in your own writing—then write revisions. A small amount of practice will alert you to the problems, make you more skillful at solving them, and generally improve your treatment of the gender issue in writing. Here are four examples for a start. Write more than one revision of each if that will help you practice a variety of techniques.

a. A responsible parent will know where his/her children are when he/she is on vacation.

b. Unless he submits to random drug tests, an air traffic controller faces suspension and possible dismissal.

c. Due to new federal regulations, a student who borrows the maximum Stafford Loan for their grade level during the 1994–95 academic year will have no Stafford eligibility for summer 1995.

d. Once a student has accepted Professor Suorogir's style, he or she finds himself or herself producing work of superior quality.

> Of the first five chapters in this book, only this one contains its own practice exercises. I have placed them here because of the specific nature of the gender-in-writing problem. For practice related to the array of writing foibles presented in Chapters 1–4 (with a few gender problems added to the mix), study and work through the material presented in Chapter 6.

CHAPTER 6

MULTIPLE-PROBLEM EXAMPLES AND EXERCISES

The examples in this chapter, most of them single sentences, contain multiple writing flaws. This is the format for each example:

Original, with keys to revision: a copy of the example in its original form, with areas to be revised bracketed and numbered.

Revision(s): a clean copy of the revision or revisions.

Comments: a list of comments, numbered to correspond to numbered brackets in the original. Comments are related to writing principles shown on the BOOKMARK { } and to material from other chapters.

You will need to study each example extensively and patiently to extract the insight it has to offer. After every four examples you will find four exercises—multiple-problem items with no revision or comment—designed for practice. Revise those on a separate sheet of paper, then refer to Appendix A: Possible Solutions to Multiple-Problem Exercises from Chapter 6.

Each example amounts to a dismemberment of one sentence (sometimes more), exposing writing flaws that have been treated more fully in preceding chapters. Comments, besides referring to writing principles and related material, in some cases refer to the effect a given flaw is likely to have on readers. That is important. You need to know not only *how* to write effective prose, but *why*. It is that reader-oriented mind-set that sustains you through difficult times—lets you dig in anew, knowing that small changes can be worth great effort.

Exercises in any writing text tend to be difficult and frustrating, because they are someone else's writing: the context is likely to be unfamiliar. Research-related examples will be particularly foreign to many of you, but they are important to readers preparing to write a thesis, monograph, or dissertation. I have marked the research-related examples with a boxed **R**. Research writers, gravitate to them; other writers, ignore those that baffle you.

Some exercises have notes or contextual material attached to give you a frame of reference. Contextual material is enclosed in brackets: [Do not revise anything that looks like this; simply use it to help yourself understand how to revise the material around it.]. Notice that the last four exercises (25–28) have no preceding examples and are all full paragraphs, each containing a sentence or sentences to be revised. Full-paragraph exercises offer valuable practice, because everyday revision commonly involves the task of making a sentence fit well within its paragraph-home.

You may want to try several revisions of each exercise, because writing is an art form: there is no right answer. In most case you will trim material, but sometimes you will need to re-arrange or even add material to bring clarity to the revision. The sentences embedded in paragraphs, particularly, tend to lack important material—material that you may find you can infer with the help of context clues from the rest of the paragraph. Just as the context of a sentence offers clues to the meaning of an unclear word, so too does a paragraph offer clues to the meaning of an unclear sentence. Once you have written your revisions, read through the corresponding exercises in Appendix A, where you can compare the original sentence with your solutions and my solution. Remember to think of each solution shown in Appendix A only as *a* solution, not *the* solution.

All the while, keep in mind that revising another person's writing is different—and more difficult—than revising your own. An excellent supplementary exercise will be to isolate sentences and paragraphs from your previous writing and revise them. In doing that you will get a more realistic feeling for revision, you will identify personal tendencies (good and not so good), and you will see growth in your writing from then to now. Also, by seeing what your writing has been, you may see more clearly what you want it to be.

In all, this chapter contains 24 examples and 28 exercises, grouped in fours. Probably four examples followed by four exercises is the most you will want to study in any one session: the work involved is intense and time consuming.

EXAMPLE 1
****

Original, with keys to revision

[Forty-one[1] surveys] were sent to [high schools[2]] in Chester and Delaware Counties.

Revision

Surveys were sent to curriculum directors at forty-one high schools in Chester and Delaware Counties.

Comments

1. When forty-one modifies surveys rather than high schools, the reader has to infer (but not know for certain) that surveys were sent to exactly forty-one high schools—one survey per school **{1, 3}**.

   RELATED MATERIAL: Ch 1 Pt 4, Disjointedness (Separation of Related Words)

2. A high school cannot respond to a survey. Let the reader know to whom the surveys were sent **{16}**.

   RELATED MATERIAL: Ch 1 Pt 3, Shortcuts (Vague Collective Noun)

Bonus Tidbit

The writer might also consider converting the sentence from passive voice to active **{14}**.

EXAMPLE 2
****

Original, with keys to revision

[If one practices the [wrong way[1] or thing][3], the learning [is][2] negative.]

Revisions

1. If one practices the wrong way or the wrong thing, the learning will be negative.

2. To learn a skill correctly, practice the right thing in the right way.

Comments

1. Any time an omission of words creates awkwardness, put the words back **{19}**.

   RELATED MATERIAL: Ch 1 Pt 3, Shortcuts (no parallel example in text)

2. If one practices refers to a consequence (future) rather than to the present; therefore, the future tense verb will be needs to replace the present tense verb is.

   RELATED MATERIAL: Appendix B Pt 1, English Usage Review (Parts of Speech: A More Detailed View—Verbs; Tense)

3. The corrections shown in Revision 1 are instructive, but the statement is much stronger in positive form, as shown in Revision 2 **{15}**.

Bonus Tidbit

In most cases you will find you can replace the word thing with a more specific, more informative term. In this case, however, the statement is so general (any kind of skill, and therefore any kind of practice, could be the subject) that the general term thing seems to work.

EXAMPLE 3
****

Original, with keys to revision

Although history is my [area of expertise][1], I am [concerned with][2] all [subject areas][1].

Revisions

1. Although history is my major subject, I am concerned about the quality of all education.

2. Although history is my major subject, I have some responsibility for all the academic subjects.

Comments

1. Area applied to anything other than physical parameters obscures exact meaning **{7, 16}**.

   RELATED MATERIAL: Ch 2 Pt 3, A Collection of Troublesome Words (area)
   Ch 4 Pt 1, Standard Terms Used as Bucket Terms (area)

2. Concerned with may mean either concerned about, as in feeling anxious (Revision 1), or involved with in some capacity (Revision 2) **{16}**.

   RELATED MATERIAL: Ch 2 Pt 1, Clarity Lost to Poor Word Choice
   Ch 2 Pt 3, A Collection of Troublesome Words (concern)
   Ch 4 Pt 1, Standard Terms Used as Bucket Terms (concern)

EXAMPLE 4
****

Original, with keys to revision

Each [individual][1] has a chance to fulfill [his][2] [potential possibilities][3].

Revision

1. Each person has a chance to fulfill individual potential.
2. Each person has a chance to fulfill his or her potential.

Comments

1. Individual, because it is applicable to both persons and objects, is not a good replacement for the specific noun person **{18}**. Think of individual as a descriptor (adjective) rather than as a label (noun).

   RELATED MATERIAL: Ch 2 Pt 3, A Collection of Troublesome Words (individual)

2. Individual now becomes useful as an adjective with which to replace the generic masculine pronoun his **{26}**. On the other hand, you may want to write Revision 2 to retain the more explicit construction.

   RELATED MATERIAL: Ch 2 Pt 2, Precision Lost to Poor Word Choice
   Ch 5 Pt 2, Gender in Writing

3. The terms potential and possibilities both represent whatever is achievable; you could use either term here, but should not use both. Potential, generally associated with human fulfillment, fits well **{9, 18}**.

   RELATED MATERIAL: Ch 3 Pt 1, Wordy Writing (Redundancy)
   Ch 2 Pt 2, Precision Lost to Poor Word Choice

EXERCISE 1.

Children are different because their physical and cultural surroundings are not the same.

EXERCISE 2.

Galton stated that there are two great forces: nurture and nature. These two are what make individuals different from each other.

EXERCISE 3.

Because of unforeseen circumstances that occurred, the testing process was disrupted in the following ways:

R

EXERCISE 4.

[English students in this study faired poorly as compared to Ugandan students.] Results of the study showed that overall, the Ugandans were in an average lead of about eight points over the English and all mean differences, except for the fourteen-year-old groups were significant ($p < .01$).

Compare your solutions with those shown in Appendix A, but remember that writing is an art form: most sentences can be written well in a number of ways.

EXAMPLE 5

****

Original, with keys to revision

[The Sensorial Level goes][1] from birth to age seven, and [the Abstract Level][1] [goes][2] from ages seven to eighteen.

Revision

Children learn sensorially from birth to age seven and abstractly from ages seven to eighteen.

Comments

1. Sensorial Level and Abstract Level are just labels for types of learning observed in children **{7}**. The issue in this sentence is not where a level goes (colloquial) **{25}**, but how children learn at particular ages **{18}**.

   RELATED MATERIAL: Ch 1 Pt 3, Shortcuts (Jargon)
   Ch 2 Pt 1, Clarity Lost to Poor Word Choice

2. If the original were kept, the verb goes would not need to be repeated in the second phrase—just as the verb learn is not repeated in the second phrase of the revision **{9}**.

   RELATED MATERIAL: Ch 3 Pt 1, Wordy Writing (Immature Writing)

EXAMPLE 6

****

Original, with keys to revision

Bruner has presented a plan [that is][1] [very][2] [crucial][3] to education [in general][1].

Revision

Bruner has presented a plan important to education.

Comments

1. The phrases that is and in general are filler; they add no information **{9}**. One might make a case for that is helping the rhythm of the sentence **{19}**; the decision is a matter of style.

   RELATED MATERIAL: Ch 3 Pt 1, Wordy Writing (Filler Phrases)

2. Because crucial means “important to the extreme,” very crucial is an overstatement, if not a redundancy **{11, 9}**.

   RELATED MATERIAL: Ch 3 Pt 2, Weak Writing (Overstatement)
   Ch 3 Pt 1, Wordy Writing (Redundancy)

3. Crucial is a questionable choice of word, as it generally applies to more specific contexts: “crucial to the winning of this case.” If education were teetering on the brink of ruination and Bruner offered the one plan that could save it, crucial would be the perfect word. Probably important is more precise here **{18}**. Then the issue of very returns. I would write very important only if I had a *very* compelling reason.

   RELATED MATERIAL: Ch 2 Pt 2, Precision Lost to Poor Word Choice
   Ch 3 Pt 2, Weak Writing (Overstatement)

EXAMPLE 7
****

Original, with keys to revision

[Intelligence][1] is [what distinguishes][2] [man][3] from [the][4] animals.

Revision

Humans differ from animals primarily in intelligence.

Comments

1. The word needing most emphasis in this statement is intelligence; placement at the end of the sentence gives it maximum emphasis **{8}**.

   RELATED MATERIAL: Ch 3 Pt 2, Weak Writing (Misplaced Emphasis)

2. In most precise terms, intelligence is not what distinguishes so much as it is the primary difference between humans and animals **{18}**.

   RELATED MATERIAL: Ch 2 Pt 2, Precision Lost to Poor Word Choice

3. Replacement of man with humans improves the sentence in two ways. First, readers who object to the generic use of man will not be offended **{26}**. Second, humans fits better than man as a parallel to animals **{13}**.

   RELATED MATERIAL: Ch 5 Pt 2, Gender in Writing
   Ch 1 Pt 5, Nonparallel Construction (Nonparallel Terms)

4. The is at best needless, and could be considered misleading (which animals?) **{9, 7}**.

   RELATED MATERIAL: Ch 2 Pt 2, Precision Lost to Poor Word Choice
   Ch 2 Pt 3, A Collection of Troublesome Words (the)

EXAMPLE 8

****

Original, with keys to revision

[This is a stage][1] [where][2] the child [starts][3] [to use][4] inference learning.

Revision

At this stage, the child begins to learn by inference.

Comments

1. The opening declaration emphasizes stage, which is less important than either child or inference. Notice in the revision that the child, by following an adverb phrase, is at the functional beginning of the sentence—a strong placement; the child's action, learn by inference, is at the end of the sentence, an even stronger placement **{8}**.

   RELATED MATERIAL: Ch 3 Pt 2, Weak Writing (Misplaced Emphasis)

2. Where denotes location, and the stage is not a location (except in show business). This is a stage, if it were retained, would be followed by at which **{18}**.

   RELATED MATERIAL: Ch 1 Pt 4, Disjointedness (Misused Conjunction or Preposition)
   Ch 2 Pt 3, A Collection of Troublesome Words (where)

3. Start has a connotation of immediacy, as in starting an engine or starting a race. Begin means simply to "perform the first or earliest part of some action" **{18}**.

   RELATED MATERIAL: Ch 2 Pt 2, Precision Lost to Poor Word Choice

4. To use implies conscious engagement of a tool, as to use a gun or to use language. A child's early experiences with inference, by contrast, are unconscious. The child is not using; the child is learning **{18}**.

   RELATED MATERIAL: Ch 2 Pt 2, Precision Lost to Poor Word Choice

EXERCISE 5. **R**

[Two schools from each of the five regions created a sample of ten schools to represent the overall population.] Two other schools were randomly selected at large using the random table to serve as substitutes.

EXERCISE 6. **R**

Thirty minutes of twelve consecutive rehearsals will be allotted for each composition.

EXERCISE 7.

The large enrollment forced Mr. DeDworc to deal with too many students for the size of the room.

EXERCISE 8. Note: You may want to turn to Appendix A rather than spend a great amount of time on this exercise. It is nearly indecipherable. Sadly, paragraphs similar to this are not uncommon in dissertation writing. If you are unfamiliar with the presentation of statistics, even the Appendix A solution may appear cryptic. **R**

Results showed that 1) all six subtests of PRRT, when correlated with each other, were statistically significant at the .05 level of significance; 2) a child's pitch and rhythm responses correlated with the combined environmental variables for each subtest beyond the .01 level of significance; 3) having and hearing musical instruments played in the home, having parents and siblings who participated or participate in musical activities, having parental help to sing in tune, and having an opportunity to hear various kinds of recorded music were positively correlated with a child's ability in pitch and rhythm and statistically significant at the .05 level of significance, with the correlation between pitch and parental help being significant at .01.

Compare your solutions with those shown in Appendix A, but remember that writing is an art form: most sentences can be written well in a number of ways.

R

EXAMPLE 9

****

Original, with keys to revision

[This researcher discovered that][1] all [studies][2] [examined][3] [separated][4] results by gender.

Revision

All previous researchers reported results by gender.

Comments

1. Implicit in any written information about previous studies is that the writer found (discover is imprecise) the information by examining those studies; words to that effect are unnecessary **{9}**.

   RELATED MATERIAL: Ch 2 Pt 3, A Collection of Troublesome Words (discover)
   Ch 3 Pt 1, Wordy Writing (Immature Writing)

2. Studies did not separate results: previous researchers did **{6}**.

   RELATED MATERIAL: Ch 1 Pt 8, Personification

3. Placement of two verbs next to each other, one applying to the writer (examined) and the next to the writer's subject (separated), is awkward and temporarily disorienting **{19}**.

   RELATED MATERIAL: Ch 3 Pt 3, Ungainly Writing (Ungraceful Rhythm)
   Ch 1 Pt 6, Vague or Tangled Construction (Confusion/Contradiction)

4. The verb reported is more precise than the verb separated to describe previous researchers' dissemination of results **{18}**.

   RELATED MATERIAL: Ch 2 Pt 2, Precision Lost to Poor Word Choice

EXAMPLE 10

****

Original, with keys to revision

[Once][1] a medical doctor wanted to learn to play [a][1] piano [so as to be able to][2] provide simple chordal accompaniments for family singing.

Revision

A medical doctor wanted to learn to play piano so he could provide simple chordal accompaniments for family singing.

Comments

1. The terms once and a are overly restrictive. Once implies that never before or since has a medical doctor had such a desire, and a implies that the doctor wanted to learn to play a particular piano **{7}**. The style sounds immature (Once upon a time . . .) **{9}**.

   RELATED MATERIAL: Ch 2 Pt 2, Precision Lost to Poor Word Choice
   Ch 3 Pt 1, Wordy Writing (Immature Writing)

2. So as to be able to is a wordy version of so he could (or so she could had the doctor referred to in this writing been female) **{9}**.

   RELATED MATERIAL: Ch 3 Pt 1, Wordy Writing (Filler Phrases)

Bonus Tidbit

If the writer were referring to a specific person, a stronger construction would have been use of the person's name with the profession placed appositively: Matthew Coles, a medical doctor, wanted. . . .

EXAMPLE 11
****

Original, with keys to revision

[Most learning at this stage is intuitive][1] as opposed to analytic, which involves a [logical step-by-step process][2].

Revision

In contrast to logical, step-by-step analytic learning, most learning at this stage is intuitive.

Comments

1. The emphatic statement that opens this sentence will carry greater weight at the end, while the parenthetic phrase that ends it deserves less prominent placement **{8}**.

   RELATED MATERIAL: Ch 3 Pt 2, Weak Writing (Misplaced Emphasis)

2. Phrase order not only weakens the sentence, but causes ambiguity. The phrase <u>logical step-by-step process</u> could describe either intuitive learning or analytic learning, depending on whether it modifies the single word before the comma or the entire phrase before the comma. Reasonably bright readers will know the answer is analytic, but the writer should not depend on that. The writer's job is to tell **{1, 3}**.

   RELATED MATERIAL: Ch 1 Pt 4, Disjointedness (Within-Sentence Disjointedness)

EXAMPLE 12
****

Original, with keys to revision

[It is important to realize][1] that [temperament and intelligence][2] are two [different][3] attributes that [independently affect][4] classroom behavior.

Revision

Teachers need to realize that student temperament and student intelligence affect classroom behavior independently.

Comments

1. As a sentence opener, the passive it is telegraphs weakness and vagueness to come; what is important to whom? Teachers need to realize orients readers to all that follows **{10, 3, 6}**.

   RELATED MATERIAL: Ch 3 Pt 1, Wordy Writing (Filler Phrases)
   Ch 3 Pt 2, Weak Writing (Passive Structure)

2. As written, the sentence could apply to the temperament and intelligence of either students or teachers. In the revision, student modifies those two key terms **{6, 7}**.

   RELATED MATERIAL: Ch 1 Pt 4, Disjointedness (Within-Sentence Disjointedness)

3. Readers will know that temperament and intelligence are not the same, so the two need not be labeled different **{9}**.

   RELATED MATERIAL: Ch 3 Pt 1, Wordy Writing (Redundancy)
   Ch 2 Pt 3, A Collection of Troublesome Words (different)

4. Relocation of independently strengthens the sentence in two ways. First, the subject and verb are brought together: student temperament and student intelligence affect **{3}**. Second, the primary message of the sentence is strongest with the key word (independently) in a position of strength—at the end **{8}**.

   RELATED MATERIAL: Ch 1 Pt 4, Disjointedness (Separation of Related Words)
   Ch 4 Pt 5, Unusual Word Arrangement

EXERCISE 9. (Hint: The term <u>concluded</u> is key to the problem.) **R**

Moore concluded that young children living in an environment which provided them with a constant exposure to music demonstrated higher levels of musical development than children who did not live in such an environment.

EXERCISE 10.

She was assisted by the classroom teacher in distributing and collecting testing material.

EXERCISE 11. **R**

[Children in Trinidad grow up singing, dancing, and hearing music everywhere—at home, in school, and in the streets.] The sum total of all these musical experiences of a child in the Trinidadian culture can be expected to influence his music aptitude during the developmental years.

EXERCISE 12. **R**

Second graders in three separate classes will be involved twice a week for approximately a six-month period.

Compare your solutions with those shown in Appendix A, but remember that writing is an art form: most sentences can be written well in a number of ways.

R

EXAMPLE 13
****

Original, with keys to revision

[When comparing][1] the performance skills [of][2] competing and noncompeting [bands][3], [[there was][4] no significant difference][5].

Revision

(Anderson) found no significant differences in performance skills between students from competing bands and students from noncompeting bands.

Comments

1. When comparing is an awkward qualification considering that the lack of difference in skills would be true even when not comparing **{7}**.

   RELATED MATERIAL: Ch 1 Pt 7, Misleading Construction

2. There was no comparison of X and Y, as if to a third factor, but rather between X and Y (or X with Y) **{18}**.

   RELATED MATERIAL: Ch 1 Pt 4, Disjointedness (Misused Preposition or Conjunction)

3. By lumping subjects into bands, the writer implies group comparisons; in reality, comparisons were made between individual students **{7}**.

   RELATED MATERIAL: Ch 1 Pt 3, Shortcuts (Missing Information)

4. At the location of there was—if the opening phrase were maintained—the reader should find the subject of that phrase (the study's author) **{6}**.

   RELATED MATERIAL: Appendix B Pt 1, Parts of Speech: A More Detailed View (Verbs; Form; Participle)
   Appendix B Pt 2, Grammar (Misplaced Subject)

5. Research protocol demands caution. Differences are not necessarily absent simply because they are not found **{11}**.

   RELATED MATERIAL: Ch 1 Pt 7, Misleading Construction

EXAMPLE 14
****

Original, with keys to revision

[Gordon][1] [goes][2] from [aural/oral][3] through [symbolic][3] before approaching [theory][3].

Revision

Gordon recommends that learners progress from aural/oral learning through symbolic learning before approaching theoretical learning.

Comments

1. What Gordon, a learning theorist, does is irrelevant to the point the writer is trying to make. Gordon is a shortcut for Gordon recommends that learners . . . **{1, 7}**.

   RELATED MATERIAL: Ch 1 Pt 3, Shortcuts (Missing Information)

2. Students do not go through learning levels, as through a doorway, but rather progress from one level to the next by virtue of accomplishment. The word goes is a colloquial expression as used here **{25, 18}**.

   RELATED MATERIAL: Ch 1 Pt 3, Shortcuts (Jargon)

3. Another shortcut is the use of aural/oral, symbolic, and theory to designate levels of learning without saying so explicitly. Persons unfamiliar with the jargon may not understand **{1, 25 }**.

   RELATED MATERIAL: Ch 1 Pt 3, Shortcuts (Jargon)

EXAMPLE 15
****

Original, with keys to revision

That is the time the child's intelligence is being formed. [But not only[1] [his][2] intelligence; [the full totality][3] of [his][2] psychic powers.]

Revision

That is the time the child's intelligence is being formed, but not only intelligence: a full range of psychic powers develops at the same time.

Comments

1. Two incomplete sentences joined by a semicolon become a compound incomplete sentence, not a complete sentence. I could have used a semicolon in the revision, but the nature of the last phrase (explanatory) gives license to use the stronger mark **{20}**.

   RELATED MATERIAL: Appendix B Pt 3, Punctuation (Semicolons; Colons)

2. His, a generic masculine pronoun, can be avoided without encumbering expression **{26}**.

   RELATED MATERIAL: Ch 5 Pt 2, Gender in Writing

3. Because partial totality is inconceivable, full totality is redundant. Usually the adjective is at fault in this type of construction, but here the writer's intent probably will be represented best by keeping the adjective and replacing the noun: full range **{18}**.

   RELATED MATERIAL: Ch 3 Pt 1, Wordy Writing (Redundancy)
   Ch 2 Pt 2, Precision Lost to Poor Word Choice

EXAMPLE 16

****

Original, with keys to revision

[Judgment of any art rests in our [knowledge][2] [4] of the nature [of the work][1] and [using][2] our [cognitive faculties][3] [to formulate a judgment.][1]]

Revision

Judgment of any art rests on our understanding its nature and applying valid criteria.

Comments

1. Baggage abounds. Omit the empty prepositional phrase of the work and the prepositional phrase to formulate a judgment, redundant to the first word of the sentence **{9}**.

   RELATED MATERIAL: Ch 3 Pt 1, Wordy Writing (Filler Phrases; Redundancy)

2. Knowledge is a thing possessed; using is an action taken. State the two criteria for art judgment in the same form (understanding and applying) **{13}**.

   RELATED MATERIAL: Ch 1 Pt 5, Nonparallel Construction (Nonparallel Terms)

3. Applying valid criteria is more concrete and easier to understand than using cognitive faculties, and the underlying meaning is the same **{16, 17}**.

   RELATED MATERIAL: Ch 2 Pt 1, Clarity Lost to Poor Word Choice

4. Excessive prepositional phrases flatten rhythmic flow. Read the two versions aloud and note that the revision is more pleasing to the ear and easier to digest **{9, 19}**.

   RELATED MATERIAL: Ch 3 Pt 3, Ungainly Writing (Ungraceful Rhythm)

Bonus Tidbit

To my ear, judgment is more likely to rest on than in.

EXERCISE 13.

Posters raise the level of awareness of students regarding research opportunities.

EXERCISE 14.

At this present time, it is hopeful that we can achieve our goal.

R

EXERCISE 15.

The problem of this study is to compare the effects of teaching a collegiate wind band quality literature with two different methods of instruction and investigate the level of musicianship attained with each method.

R

EXERCISE 16.

Results of this study showed that firstly, Chinese test-retest reliabilities were lower than the American test-retest reliabilities. Secondly, American students' mean scores were slightly lower than the Chinese students' mean scores. However, the difference was not large enough to be statistically significant.

Compare your solutions with those shown in Appendix A, but remember that writing is an art form: most sentences can be written well in a number of ways.

EXAMPLE 17
****

Original, with keys to revision

[Performing[1] ensembles] can [incorporate educational[2] objectives] if [they[3]]
[relate to the performing[4] ensemble].

Revision

Conductors of performing ensembles—if they recognize learning opportunities—can teach while they rehearse.

Comments

1. Conductors of the ensembles—not the ensembles themselves—would be responsible for educational objectives **{7}**.

   RELATED MATERIALS: Ch 1 Pt 8, Personification

2. A simpler version of incorporate educational objectives is teach **{17}**.

   RELATED MATERIALS: Ch 3 Pt 1, Wordy Writing (Academically Inflated Writing)

3. Whether the antecedent of they is objectives or ensembles is clear only in retrospect **{6}**.

   RELATED MATERIALS: Ch 1 Pt 4, Disjointedness (Within-Sentence Disjointedness)

4. Readers will easily and rightfully assume, without being told, that whatever teaching and learning takes place in an ensemble rehearsal will relate to the performing ensemble.

   RELATED MATERIALS: Ch 3 Pt 2, Weak Writing (Empty Language)

Bonus Tidbit

"Write concisely" is good advice **{9}**, but concision can be overdone. A major problem with this sentence is lack of information needed to make its meaning clear **{1, 7}**.

EXAMPLE 18
****

R

Original, with keys to revision

[Research has shown][1] [that there is][2] [very][3] [little][4] relationship between a [student's][2] athletic activities in school and [his][2] later preferences for sports.

Revision

Researchers report a weak relationship between participation in school athletic activities and later preferences for sports (Satorio, 1986; Black, 1991; Lee, 1995).

Comments

1. This common phrase is not as blatant as some personification seen in research reports ("This paper is concerned with . . ."). Still, a direct link between actor and action invigorates writing (Researchers report) **{6}**; also, citations of specific sources [fictitious] give the writer's claim credibility **{24}**.

   RELATED MATERIAL: Ch 1 Pt 8, Personification

2. The phrase that there is adds needless words. Also, student's (and therefore his) can be left to inference: who else partakes of athletic activities in schools **{9}**? Of course those changes also carry with them the advantage of eliminating a generic masculine pronoun **{26}**.

   RELATED MATERIAL: Ch 3 Pt 1, Wordy Writing (Immature Writing; Filler Phrases)
   Ch 5 Pt 2, Gender in Writing

3. The qualifier very is impotent and irritating **{11}**.

   RELATED MATERIAL: Ch 3 Pt 2, Weak Writing (Overstatement)

4. Relationships are thought of as strong/weak or close/distant, not much/little **{18}**.

   RELATED MATERIAL: Ch 2 Pt 2, Precision Lost to Poor Word Choice

EXAMPLE 19

****

Original, with keys to revision

Shuler (1992) [found math scores][1] to be significantly [correlated][2] with hyperactivity[.][3] Borgman (1994) **[**found significant [associations][2]**]**[1] between math scores and eight emotional deficiency ratings.

Revision

Researchers have found significant correlations between math scores and hyperactivity (Shuler, 1992) and between math scores and eight emotional deficiency ratings (Borgman, 1994).

Comments

1. Present parallel factors from the two studies in the same order rather than begin with found math scores for one (Shuler) and found significant associations for the other (Borgman) **{13}**.

   RELATED MATERIAL: Ch 1 Pt 5, Nonparallel Construction (Nonparallel Sentence Construction)

2. Use terms consistently: compare correlations with correlations, not with associations **{5}**.

   RELATED MATERIAL: Ch 1 Pt 5, Nonparallel Construction (Nonparallel Terms)

3. The two studies have one train of thought in common: correlation between math scores and emotional anomalies. When that common ground is used to combine the sentences into one, the relationships between the two studies and the overriding message that the two carry become clear for the reader: Shuler's work amounts to one piece of a puzzle to which Borgman added several pieces two years later **{7}**.

   RELATED MATERIAL: Ch 1 Pt 4, Disjointedness (Between-Sentence Disjointedness)

EXAMPLE 20
****

Original, with keys to revision

He [employs][1] [tonal and rhythm patterns][2] [(ranging from [two-note to short phrases][3] for the tonal and [4-beat to phrasal][3] for the rhythm).][4]

Revision

He uses tonal patterns and rhythm patterns. Tonal patterns range in length from two pitches to complete phrases, and rhythm patterns from four beats to complete phrases.

Comments

1. Employ is fancier than use, and a bit less precise **{17, 18}**.

   RELATED MATERIAL: Ch 2 Pt 2, Precision Lost to Poor Word Choice

2. Tonal and rhythm patterns is a shortcut for tonal patterns and rhythm patterns. The latter makes clear to the reader that the writer is referring to two types of patterns—a tonal type and a rhythm type—rather than to musical patterns having tonal elements and rhythm elements combined **{1}**.

   RELATED MATERIAL: Ch 1 Pt 3, Shortcuts (Missing Information)

3. Shortcut jargon used to describe phrase length makes the information nearly incomprehensible. Does two-note refer to phrases? If so, would a two-note phrase not be a short phrase **{7}**? As if more complication is needed, the writer has described tonal phrases and rhythm phrases in nonparallel form: phrases compared to phrasal and two-note compared to 4-beat **{13}**.

   RELATED MATERIAL: Ch 1 Pt 3, Shortcuts (Jargon)
   Ch 1 Pt 5, Nonparallel Construction (Nonparallel Terms)

4. The writer inexplicably encloses the meat of the statement between parentheses. Use parentheses sparingly, and only when material is truly parenthetic (functioning as an aside to the primary statement) **{8, 20}**.

EXERCISE 17.

American music is often divided into periods with wars serving as convenient demarcations.

EXERCISE 18. **R**

[Four judges each used a three-dimensional scale—precision, efficiency, and style—to rate the subjects' performances.] Test-retest correlation coefficients were calculated for each dimension and for the three dimensions combined for one judge to measure reliability.

EXERCISE 19. **R**

[A comparison of standardized test scores between the groups will reveal whether there is a statistically significant difference between the two. Still, statistically significant differences do not necessarily indicate practical significance.] To assess the practical significance of the results, the means of the standardization sample can be used for comparison.

EXERCISE 20. **R**

[Madsen and Darrow's approach to investigating test validity for blind students, in contrast to Anderson's mixed-response approach, was to have students use a single method of response from beginning to end for each test.] They used two methods of recording responses. The oral response method was applied to MAT, but a Braille answer sheet was used with the Walker Test.

Compare your solutions with those shown in Appendix A, but remember that writing is an art form: most sentences can be written well in a number of ways.

EXAMPLE 21
****

Original, with keys to revision

[The object of visual[1] aesthetics] is [not [so much[2]] the study[3]] into the nature of art [[but[2]] into the[3] feelings] art stirs in the viewer.

Revision

The object of study in visual aesthetics is not so much the nature of art as the feelings art stirs in the viewer.

Comments

1. The object at issue in this sentence is not the object of visual aesthetics, but the object of study. Visual aesthetics is the discipline within which the study occurs **{7}**.

   RELATED MATERIAL: Ch 1 Pt 4, Disjointedness (Separation of Related Words)

2. So much needs to be followed by as rather than by but **{18}**.

   RELATED MATERIAL: Ch 1 Pt 4, Disjointedness (Misused Preposition or Conjunction)

3. The form of this statement is "not so much X, but Y," a form that begs for parallel construction. Replacing X and Y with the author's words reveals nonsense: not so much the study . . . but into the feelings. The two coordinate ideas needing to be expressed in similar form are the nature of art and the feelings art stirs **{13}**.

   RELATED MATERIAL: Ch 1 Pt 5, Nonparallel Construction (Nonparallel Sentence Construction)
   Ch 1 Pt 4, Disjointedness (Separation of Related Words)

EXAMPLE 22
****

Original, with keys to revision

DaVinci [believed that it was impossible for][1] [the student][2] to [judge what is good in art][1] if [one][2] does not [practice art, and gain an understanding of [the nature of artistic quality][4]][3]. (5 = The Total Sentence)

Revision

DaVinci believed that students need to practice art to understand enough about it to judge artistic quality.

Comments

1. Believed that it was impossible for is indirect and wordy; judge what is good in art is also wordy **{9}**, and it is less precise than judge artistic quality: one judges both what is good and what is not good **{18}**.

   RELATED MATERIAL: Ch 3 Pt 1, Wordy Writing (Immature Writing; Filler Phrases)

2. The shift of reference from the student to one is jarring, and forces the reader to infer that the two are the same **{5, 6}**.

   RELATED MATERIAL: Ch 1 Pt 5, Nonparallel Construction (Nonparallel Terms)

3. For cohesiveness, the sentence needs an explicit statement of the relationship between practice and understanding: need to practice . . . to understand **{7}**.

   RELATED MATERIAL: Ch 1 Pt 4, Disjointedness (Within-Sentence Disjointedness)
   Ch 2 Pt 3, A Collection of Troublesome Words (and)

(continued next page)

(Comments for Example 22, continued)

4. The nature of artistic quality is hardly strong enough to merit placement at the end of the sentence; better to emphasize the topic of the sentence: judge artistic quality **{8}**.

    RELATED MATERIAL: Ch 3 Pt 2, Weak Writing (Misplaced Emphasis)

5. Rather than state that good judgment is impossible for a person who has not practiced, state that a person needs to practice to acquire good judgment. Positive form is stronger than negative form because it is direct, clear, and usually more concise **{15, 9}**.

    RELATED MATERIAL: Ch 3 Pt 2, Weak Writing (Negative Form)

EXAMPLE 23
****

Original, with keys to revision

From this analysis we will see [the][1] need for [a great deal of][2] improvement in [the present][3] science curriculum, and we will examine Schmidt's learning theory, comparing it to [the mold that we will inevitably form][4]. (5 = The Total Sentence)

Revision

From this analysis we will see a need for substantial improvement in the science curriculum, and we will examine Schmidt's learning theory as a potential foundation for that improvement.

Comments

1. The language needed here is a rather than the, allowing for the probability of more than one need **{11, 18}**.

    RELATED MATERIAL: Ch 2 Pt 2, Precision Lost to Poor Word Choice
    Ch 2 Pt 3, A Collection of Troublesome Words (the)

(continued next page)

(Comments for Example 23, continued)

2. Replace a vague, inefficient, four-word phrase with one descriptive word; substantial is a good candidate **{9, 16}**.

   RELATED MATERIAL: Ch 3 Pt 1, Wordy Writing (Immature Writing)

3. No one would propose changes in a curriculum that is out of use (past) or not yet formulated (future), so the present is redundant by implication **{9}**.

   RELATED MATERIAL: Ch 3 Pt 1, Wordy Writing (Redundancy)

4. The mold that we will inevitably form sounds more poetic than factual. Beyond the style problem is a problem of overstatement. Bright readers will not buy the inevitability of "forming a mold" **{11, 17}**.

   RELATED MATERIAL: Ch 3 Pt 2, Weak Writing (Overstatement)

5. The first phrase relates to the second and the second to the third, but first to second to third rambles into reader overload. The solution I chose, because of the fluffy last phrase, was to make the sentence more compact rather than divide it into two **{2}**.

   RELATED MATERIAL: Ch 1 Pt 1, Overstuffed Sentences

EXAMPLE 24
****

R

Original, with keys to revision

The numbered list of the schools was divided into five sections: 1–99, 100–199, 200–299, 300–399, and [1 400–], which [2 were matched with the numbers in the random table.] One school from each section was then selected randomly [3 by using the blind pointing method] to arrive at a row from which to begin. The numbered list was [4 completed in order that there might be an equal geographical and ethnic distribution of the country]. (5 = The Total Paragraph)

(continued next page)

(Example 24 continued)

Revision

To ensure an equal geographic and ethnic distribution among sample schools, the researcher divided the list of the country's schools into five sections by location: 1–99, 100–199, 200–299, 300–399, and 400–487. Using a table of random numbers, she selected one school from each section, using the blind pointing method to arrive at a row from which to begin.

Comments

1. Use of a dangling hyphen (400–) deprives the reader of information that is available.

   RELATED MATERIAL: Ch 1 Pt 3, Shortcuts (Missing Information)

2. The phrase were matched with the numbers in the random table refers to procedures not unique to this study, apparently in an awkward and unnecessary attempt to describe standard use of a table of random numbers. Also, the passivity of the phrase leaves the reader to infer, but not know for sure, that the researcher did the selecting **{9, 14, 6}**.

   RELATED MATERIAL: Ch 1 Pt 6, Vague or Tangled Construction (Vague Language)
   Ch 3 Pt 2, Weak Writing (Passive Structure)

3. Schools were selected randomly by use of a table of random numbers, not by use of the blind pointing method—a simple technique that precedes the selection process itself **{7}**.

   RELATED MATERIAL: Ch 1 Pt 7, Misleading Construction

4. Geographic balance was attained not by completing the list, but by dividing it into five sections to prevent selection of multiple schools from one area **{7}**.

   RELATED MATERIAL: Ch 1 Pt 6, Vague or Tangled Construction (Confusion/Contradiction)

5. The muddled feeling of this paragraph begins with failure to inform the reader at the beginning about the premise underlying the unique selection process: geographic and ethnic balance **{3}**.

   RELATED MATERIAL: Ch 1 Pt 4, Disjointedness (Between-Sentence Disjointedness)

EXERCISE 21. (Note: Subjects of the study were hearing-impaired.) **R**

Limited research pertaining to the present study is available. However, research has been conducted with visually handicapped individuals and tests have been adapted for administration to specific handicaps.

EXERCISE 22. **R**

A total of 23 students participated. The sample represents a population of first graders, second graders, and third graders from a cross-section of socioeconomic backgrounds.

EXERCISE 23. **R**

One week after group administration, each student was individually tested at Cedarbrook School.

EXERCISE 24. **R**

The researcher obtained the means and standard deviations for the group administration and individual administration of MRT. The mean differences between Adapted MRT and MRT were calculated for each grade level and all grades combined. Results are shown in Figure 7.

Compare your solutions with those shown in Appendix A, but remember that writing is an art form: most sentences can be written well in a number of ways.

EXERCISE 25.

Still another threat to school funding needs to be taken seriously. An aging population is infusing each community with a growing percentage of "empty nesters," meaning older people who have no children at home. Educators, administrators, and board members of public schools should be alarmed that seventy percent of their constituents are now "empty nesters" whose support is allegedly declining.

EXERCISE 26.

Public education will have to maintain excellence while coping with language barriers and conflicting values among various minority groups. The Bill of Rights, the branches of government, the Constitution, and our system of education were all formed on a monocultural basis. Strategic planning is about being creative instead of adaptive during such a transition; thus, strategic planning means being proactive rather than reactive.

EXERCISE 27.

Shinichi Suzuki was born in Nagoya, Japan, in 1898. As a child, he grew up in an environment conducive to his becoming acquainted with the workings of stringed instruments. He worked in the first violin factory that was founded in Japan by his father.

EXERCISE 28.

[The final Inner Game skill is Trust. Trust in the Inner Game sense is not blind, but rather is preceded by well-laid groundwork through practice and hard work. Trust is essential to one's entering the requisite state of relaxed concentration.] Unfortunately, barriers to trusting exist; however, for ease of identification, Green has articulated three barriers to trust: worrying what others will think of you, the feeling of being out of control, and fears about your own ability.

> Compare your solutions with those shown in Appendix A, but remember that writing is an art form: most sentences can be written well in a number of ways.

CHAPTER 7

THE LARGER PICTURE

Some writing issues are too broad to cover with writing principles: paragraph function, paragraph order, form, focus, flow. I can talk about those issues best by working from good writing rather than from flawed examples, so you will read four well-written pieces in this chapter. After each piece you will read comments about its strengths and about specific choices the writer made. To illustrate particular points, I have incorporated less effective versions of some passages into the comments.

I chose the four examples in this chapter to represent a cross-section of writing assignments that readers of this book might encounter: one partial essay in a conventional form, one full essay in an unconventional form (with some dialogue), one literary review, and one dissertation abstract. The dissertation abstract, taken from a typical piece of quantitative research, will be particularly valuable to you if you are engaged in research. If you are unfamiliar with research writing and find technical aspects of that example perplexing, you may either skip over it or generalize some of its characteristics to your nonresearch writing.

Though the primary purpose of this chapter is to comment on the larger picture of writing, along the way I will take opportunities to reinforce earlier material. As in previous chapters, bold numbers enclosed in wavy brackets **{ }** refer to writing principles shown on the BOOKMARK.

1. Partial Essay: Conventional Form

The basic unit by which a good piece of writing is organized is the paragraph; each paragraph should have a clear, definite function. That is the case in the prison-reform essay below. Paragraph one states the problem and reveals the writer's status, paragraph two introduces the idea for a two-level system, and paragraphs three and four describe the two levels respectively.

A CITIZEN'S IDEA FOR PRISON REFORM

The large number of persons who oscillate from prison to freedom to prison indicate that we manage our criminal population poorly. Aggravating the problem are early-release programs that allow overcrowded, financially-strapped prisons to set felons free simply for lack of a place to keep them. The system is broken. I would like to offer, as a layman, one commonsense idea for criminal justice professionals to consider as they try to repair it.

At the heart of prison reform should be recognition that we have more than one level of criminal, and therefore need more than one level of imprisonment. In simple terms, there are criminals who have gone wrong and whom we have hope of inducing to go right, and there are criminals who have gone very wrong—or who have gone wrong repeatedly—and who need to be separated permanently from noncriminal society.

For the first category of prisoner we need a *rehabilitation level* of imprisonment (R-level), which would approximate the present system. R-level imprisonment would be designed to reform prisoners—to give them the mind-set and skills needed to walk away from criminal behavior and join the noncriminal population. Rehabilitation is expensive: it entails education programs, libraries, recreation facilities, mental-health professionals, social workers, job-training and placement, and other appointments common in today's prisons. Those goods and services inflate the cost of incarceration considerably, but the money is well spent when it enables parolees to assume noncriminal lives.

For the second category of prisoner we need a *storage level* of imprisonment (S-level), which would approximate the prerehabilitation-era prison system. S-level imprisonment would be designed solely to warehouse prisoners—to keep them separated from the noncriminal population. Storage would require little space and little expense: a small cell, a bed, a toilet, food, and medical care. The Spartan S-level appointments would be imposed neither to punish prisoners nor to exercise vindictiveness, but simply to give innocent, honest, productive citizens safety and peace of mind at a reasonable cost—because they deserve it.

(Reminder: this is only the first half of an essay.)

One key to writing a paragraph that has a specific, identifiable function is to arrange material in the most fruitful order **{3}**. For example, read this lesser version of paragraph one:

> I would like to offer, as a layman, one commonsense idea for criminal justice professionals to consider as a way to fix our broken prison system. We manage our criminal population poorly, judging by the number of persons who oscillate from prison to freedom to prison. Early-release programs that allow overcrowded, financially-strapped prisons to set felons free simply for lack of a place to keep them aggravate the problem.

The first sentence sounds audacious as an opening statement, and the last sentence leads nowhere. Also, reordered material in the second and third sentences separates two phrases whose proximity had oriented readers well to the original paragraph's content: *we manage our criminal population poorly* and *aggravating the problem.*

Before leaving the opening paragraph, I should note two subtleties that help pull the reader into everything that follows. First, the writer gives readers a foundation for material to come by referring to three specific subproblems—repeat offenders,[9] overcrowding, and cost. Second, the writer manages to create some sense of credibility by neither pretending expertise (<u>as a layman</u>) nor apologizing for the lack of it (<u>one commonsense idea</u> . . . <u>to consider</u>).

As important as order within paragraphs is order between paragraphs. Paragraph two sets up paragraphs three and four by describing the basic prison-reform plan and giving a rationale: the prison system should be reorganized into two distinct levels of incarceration because it houses two distinct levels of prisoner. The writer was wise not to launch into details until after stating, in a separate paragraph, the basic premise underlying those details. Notice how economically that was done. One of the most difficult paragraphs to write in an essay is the one that states an opening position; overwriting and lack of form are common, as in this version of the second paragraph **{9}**:

> An important aspect of crime and punishment to be recognized is that we have in our society more than one level of criminal. To respond to multiple-level criminals with one level of imprisonment is inappropriate. For example, some crimes are committed by offenders who have gone wrong, but who can be turned around with rehabilitation. Others crimes are committed by hardened criminals who will never be essentially different than they are, or by habitual criminals who will continue to endanger noncriminal society regardless of repeated efforts at rehabilitation. We need to do our best to reform the criminal who can be rehabilitated, but we need to simply keep the incorrigible criminal separated permanently from noncriminal society.

The version above is not disastrous, but it is bloated **{9}**, and it lacks the symmetry of the original:

> —more than one level of criminal; more than one level of imprisonment
> —have gone wrong; have gone very wrong; have gone wrong repeatedly **{13}**

The combination of brevity and symmetry in the original keeps readers out of the fog, but it does more than that; it carries readers along with a graceful rhythm. To appreciate the differences fully, read each version aloud **{19}**.

Paragraph three and paragraph four are each devoted to one of the two levels of imprisonment endorsed by the writer. To present the elements of a piece (paragraph 2) and then describe each of those elements with a paragraph of its own (paragraphs 3 and 4)—in the same order they were presented—creates an easy flow. It also prepares readers well for the develop-

---

[9] Word-Choice Note No. 1: The writer used *recidivism,* a shorter and more precise term, in an earlier draft, then retreated to *repeat offenders* to avoid distracting readers unfamiliar with the term *recidivism.* That is a typical word-choice judgment that writers have to make.

ment of thoughts based on those elements (not shown in this partial essay). Take particular note of these techniques if you will be writing a thesis or dissertation proposal. This type of paragraph sequencing is indispensable to any kind of proposal writing.

Finally, notice the extent to which the writer has constructed paragraph four parallel to paragraph three **{13}**. That scheme helps readers see similarities and differences between the two levels of imprisonment. Suppose the writer had begun paragraph four like this: "Before rehabilitation days, prisoners had a cell, a bed, a toilet, and medical care, and that was all." The reader's mind would have been cast away temporarily, and reeled back only when the writer got around to mentioning "second category of prisoner," and "storage level (S-level)." Contrary to popular opinion, reading comprehension begins *not* with the reader, but with the writer.

2. Full Essay: Unconventional Form

The story-like opening of *Villagers and Children* is unconventional in essay writing. Good writers choose the most effective form for a piece, regardless of how unorthodox.[10]

VILLAGERS AND CHILDREN

The little girl I saw in a restaurant booth last week was about five or six. Her mother had just chided her for putting a piece of paper where the plate belonged, and the little girl looked ambivalent about whether to obey her mother or continue to gaze at the paper. It was filled with a colorful scene in crayon: grass and trees, bright flowers, sky and clouds, and a few birds. I wanted to talk to the mother: *Look at the beauty in that picture. Look at the beauty in the child who created it—your child! Appreciate that beauty; help it flourish.*

A man in the booth next to theirs had been watching, too. When he stood to pay his bill he made a point to notice the picture and comment on it.

"That's beautiful. Did you make it?"

"Yes, I did." The little girl was cheered by his attention. Then the man gently picked up the picture to get a closer look.

"I'm impressed. Those trees look almost real; and I love that bird. And the colors you've chosen for the flowers couldn't be better." As he handed the picture back to the little girl, he added "You might be a famous artist some day with talent like that." She beamed and thanked him. The picture was truly exceptional. She was not just another cute child being gushed over by an ingenuous adult, but a talented little girl who deserved praise and encouragement.

(continued on next page)

[10] Word-Choice Note No. 2: In an earlier draft, the writer chose *ambivalent* over *torn* (second line) because of the proximity of the word *paper* and its association with *torn*—a matter of protecting the reader from distraction.

When the man returned to his table to leave a tip, the little girl thrust the picture at him with a smile. "I want you to have it," she said.

"But if I take it you won't have it to look at."

"That's OK. I can make more!" I heard pride and confidence in her voice.

"Thank you," said the man graciously. Then he took the picture and bade her good-bye with the words "You've made my day." Anyone watching knew the reverse was also true, and more powerfully so: the man had made the little girl's day. One could easily imagine her going home and beginning to draw pictures with gleeful fury.

As the restaurant door swung shut behind the man, I realized I had just seen him act out a long-held, well-known adage: *It takes a village to raise a child.* The child's mother had received the man's actions warmly and gratefully, as if to say "I was distracted, and I missed something important; thanks for picking up the slack." The next day she might pick up the slack for another parent. A healthy village works that way. Parents are responsible for raising their children, but the load parents carry is lightened by villagers who act as the man in the restaurant did.

Adults who do not give the best of themselves to children probably underestimate their own effect on the village. They feel less visible—less potent—than they are. All villagers need to understand that children live with developmental radar fine-tuned to the sights and sounds around them. Adults are models, willing or not: models of whatever behavior they exhibit. Their glances can be friendly or menacing; their words soothing or cutting; their actions benevolent or selfish. Everything is seen by little eyes, heard by little ears, and stored in little minds. Where adults consciously influence all children for the better, a village becomes a wonderful place to live. Parents raise children more easily, children tend to become better models themselves, and a happy cycle is locked into place.

Of course none of this is new; the formula for nurturing the next generation has deep roots. John Donne, when he wrote *No Man Is An Island,* announced "I am involved in mankind," and his words still ring like a trumpet call four hundred years later. They rang through the restaurant last week when a man engaged a little girl in conversation. ***I am involved in mankind.*** As simple as that statement is on the surface, and as dated as its wording will sound to some, it may be the highest calling to which any of us can aspire.

Usually essay writers are trying to attract readers to their viewpoint regarding a particular issue. The writer of *Villagers and Children* used a cryptic title and a personal anecdote to pique the reader's interest, linked the title and anecdote to a well-known adage, and then began to build arguments only after reader and writer were looking through the same lens. Notice how an explicit title and a more conventional approach drain life from the first part of the piece.

IT TAKES A VILLAGE TO RAISE A CHILD

Child-raising is a complex responsibility. Even competent, committed, loving parents make mistakes with their children, and fail periodically to capitalize on ready-made opportunities to teach or to encourage them. That is why parents need help from other adults, even strangers, who have contact with their children. As stated in a long-held, well-known adage, *It takes a village to raise a child.*

I saw an example in a restaurant just last week. A girl about five or six years old was preoccupied with a crayon drawing she had made, and her mother told her to remove it from the table. I was wishing that the mother would appreciate the picture more, and a man at the table next to theirs apparently had similar thoughts. He made the girl happy by praising the picture when he stood to leave, and the girl was so flattered that she gave the picture to him.

These paragraphs are concise and well-written, and they contain the basic information to be imparted, but their impact is no match for the impact of the original.

The writer of *Villagers and Children* seems passionate about the subject of the essay, which reminds me to warn you that passion is a two-edged sword: it stirs the fires and keeps writers writing through fatigue and discouragement, but it also lures writers to insert pet ideas and slavishly-crafted sentences where a cooler head would say "no, that damages the focus of this piece"**{2}**. During an early stage of writing, *Villagers and Children* lost its focus when the writer—irritated at the thought of government officials trying to skew the meaning of the original adage—wrote this into the third-to-last paragraph, right after the adage:

> Furthermore, this was a genuine village at work—not a paternalistic government-run village administered by inefficient bureaucrats and paid for by unwilling taxpayers.

The writer may have fallen into that little side trip (later revised out) partially because of the essay's unconventional form. One advantage of the more conventional opening you saw in the prison-reform piece is that the writer creates some clear self-instruction to follow regarding purpose and focus.

Closing an essay is as critical as opening it. The writer of *Villagers and Children* wanted to finish with two points: 1) villagers helping to raise each other's children is an age-old idea, and 2) positive involvement in the lives of others is a high calling. John Donne's *No Man Is An Island* came to mind as one of the writer's favorite poems related to the topic, and a tug-of-war began; in the first few drafts the information about John Donne and his poem looked tacked on and disjointed. Wanting very much to make the Donne connection work, the writer identified problems and found solutions: a transition sentence was needed to tie Donne to the next-to-last paragraph **{4}** ("Of course none of this is new; the formula for nurturing the next generation has deep roots."); readers unfamiliar with Donne needed a time frame ("words still ring . . . four hundred years later"); and Donne had to be connected to the opening story about the little girl ("they rang through the restaurant last week").

A writer who tries to stitch new material into a piece, then finds bumps in the form and flow, needs to ask several questions. How valuable is the material to the writing objective? Would something else do as well and fit more naturally? How much time is the writer willing to invest to fit a less-than-round peg into a well-rounded hole? In the midst of these questions a writer begins to understand fully the statements about revision in the introduction of this book: ***Writing is revision. First drafts are tomorrow's trash; second and third drafts are momentum toward a good final copy.***

3. Literary Review

Suppose you were given this writing assignment: In just 500 words, give the essence of two audiobooks spanning 22 tapes, give your assessment of their quality, and tell readers how to locate the tapes and what the cost will be to buy or rent. That is typical of the challenge set before book reviewers every day: say much in a small space, and say it well. The nature of the challenge makes any good literary review an excellent display of writing skill.

Had you been given Gayle Sims's assignment, below, how might you have begun? Feeling the heat of limited space on the back of your neck, you might have used as few words as possible to get into the content of the first tape, something like this:

> I recommend highly **Coming Out of the Ice: An Unexpected Life** by Victor Herman (Blackstone Audiobooks, 800-729-2665, unabridged in 10 cassettes, purchase $69.95, rental $13.95). The heartening memoir of Herman, a young American . . .

Gayle Sims did not. She used 100 words—20 percent of her total space—just to introduce the review; but notice how well she used those words. Knowing the value of selling readers on quality before launching into content, she endorsed the first audiobook obliquely with "I recommended . . . to a friend"; then she used her friend's words, "I want to listen to another book as important as that," to imply that the book was uncommonly good; and finally she bolstered her endorsement with the friend's credentials as a bookstore owner and lover of fine literature. By then she had impelled even the most skeptical reader to continue reading, an accomplishment well worth 100 words.

AUDIO BOOKS

Gayle Sims, *Philadelphia Inquirer*

I recommended **Coming Out of the Ice: An Unexpected Life** by Victor Herman (Blackstone Audiobooks, 800-729-2665, unabridged in 10 cassettes, purchase $69.95, rental $13.95) to a friend. It not only hooked her for life on spoken books, but it also became her standard for all others. "I want to listen to another book as important as that," she repeatedly says.

My friend is an artist of Jewish-Russian ancestry who grew up hearing tragic stories of her family's suffering under Stalin. She is a gifted potter (who listens while working), an owner of a rare-book store, and a lover of great literature. The heartening memoir of Herman, a young American who moved with his family in 1931 from Detroit to the Soviet Union, where his father set up an auto plant for the Ford Motor Co., had a haunting effect on her.

Herman, a teenager who adored his Jewish Russian-born father, at first thrived in the Soviet Union as an outstanding athlete. He became a celebrity and was called "the Lindbergh of Russia" after setting a world record for parachute jumps. When he refused to sign a document stating he was a native of the U.S.S.R. in 1938, he was thrown into prison for 18 years, beginning a nightmare of starvation and torture.

(continued on next page)

> Herman was one of the few prisoners who survived Stalin's 30-year reign of terror that resulted in the deaths of tens of millions of people.
>
> The rich, mellifluous voice of narrator Christopher Hurt personalizes Herman's daily endurance in the prisons and camps where he ate rats to keep from starving and was never given a reason for his imprisonment. After he was released from prison, he was exiled to Siberia, where he met and married a beautiful Russian gymnast. They lived with their baby in the forest in a cave chopped out under the ice. Theirs is a torturous love story of the power of the human spirit.
>
> After 45 years, remarkably, Herman returned to Detroit. He wrote his memoir while waiting for his wife and two daughters to come to the United States.
>
> *Coming Out of the Ice* inspired me to listen to **Stalin: Breaker of Nations** by Sovietologist Robert Conquest (Recorded Books, 800-638-1304, 12 cassettes, purchase $97.00, rental $18.50). I studied some Russian history in college, but I wanted to know more about the powerful maniac who used murder and torture to resolve difficulties and maintain power. He is quoted as saying, "No man, no problem." He used this policy to liquidate entire classes of people.
>
> Stalin concealed his monstrous instincts behind a mask of charm and sickened the spirit of millions of cowering Russians.
>
> Stalin also deceived some leaders in democratic countries, including President Franklin Roosevelt, and his own mentor, Lenin, who realized Stalin's insanity too late. Shortly before his death, Lenin oddly described Stalin's worst quality as "rudeness."
>
> This biography is read by the superb narrator Nelson Runger, who has a talent for making even pedantic history come alive with his remarkable voice.
>
> These two haunting audio books evoke tremendous feeling: admiration for Victor Herman and revulsion for Joseph Stalin.

Notice next a skillful third-paragraph synopsis of the storyline in about 70 words. We have all read sentences longer than that paragraph, yet in those 70 words Gayle Sims takes readers through the essential run of the story quickly and clearly. My sense is that not a word could be moved or removed without damaging the whole—the essence of writing for efficient reading.

With a few well-chosen details in the fifth paragraph, Sims puts enough specific meat on the bones of the third paragraph to irrevocably hook readers who at that point are leaning toward the book. Who could resist "eat rats to keep from starving," and "lived with their baby . . . in a cave chopped out under the ice"? Skillfully, Sims also slipped in praise of the oral delivery of the story by announcing the fifth-paragraph specifics through the "rich, mellifluous voice of narrator Christopher Hurt."

Gayle Sims avoided introducing the second review with a hackneyed phrase ("Another audiobook I have enjoyed recently . . .") by choosing books so closely related in content that the first essentially introduces the second by segue. Also, she found she could do without an elaborate endorsement of the second book. Her endorsement of the first was so powerful, and the two books so easily associated with each other, that the reader's confidence in the quality of *Coming Out of the Ice: An Unexpected Life* spills over to *Stalin: Breaker of Nations*. Be careful not to create such a "halo effect" inadvertently, because it is deceiving; at the same time, Sims used the effect well to endorse a book she admires without spending valuable word space.

Knowing that documentary-type books have a reputation for blandness, Gayle Sims inserted into the second review a few tidbits about Stalin's maniacal nature and heinous acts, then chose a Stalin quote that offers both power and brevity: "No man, no problem." To neutralize further the reader's possible fear of blandness, she cited narrator Nelson Runger's talent for "making even pedantic history come alive." She neatly recommends and reviews simultaneously.

One compromise that seems inescapable when putting so much information in so short a space is indulgence in the one-sentence paragraph, supposedly anathema to good writing: notice paragraph four and some of the later paragraphs. Maybe Sims could have found a way to reduce the number of one-sentence paragraphs, but that mechanical detail pales in the shadow of her fine and superbly compact writing accomplishment. In the last paragraph, for example, she summarizes in one 17-word sentence—in a way that makes the reader want to partake of both books—the effectiveness of the two in relation to each other. I can think of no better closing.

4. Dissertation Abstract

Readers of research abstracts want four pieces of information: the purpose of the research, the subjects, what was done, and what was found. That information needs to be presented very clearly and economically in dissertation and journal-article abstracts.

PERSONAL TEMPO AND MUSIC SYNCHRONIZATION ABILITY IN PRIMARY-AGED CHILDREN

The purposes of this study were to 1) investigate the personal tempos of primary-aged children for within-child consistency and between-child variability, and 2) identify relationships between personal tempo and a primary-aged child's ability to synchronize movement with music at a variety of tempos. Ninety-six randomly-selected subjects in grades K–3 were distributed equally by sex and grade level.

Subjects were measured four times for personal tempo (PT): initial measurement, five minutes later, one week later, and another week later. The activity measured was a series of two-handed lap pats, self-initiated without aural stimulation, "in a steady beat that feels good to you." Within-subject SD for the four PT measurements was 10 beats per minute; between-subject SD was 30. Seventy-eight subjects with a coefficient of variation (CV) less than .17 were labeled Consistent PTs; 18 subjects with a CV between .17 and .47 were labeled Inconsistent PTs. Only the data for consistent PTs was included in the analysis.

Between-subject PTs ranged 500 percent, MM 40 to MM 210, compared to the maximum within-child range of 47 percent, evidence that the condition of within-child consistency and between-child variability of PT does exist in children of grades K–3. The mean PT was 107. Differences were found in mean PT between grades, but high between-subject variability kept the differences from being statistically significant. Specifically, mean PT decreased in beats-per-minute as grade level increased.

(continued on next page)

Subjects were administered the *Primary Measure of Kinesthetic Response to Tempo in Music*, created for this study by Professor James O. Froseth of the University of Michigan School of Music. This test contains 14 tape-recorded musical items for synchronization, ranging in tempo from MM 57 to MM 130, and shall be referred to here as the *synchronization test* or *synchronization scores*. Subjects showed synchronization ability for each item by coordinating two-handed lap pats with the sound of the music.

The highest mean synchronization score collectively was for the item at or nearest each subject's personal tempo. Scores generally decreased as items diverged, either faster or slower, from PT. The falloff of synchronization scores was more consistent and more severe with movement to the slow side of personal tempo than with movement to the fast side. Directions of error were consistently toward PT.

Differences in synchronization scores were significant between grade levels, between percentile rankings on the rhythm subtest of the *Primary Measures of Music Audiation*, and between children of greater prior musical influences and children of lesser prior musical influences ($p < .01$). Differences between male and female subjects were not statistically significant ($p > .05$).

A comparison of mean synchronization scores between the 78 Consistent PTs and the 18 Inconsistent PTs whose scores had been excluded from analysis revealed a surprise: the Inconsistent PTs scored consistently and significantly higher on the synchronization test than did the Consistent PTs.

Research writing is technical, complex, and jammed with information—and therefore difficult to read. Its richness challenges writers all the more to produce readable copy. For example, the original terms used in this study for *within-child* and *between-child* were *intraindividual* and *interindividual*. Meaning is the same; the difference is in how intensely the reader has to think to assimilate the meaning. ***Never choose high-sounding terms over easily understood terms simply to sound academic*** {17}.

Standard procedure in research writing is to attach a symbol in parentheses after the first appearance of a technical term (PT; CV). The writer can then use the symbol subsequently so readers will not have to keep rereading the full term. Sometimes the term and the symbol are used interchangeably to save reading time while keeping the meaning of the symbol in the reader's mind; the term *personal tempo* and the symbol *PT* are used that way in this piece.

In research reports, tests are commonly abbreviated with their initials, but the writer chose not to do that for either of the tests cited in this abstract. *Primary Measures of Music Audiation* is commonly written *PMMA*, but that was unnecessary because the test is cited only once. *Primary Measures of Kinesthetic Response to Tempo in Music* is cited multiple times, but *synchronization test* and *synchronization scores* are easier terms for readers to interpret in subsequent paragraphs than would be *PMKRTM,* an awkward acronym. Writers should write what readers need.

Symbols can be used without explanation so long as their use is common among potential readers. For example, musicians know that MM signifies metronome marking, i.e., beats per minute, and consumers of research know that SD signifies standard deviation and $p < .01$

signifies the probability of a chance occurrence as less than one in 100. The key is to know your audience and assume only as much as is reasonable to assume.

Wise paragraphing is particularly important to the ease of reading a research abstract or research report. The paragraph functions in this abstract are clear and sensible:

¶ 1: Purpose and subjects
¶ 2: PT measurement; within-subject PT results
¶ 3: Between-subject PT results; conclusion about problem 1
¶ 4: Synchronization measurement
¶ 5: Synchronization test results relative to problem 2
¶ 6: Relationships between synchronization ability and other factors
¶ 7: A surprise sidebar to the results of the study

Resist the temptation to blend material together into larger paragraphs in research writing, particularly in abstract writing. Paragraphs help you place highly related pieces of material together and isolate them from unrelated or more distantly related material. That is a boon to comprehension, especially for readers who find themselves in a tight spot.

Finally, if you have a penchant for flowery phrases, be vigilant about your research writing: cool, dispassionate, razor-sharp expression is important. Beware research writing with sentences that roll and tumble like the sentences of a romance novel:

> This study has sought to investigate the consistency with which a given primary-aged child expresses himself or herself temporally when self-expression is unimpeded by suggestion, and contrarily, the extent to which such free expression varies from one child to another. This study has sought further to discover the extent to which said personal tempo impinges upon the primary-aged child's efforts to synchronize movement to music at a variety of tempos.

A Closing Note

Of course *The Readable Thesis* is meant to help you write full documents—larger tasks than anything shown in this chapter. Alas, in choosing examples I must draw the line somewhere to retain a hint of slimness or I would never induce you to pick this book up—and then where would we be? I do want to give you one more piece of help with large writing projects, however, so I have written Chapter 8, *How I Write.* There you will read—as closely as I can represent it on paper—an account of how I go about creating a piece of writing. I hope you find it helpful.

Note: Except for the literary review by Gayle Sims, Darrel Walters is the author of all examples shown in this chapter.

HOW I WRITE

In this final chapter I want to just talk to you about writing—about what I believe, how I think, how I feel, and what I do when I write. There is no single best way to go about writing, but if I tell you what works for me you might be able to take from it a few things that work for you. The form of the chapter is direct advice from me to you, based on my experience. The aim of the chapter is to answer questions you might ask if we had a chance to sit down together and visit about the subject of writing:

- When a writing project is big, how do you know where to start?
- What kinds of problems do you encounter while writing, and how do you solve them?
- What kinds of thoughts and feelings come to you as you write?
- At what point do you revise, and how much?

There are three sections to this chapter, each containing a few subsections.

1. Preparing to Write
2. Writing
3. Revising

Before starting Section 1 I need to tell you about two principles in which I believe firmly. You may believe differently, but you need to know my attitude toward writing to make the most sense of what I have to say. First, I believe your writing represents you. It tells readers something about who you are before it tells them what you have to say. When you write just well enough to get by, you not only hamper readers but you represent yourself poorly. Second, I believe you have specific responsibilities when you write. You should not be reckless with facts, deceptive in argument, or irresponsible about citing other persons in context **{24}**. Further, your responsibility grows as you learn to write better, because skillful writing wins more readers. Know the power of the tool you are honing, and use it honestly and ethically.

1. Preparing to Write

This section is more than just an introduction to Sections 2 (writing) and 3 (revising). As much as half the effort expended on a writing project and half the quality of the final copy can be accounted for by preparation. Preparing to write is generally less gratifying than writing and revising—just as preparing a rough surface for painting is less gratifying than painting it—but preparation affects the final product profoundly. That is especially true for a thesis or dissertation proposal, but it is true for every other type of writing project as well, down to the simple one-page paper.

Having the Goods

The first step toward writing well is having something to say. Long before you conceive of a specific writing project you will be preparing for it by listening to other people, asking probing questions, contemplating ideas, and perhaps keeping notes about thoughts and pieces of information important to you. I recommend highly that you keep a file of thoughts, ideas, and topics, preferably on a computer disk. That file becomes a preserve for the occasional poignant thoughts that come to you and would otherwise dissipate with time. It gives you a kind of window to your own mind, which you can open at will, peer into, and apply to writing tasks. I began such a file years ago, and I draw on it frequently. Just remember that a computer disk is to thoughts and information as an attic is to household items: it lets you save a great amount of material against its day of usefulness, but you need to sort, discard, and relabel periodically to know what you have and how to put it to use.

If you plan to write a master's thesis, a doctoral dissertation, or a monograph, you need to be particularly diligent about this reading/thinking stage. Such projects are preceded by a proposal, which is preceded by a review of literature, which is preceded by exploratory thoughts and conversations. I encourage students to begin prewriting machinations as much as a year before starting to write the proposal, and certainly no less than six months before. Seek persons whose thinking you respect—persons whose experiences and knowledge coincide with potential topics—and engage them in conversation. Ask them to recommend material to read, then read it. Let the bibliographies launch you into your review of literature.

If you are writing a term paper, or even a smaller assignment, thought and conversation will be valuable to you, too. Participate in class discussion and steer it toward topics you may be interested in developing into papers. Talk to teachers, friends, and relatives about ideas, take notes, and when an idea catches your interest, do a little exploratory writing to see where it leads. Have someone read your exploratory writing and respond to it. Then if you find yourself impatiently explaining and defending what you wrote, try to think and write more clearly. That type of preliminary activity may sound like overkill, but it will give you an exhilarating head start on a paper. If you have ever found yourself sitting and thinking about what to write—trying to begin a writing assignment from a dead standstill—you will appreciate the value of such a head start.

Working with Timetables

To follow the preceding advice is to take the first step toward setting a timetable for your project, and that is important whether you are writing a thesis proposal or a five-page paper. Doom begins to hover over most substandard pieces of writing weeks before the writer begins work; that is, at the point the writer *should* have begun work. I see students, particularly undergraduate students, begin pulling thoughts together for a major paper only a few days before the deadline. I know before the first word is written that the product will be mediocre at best. You can make no stronger statement about your commitment to quality in a writing project than to allot enough time to read, think, collect material, write, and revise. A paper that needs five or six weeks of work and is given one will be as palatable as a cake that needs 25 to 30 minutes of baking time, but is taken out of the oven after five.

Conceiving Your Audience

Another important aspect of preparing to write will be your conception of an audience. Will your topic interest secondary school principals, social workers, parents of young children, high school students, psychologists? You will write best when you know your audience and envision the effect your piece might have on them.

Of course the audience-conception approach does take away a popular option—writing to the instructor as audience—but that loss only reduces the chances of your writing a piece of embarrassing, pandering nothingness. To write what you think an instructor wants to read is to risk feeding back familiar classroom material, maybe even a rewording of something the instructor said. That is hardly impressive. Good instructors treasure original thought in student papers. How ironic that writing to please an instructor is one of the least reliable ways to please an instructor!

A good mind-set is to think in terms of publication, whether you intend to publish or not. Think of a journal whose readership would be interested in your topic. Imagine preparing an article for submission, and envision the readers whom you want to inform and influence. That will motivate you to get to work, and it will invigorate your writing.

Organizing Your Information

Before you begin to write, you need to transform the material you have collected into manageable compartments of like information and ideas. For large projects, that material can be a mountain. How you do that is up to you. Some writers make detailed outlines; I find them constricting. Some pull from the mountain as they write; I find that chaotic, frustrating, and nerve-wracking.

Before I became reliant on the use of a word processor,[11] I organized material for a writing project by physically stacking news clippings, published articles, notes to myself, and so forth into piles that represented what I considered to be sections of the project. Then I read through the material, sometimes divided the material further into subsections, and labeled each piece clearly. I used a numbering system if the project was large. In effect, I built an outline of the materials. I find freedom and creativity in building an outline of sorts from the material rather than writing an outline and then trying to fulfill it.

I still organize hard-copy material into stacks (books and articles in particular), but I am more likely now to have some material in a computer file. In the numbered entries below, you will read an account of the organizing steps that I generally follow, but do not think of these steps too rigidly. In reality, all the time you work on a written project you will find that you move from hatching ideas to refining specifics to incorporating supporting material to hatching more ideas—ideas relative to both your content and your presentation.

1. I have essays and articles (mine and others), notes to myself, and so forth stored in computer files. Sometimes a sentence or paragraph from one of those pieces has a place (maybe with variation) in the current work. I copy those items into the file in which the current piece will be written, trying to clump them by topic.

2. After finishing the electronic transfers, I turn to paper sources (books, articles, essays). I type into logical places in the file anything that is short and highly likely to become part of the piece. Then I set the corresponding hard copy aside.

3. As I carry out steps 1 and 2, thoughts occur to me about how to introduce material or tie material together, or how to use it to support an argument. I type notes to myself that range from a few words of reminder to nearly polished sentences. Sometimes I put reminder notes in parentheses.

---

[11] Word processor: a marvelous tool stuck with an ugly, inappropriate name.

4. As I see the clumps of material suggest sections within the piece, I insert section titles in bold type. Within those sections, I move material around so it gradually assumes a sequence that seems to make sense for the project. In some cases I create subsection names.
5. I arrange the remaining paper material (books, articles, etc.) into stacks to coincide with the sections and subsections I have created in the project file. The stacked material at that point amounts to whatever is too extensive or too tentative for me to type into the file during the preparation stage.
6. I label the stacked materials according to the sections in the file where they are likely to come into play, then type author names into the file as reminders to check hard copy at particular points. (I use underlining or bold type to make reminders easy to spot as I write.)

Once I have prepared my materials in this way, I am ready to begin writing.

2. Writing

I do most of my writing at a computer, a common practice among writers now. If you write by hand or typewriter you will need to adapt some of my comments, but most of what I have to say involves not so much mechanics as mind-set, self discipline, and feelings about writing.

Getting Started

I scan my material to get ideas flowing for the most difficult part of the assignment, the opening. If I feel adrift I may even print my preliminary pages. Reading hard copy and making pencil marks tends to get my mind into motion. Then I begin work on the opening, which may be one paragraph or several. I have two goals for the opening: 1) Orient readers to what I am writing about and how I have organized it; 2) Interest readers in continuing to read. A good introduction makes the rest of the piece easier to write by giving self-direction and by reducing the reader's need for explanations and transitional sentences. It also makes the reader more receptive to what I have to say.

You need to know that writing the first paragraph or two of a piece is time consuming: I may spend hours getting a piece started, and still have an opening that I will revise heavily later. Sometimes I essentially give up on the opening—leave it in disarray—until I have learned enough about my own piece to come back and do a better job. I once abandoned several openings for a chapter titled "Sequencing for Efficient Learning" (1992). After writing the entire chapter, I hit upon an idea. Rather than introduce learning theories and the structure of the piece right away, I opened with anecdotes that might seize the reader's attention. The editor agreed with the approach.

> Arthur Pryor, internationally acclaimed trombonist with the Sousa band, is said to have credited his musicianship to "a little town in Missouri where there were no teachers to get in my way." More recently, neurologist and amateur musician Frank Wilson, commenting about the impatience of music students, said that "beginners tend to resent the learning process, as though it were some sort of obstacle in their way" (1986, 191). The last thing you will want as a teacher is to become an obstacle—to obstruct learning by presenting students with poorly sequenced learning experiences. Good teachers think about more than what to teach and how to teach; they think about when and when not to teach particular lessons.

True confession time: that is not the paragraph I published in 1992. It is today's revision. Compare the underlined parts of the original (below) with today's revision, and you will see that I have made a shift toward simpler, more personal language in the last few years.

> Arthur Pryor, internationally acclaimed trombonist with the Sousa band, <u>allegedly attributed</u> his musicianship to <u>having come from a little town in Missouri where there were</u> "no teachers to get in my way." More recently, neurologist and amateur musician Frank Wilson, commenting about the impatience of music students, <u>observed</u> that "beginners tend to resent the learning process, as though it were some sort of obstacle in their way" (1986, 191). The last thing <u>a teacher wants to do</u> is obstruct learning by presenting students with poorly sequenced learning experiences. Good teachers think about more than what to teach and how to teach; they think about when and when not to teach particular lessons

Writing style grows constantly for anyone who writes and thinks about writing.

Now you may be thinking, "I know what he means about writing an opening" or you may be thinking, "He can't be serious; that sounds like a huge job." Your view will depend on the extent to which you have developed a feel for the task of writing.

A Feel for Writing

If you play baseball you know the feeling of standing at the plate and trying to hit a pitched ball, and you know the feeling of fielding a hard grounder to your left. If you play violin you know the feeling of tucking the instrument securely under your chin, tightening the bow hairs to exactly the right tension, tuning the strings, and coordinating movement between fingers and bow arm. Writing is like other skills: the more you write the more you acquire a feel for it—a feel that lets you predict what lies ahead, judge the formidability of various segments of the process, and react to difficulties without overreacting to them. That is why I suggested earlier that you write short pieces, aside from formal writing projects, then discuss them with others. You can stimulate your feeling for writing all the more by extending those exercises to off-topic writing: pieces completely unrelated to anything you expect to pursue formally. I write poetry and children's literature, for example, and share it with friends. My academic writing then benefits from my having expanded my imagination, wrestled with word choice and sentence structure in another dimension, and refreshed the writing corner of my brain.

Patience and Thought

When you want instant gratification, you will have to turn to something other than writing. To write well you need to take time to think deeply and clearly about your purpose, about what to say, and about how to say it. ***Writing is thought made visible,*** so you cannot expect to write more clearly than you think.[12]

Writing without sufficient thought behind it is usually a sign of impetuousness. If you are an impetuous writer, one who begins striking keys before assembling thoughts, try this exercise in patience. It is artificial in that you could never do all your writing in this fashion, but as an exercise it will build writing muscles much as ankle weights build running muscles.

1. Construct a sentence mentally. Speak it aloud to give yourself a chance to hear what works. Fix inconsistencies, redundancies, vague expression, and so forth in your mind.
2. When you have recited a good sentence, put it on paper. Construct a whole paragraph by this method, sentence-by-sentence, then take a little time away from it.
3. When you come back, read the paragraph aloud. Ask yourself questions about spots that sound awkward or unclear. Work specifically to remove needless words and to use the best words. Repair problems with a pencil, then type a clean copy.
4. The next day, read the clean version and look back at the penciled version to see what thought processes you went through. Make a new revision based on whatever comes to mind with the fresh look.

---

[12] On the other hand, lack of mechanical skill and experience can cause writers to write *less* clearly than they think.

You may be pleasantly surprised at how time and thought improve your writing. If you like what you see, remember how you achieved it.

Writers sometimes make the mistake of using outside information as a substitute for thinking. Never insert a citation into your writing as if it has the strength to mean something in isolation from your message and your structure. When you do that, you pass responsibility to the other author. That means you have lost control over your own work. If a powerful, stimulating citation tempts you to alter your paper fundamentally, inspect all your other material relative to the changes you contemplate. Ask yourself if the new inspiration truly has the strength and validity to override all you have planned. If you decide to restructure the piece, do it thoroughly, from the roots up. You will need to retrench back to the preparation stage to be sure everything fits together well.

The relationship between thinking and writing is itself interesting food for thought; in that vein, allow me one brief side trip from the purpose of this chapter. If good thinking is important to good writing, will a commitment to good writing encourage and help develop good thinking? If so, teachers who ask children to write only from a stream of consciousness may not be achieving their aims at all. Teachers of that persuasion sometimes argue that they encourage students to think by valuing content and ignoring structure. As an occasional exercise, or as a gimmick with which to get a project started—a kind of brainstorming session—the approach has merit. Used regularly, though, a stream-of-consciousness approach may hold back development of thinking skills by keeping students mired in shallowness.

Dimensions of Writing

These four statements and the elaborations that follow will tell you how I think about specific dimensions of writing.

- The document is the unit of purpose.
- The paragraph is the unit of composition.
- The sentence is the unit of expression.
- The word is the unit of meaning.

The document is the unit of purpose: Every piece you write has a purpose behind it; in most cases you will want to state that purpose clearly for the reader. When detail later distracts you from the purpose, as it will for periods of time, reread your purpose statement to be sure you stay on track. When you read the total piece for effect during post-writing revision, purpose will return to the forefront of your thinking.

The paragraph is the unit of composition: Your larger mission—to write a paper, or an article, or a chapter—consists of many smaller missions: to write paragraphs that organize material by topics or by trains of thought for the reader. Paragraphs generally need a strong topic sentence to declare their business. Usually the topic sentence introduces the paragraph, telling the reader "in a nutshell, this is what the paragraph will be about." At other times it follows a sentence or two—material that might be introductory or transitional. In still other circumstances, the topic sentence ends the paragraph; it takes on a summary role, tying together the preceding sentences and telling the reader "in a nutshell, this is what the paragraph has been about."

Examine a few of the paragraphs in this chapter and notice that each is a short composition unto itself. Each contains two or more sentences that play off from each other and together form a unit.[13] Paragraphs are nearly always shorter than a page, usually much shorter, if for no reason other than to let the reader up for air. A legitimate writing technique is to force a paragraph where it is acceptable but not needed, simply to break the page visually for the reader.

The sentence is the unit of expression: When I write, I mold sentences much as potters mold bowls—choosing the type and the amount of material, massaging that material and moving it around, evaluating how it looks in one shape versus another, and finally settling on the most pleasing expression. Your obligation as a writer is to be sure each sentence is palatable and comprehensible to the reader. You will accomplish that by writing clear, precise, well-focused expressions of exactly what you want to say, and by presenting them with a minimum of words and a maximum of gracefulness. Any thought can be presented in dozens if not hundreds of ways.

- We have to delay the testing for now, and just do the interviewing by following the schedule that we had planned originally.
- We can go ahead and interview according to the original schedule, but we have to do the testing some other time.
- The interview schedule works well as planned, but we need to delay the testing.

Serious writers write multiple versions of most sentences en route to the final draft. Why is the third of the three sentences above better than the others? It sends a clear, direct mes-

[13] Occasionally a single sentence stands alone (perhaps as a transition statement), but a single sentence technically is not a paragraph.

sage and has a comfortable rhythm. It is also shorter, and it ends with an emphatic statement of the main point. While I write by feel and sound now more than by consciously building specific characteristics into a sentence, I find those characteristics present whenever I analyze a good-feeling, good-sounding sentence.

That brings us back to the writing principles shown on the BOOKMARK. I tied the examples in this book to those writing principles because I believe you will master the unit of expression—the sentence—only by studying systematically what makes sentences work well.

<u>The word is the unit of meaning</u>: I enjoy what William Zinsser (1994, p. 34) has to say about words:

> . . . you will never make your mark as a writer unless you develop a respect for words and a curiosity about their shades of meaning that is almost obsessive.

Be vigilant about word choice. Value precision. Do not write about *expanding* a policy to another department, or *enlarging* a narrow view, or *extending* a room you have outgrown. More precisely, you will *extend* the policy, *expand* your view, and *enlarge* the room. When a term that comes to mind is less than perfectly precise, think more deeply; you may be surprised at the power of focused thought.

- Tomato plants <u>thrive</u> in that kind of soil.
- Tomato plants <u>flourish</u> in that kind of soil.
- Tomato plants <u>proliferate</u> in that kind of soil.

The first two sentences are nearly interchangeable, because both *thrive* and *flourish* mean to grow vigorously. If I were the writer, my choice might depend on the type of energy I want to exude: *thrive* strikes me as bullet-shaped and *flourish* as fireworks-shaped. In contrast, the third sentence is not an option, because *proliferate* means to grow by multiplication. *Proliferate* is more applicable to ivy, which—while it might *thrive* or *flourish*—is known for its proliferation. An astute writer on the subject of ivy would use *thrive* or *flourish* to describe healthy ivy, but would use *proliferate* to describe ivy that returns in greater abundance year after year. Word choice, a well too deep for the bottom ever to be seen, challenges writers and exhilarates them—gives them infinite possibilities. It is the infinite possibilities that make writing an art form.

Use the dictionary freely, not just to seek definitions for words unfamiliar to you, but to read and reread definitions of familiar words that compete for placement in your sentences. Study word lists, like those in Chapter 2 and Appendix C of this book. You may be surprised at what you learn. I remember reading the definition of *peruse* after years of using it to mean "scan," and finding that it means "read through, as with thoroughness or care" (Webster, 1997, p. 1076).

Finally, keep in mind the most important question about any word. Is it needed?

Perspiration and Inspiration

Writing is work because sustained thinking is work. You may find yourself writing one moment and eating or watching television the next, without recalling a conscious decision to leave the writing. You simply fled. On one occasion you will need to hold your feet to the fire; on another you will need to give yourself a break. Only you can judge. How long you can sustain productive writing without a break and how many total hours per day you can write will depend on your temperament and on the intensity of the task.

I need to balance this oppressive picture of writing with a look at the other side of the coin. Writing can be euphoric, sometimes springing free and flowing faster than your fingers can record it. You need to seize those times. Jump from section A to section B if you suddenly have a strong feeling about how to write something that belongs in section B. Unless a deadline looms, I will even jump to a different project. While away from my writing, if I am struck by an outstanding thought or by a superb idea for constructing a sentence or a paragraph, I will leave whatever I am doing and write, if at all possible. I hate to let a golden wisp of inspiration dissipate if there is any way to capture it.

I should add one last thought about inspiration. You may be struck by an idea bursting with potential, but when you begin to write you are unhappy with your expression of it. That is no time to nag yourself about constructing pristine sentences. Write what comes to you. As a temporary technique, stream-of-consciousness writing can be valuable. You may write poorly at that moment, but you are preserving the general thought to be packaged in better form later.

Sincerity

Straining for effect is a common writing fault. When you are in a muddle you may find yourself straining to decorate a paragraph you know to be substandard. When you are on a euphoric binge you may find yourself straining from headiness and delusions of grandeur. Either way, strained writing gives an air of artificiality. Genuineness versus artificiality has a way of shining through writing as it does through personal relationships; so if you feel yourself levitating a bit, pull yourself back to Earth and take an honest look at what you have written.

Another important dimension of sincerity is honesty with yourself. You may spend a great amount of time writing a paragraph (or something larger) that you should not use. A day or two later you may need to talk frankly to yourself: "How could you have spent three hours writing something as bad as that? Trash it." Or the issue may be appropriateness rather than quality; you may need to say something like this to yourself: "I know you've worked hard on the material about X, and it reads well, but it doesn't belong in this piece. Take it out." Neither the number of hours spent writing nor the quality of the work justify using material in a piece. ***To a sincere writer, the only justification for using anything, from a single word to multiple pages, is that the piece will be poorer without it.***

Being the Reader's Friend

A last feeling I want to encourage you to court as a writer is a feeling of good will and helpfulness toward the reader. You will naturally lose readers who are uninterested in your content, or opposed to your views, or lacking the background to understand what you have written: that is expected. You should not lose readers for having burdened them with unwarranted tasks, as this writer did:

> The researcher recorded individual performances of the subjects after sixteen weeks of instruction. The researcher and an assistant evaluated the recordings.

The researcher and assistant evaluated the performances, not the recordings themselves (too much reverberation; not enough bass). Readers would have been spared the task of interpreting that second sentence had it read, "The researcher and an assistant evaluated the recorded performances." If your writing assigns the reader a task, it should be a task that leads to inquiry and insight, not a task that has the reader compensating for shortcomings in your writing. Can you always avoid giving the reader unwarranted tasks? Of course not, any more than a golfer can shoot par on every hole. All any of us can do is work on technique, approach each writing job with commitment and concentration, and keep our bad strokes to a minimum.

3. Revising

A Perspective

All writers revise—some lightly, some extensively. Each adopts an approach that lies somewhere between two extremes: 1) revise while writing, so the last word written finishes the piece, and 2) write from a stream of consciousness, never looking back until the last word is written, then begin revising. You will find your best approach some distance from either extreme. I cannot imagine writing without revising as I go, nor can I imagine foregoing post-writing revision. I will describe advantages of each from my perspective, along with dangers of carrying either too far, but first let us think for a minute about what revision is.

When you revise, you are silently asking questions of yourself, answering them, and then responding with changes. That is true whether you work on a paragraph, a sentence, or a word or two. Once finished, you want to know that you have delivered your message as clearly and concisely as possible—that others will read your piece efficiently and will understand you to be saying exactly what you believe yourself to be saying. Here are some of the covert questions you might ask yourself relative to sentences and paragraphs as you revise. There are others, but this list offers a good start.

- Is it meaningful?
- Is it completely true and accurate?
- Is it stated precisely
- Is it stated clearly?
- Is it active? Alive?
- Is it free of unneeded words?
- Is it free of unnecessarily long and complicated words?
- Does it hold together logically?
- Does it let the reader move through?

Notice that the questions are more reader oriented than writing-principle oriented. Your reader, rather than seeing an illogical arrangement of material **{3}** or a lack of parallel structure **{13}**, is likely to find your writing unclear or difficult to read through comfortably. So look for rough spots through the reader's eye, then use your mindfulness of writing principles to discover why the rough spots are rough and what type of revision is needed. You will find that approach more efficient than hunting for specific writing-principle violations, because those violations are not so much errors as warning flags—signs that readability *may be* damaged.

An example may help. I tell my students to be wary of beginning a sentence with a weak subject-verb combination: It is, There are, and the like. I call those expressions slow-start phrases, because they usually lead to longer than needed sentences in which the real subject and verb are buried **{10}**:

Slow-Start Phrase	**Revision**
It is difficult for most new teachers to feel confident in themselves when they first begin to teach.	Most new teachers need time to develop self-confidence.

On the other hand, to consider *It is* and other precarious expressions and constructions taboo is to obliterate intelligent judgment and individual style. It is and It was make fine sentence openers in some circumstances:

> You may forget your jacket or your sunglasses—or even your wallet—but whatever you do, be sure to bring your sense of humor. It is important to all of us.
>
> It was the police who stole the car.

In the first example, the pronoun *It* has a concrete antecedent: the noun phrase sense of humor from the preceding sentence. That works well. In the second, It was gives emphasis: as opposed to other persons one might suspect, it was the police who stole the car.

You will make hundreds of intelligent and creative revision judgments as you compose rich prose that reflects you—that comes from your own voice. To achieve a high level of readability at the same time, read and revise your work from the reader's perspective.

Revising as You Write

I write for periods of time without looking back—maybe to the end of the paragraph or further—if sentences are flowing comfortably; but if I have just fought my way through a difficult sentence I stop and reread it. Often I find that a different word or punctuation, or sometimes a change in construction, improves the sentence markedly. To finish a piece with several such sentences unrevised would add heavily to the job of post-writing revision. Besides, a sentence that feels suspect while I am writing usually can be revised best and most efficiently while it is still warm. Also, I know that what I write now may lead in some way to what I write a few minutes from now. I will do better taking clues from good writing than from mediocre writing.

Compare the paragraph below (original version) with the paragraph above to see the kinds of changes I make when I double back.

> I double back on my writing periodically to ask myself questions about what I have written. When a sentence flows comfortably, I continue writing without looking back—maybe to the end of the paragraph or further—but if I have just struggled with a sentence I stop and reread it. Often I find that a change in word choice, punctuation, or construction improves the sentence considerably. To finish a piece with several such sentences unrevised would be unwise for three reasons. First, I would have made the job of post-writing revision larger. Second, a sentence that feels suspect while I am writing usually can be revised best and most efficiently on the spot. Third, what I write now may lead in some way to what I write later. I will be better off taking clues from good writing than from mediocre writing.

Probably the most common revisions made while writing are changes in the order of sentences or clauses **{3, 8}**, the smoothing of connections between sentences **{4}**, and adjustments in the tone and flow **{19}**. Also common, though not the case here, is a significant reduction in the number of words **{9}**.

You may see why I made the changes in the paragraph above, and you may agree with my decisions; or you may think some parts of the original are preferable. Writing judgments are highly subjective, because there are many good ways to construct a given sentence or paragraph. Poor writing comes not so much from failure to find "the" good way as it does from a lack of diligence in pursuing "a" good way.

When I resume writing after a period of time away (maybe an hour, maybe a day), I reread the last few paragraphs I wrote—sometimes more—to orient myself to what I am about to do. More often than not I revise lightly during that time. Sometimes I see need for a major change, and may spend that entire session revising rather than writing new material. Also, when I have finished a section of writing, say a few pages of a twenty-page piece, I reread that section to be sure it holds together well and flows logically from beginning to end. Usually I change a word here and there, and may reconstruct a sentence or paragraph that strikes me as awkward. Typically I make changes to the beginnings or ends of paragraphs in the form of transitions that ease the reader through.

While revising along the way I may find that I lack conviction about a change. To revise my previous writing out of existence and risk replacing it with a lesser version would be unwise. In that case I revise below the original, then read the two. Sometimes I keep one and delete the other; sometimes I write a blend of the two; sometimes I am undecided and leave both, marking the newest version to be evaluated later.

Be careful not to revise too heavily as you write. A compulsion to leave no trash strewn through a piece can keep you from unleashing your thoughts fluently. It can also cause you to destroy some good writing. A corollary to the infamous Murphy's Law states, "If you play around with a thing long enough, eventually it will break." Writers revising compulsively tend not to stop revising when the sentence or paragraph is at its best. When you sense that you can no longer distinguish between a change that improves and a change that simply changes (possibly worsens), you need to move on and let the passage cool for a time.

An unfortunate effect you may suffer from overrevising is a condition I call reader's block. Reader's block, which I find more frustrating than writer's block, is a matter of losing all ability to judge the quality of your own writing. It comes from having reread and rethought a piece or a section too extensively. When reader's block sets in, all progress stops. All you can do is let the material sit—the longer the better—and return to it with a fresh perspective.

Revising After You Write

I do my first post-writing revision at the computer screen, then print the document. I always find a few things to change as I scroll through, ranging from typographical errors to awkward sentences; had I printed them, they would have been annoyances.

With printed copy in hand, I am ready to work the piece over at a deeper level. I cross out words, write in words, circle sections, draw arrows showing relocation, cross out full sections, and sometimes handwrite extensive additions. Why not do all that revising at the computer? First, the document looks different in hard copy than scrolling through a computer screen, and the hard copy version is what my readers will see. Second, the pencil leaves a trail that shows where I have been and what I have changed. It helps me acquire a better sense of the whole—of how one change interacts with another. Sometimes I make a change that prompts me to undo an earlier change; I would have lost that perspective had I revised on screen.

When I have finished marking the first draft, I reopen the file and make changes from the marked copy. That process is almost entirely mechanical; I put faith in the thinking I did while making the pencil marks. Occasionally I see something I missed and change it on the screen, but only rarely.

When I print the next version it is not likely to be the final. I read it a day or two later and make another set of changes. Some pieces need six or seven revisions—or more—from printed copy, others only two or three. I find that with each subsequent revision I read more quickly, consciously trying to get a sense of how the pieces fit into a whole. At the last stage of revision I may repair a slightly awkward spot or two—perhaps a matter of unintentional alliteration or rhythmic clumsiness—that I have let stand several times previously out of uncertainty.

If you are revising a large work—thesis, dissertation, book—heed this advice. When you read your first full copy for revision, begin by laying out the Table of Contents, including lists of figures, tables, etc.; then check every page of the document against those pages to be certain that 1) page numbers of the sections, figures, and tables in the document correspond to the page numbers in the Table of Contents, and 2) titles of chapters, sections, subsections, tables, and figures all coincide precisely with the Table of Contents in terms of wording, capitalization, underlining, and every other detail. I usually find errors when I apply that process to student documents.

Finally, I should make a point of an important revision concept that I refer to as *fresh eyes*. A paragraph can look wholly different to you after time has passed. I remember jumping from my chair after writing a paragraph that had hit the bull's-eye: it was exactly what I wanted! The next day I read it—not to revise but to enjoy my masterpiece—and I was shocked that I could have written something so mediocre and thought it was good. *Fresh eyes.* This is why I tell students that to finish a paper at night and submit it the next day is to guarantee substandard work.

Of course the freshest eyes belong to someone else. I no longer consider anything a final version until at least one other person has offered suggestions for revision. One of the best ways to improve your writing is to make a pact with a friend that you will read each other's work and make frank comments. The outside-reader approach is not a matter of a better writer helping a lesser writer; it is simply a matter of fresh eyes. Anyone can learn from almost anyone if communication is honest and if minds are open.

I wish you well in your pursuit of skillful writing. As you improve, you will find fewer and fewer basic flaws in your early drafts. That will free you to make higher-level revisions, which in turn will lead to documents that please both you and your readers more than you had ever thought possible. That is the ultimate reward for a diligent approach to writing—a reward I hope you will reap and enjoy.

APPENDIX A

POSSIBLE SOLUTIONS TO MULTIPLE-PROBLEM EXERCISES FROM CHAPTER 6

Here you are on your own to identify writing problems. I have neither made extensive comments nor linked my solutions to writing principles as I did in Chapter 6, though I have added short notes in *italics* to some exercises.

Important: Think of each solution given as *a* solution, not *the* solution. I find myself writing different versions of the sentences each time I try, because writing is an art form: most sentences can be written well in a number of ways. Do not be impatient or discouraged if you find the writing of solutions time consuming and difficult. Just seeing problems in the sentences, regardless of the solutions you write, will raise your consciousness of specific dangers—and that alone will improve your writing. To acquire still more insight, try to identify writing principles that apply to the problems you see.

EXERCISE 1

Original

Children are different because their physical and cultural surroundings are not the same.

Revision

Children are different from one another, in part, because their physical and cultural surroundings are different.

Note

In part acknowledges that some differences are attributable to factors other than physical and cultural surroundings.

EXERCISE 2

Original

Galton stated that there are two great forces: nurture and nature. These two are what make individuals different from each other.

Revision

Galton attributed differences between persons to two primal forces: nature and nurture.

Note

A subtlety: nature and nurture is a more logical sequence than nurture and nature.

EXERCISE 3

Original

Because of unforeseen circumstances that occurred, the testing process was disrupted in the following ways:

Revision

1. Testing was disrupted by three unforeseen circumstances: 1) . . . , 2) . . . , and 3) . . .
2. Two unforeseen circumstances disrupted testing: 1) . . . , and 2) . . .

EXERCISE 4

R

Original

[English students in this study faired poorly as compared to Ugandan students.] Results of the study showed that overall, the Ugandans were in an average lead of about eight points over the English and all mean differences, except for the fourteen-year-old groups were significant ($p < .01$).

Revision

Ugandan scores were significantly higher than English scores at all age levels except age fourteen ($p < .01$), with an overall mean difference of about eight points.

Note

The problem of wordiness is compounded by the writer's careless use of commas (see <u>*Commas*</u> *in Appendix B, Part 3.) Also,* <u>*in an average lead*</u> *makes the tests given sound more like an athletic contest than a study of educational outcomes.*

EXERCISE 5

R

Original

[Two schools from each of the five regions created a sample of ten schools to represent the overall population.] Two other schools were randomly selected at large using the random table to serve as substitutes.

Revision

Using a table of random numbers, the researcher selected two additional schools to serve as substitutes.

Notes

Separation of related words is the principal problem with the original, but notice how active voice also adds strength.

EXERCISE 6

R

Original

Thirty minutes of twelve consecutive rehearsals will be allotted for each composition.

Revision

Each composition will be rehearsed for thirty minutes at each of twelve consecutive rehearsals.

EXERCISE 7

Original

The large enrollment forced Mr. DeDworc to deal with too many students for the size of the room.

Revision

The large enrollment forced Mr. DeDworc to choose between finding another room and asking some students to drop the class.

EXERCISE 8

R

Original

Results showed that 1) all six subtests of PRRT, when correlated with each other, were statistically significant at the .05 level of significance; 2) a child's pitch and rhythm responses correlated with the combined environmental variables for each subtest beyond the .01 level of significance; 3) having and hearing musical instruments played in the home, having parents and siblings who participated or participate in musical activities, having parental help to sing in tune, and having an opportunity to hear various kinds of recorded music were positively correlated with a child's ability in pitch and rhythm and statistically significant at the .05 level of significance, with the correlation between pitch and parental help being significant at .01.

Note: This example will make no sense to persons unfamiliar with the language of written research.

(continued on next page)

Revision (Point 3 only)

	Rhythm	Instruments	Family Music	Parent Help	Recordings
Pitch	.46	.63*	.62*	.81**	.65*
Rhythm	1.00	.61*	.67*	.73*	.71*
Instruments		1.00	.77*	.51	.44
Family Music			1.00	.58*	.49
Parent Help				1.00	.38

* = p < .05 ** = p < .01

Notes

This type of information is nearly impossible to digest in paragraph form. Help the poor reader by expressing it in a correlation matrix or series of matrices. Mark significant coefficients with asterisks and add a key to show levels of significance. Not only will the information from the original paragraph be more clear, but the correlation coefficients will give the reader a wealth of additional, specific information. Of course each factor correlates 1.00 with itself, sometimes shown in a matrix by a — . Notice also that one row and one column of space can be saved by leaving off headings that would simply show the first and last factors correlating perfectly with themselves.

EXERCISE 9

R

Original

Moore concluded that young children living in an environment which provided them with a constant exposure to music demonstrated higher levels of musical development than children who did not live in such an environment.

Revision

The writer needs to decide whether this is a statement of results or a conclusion.

Results: Moore found higher levels of musical development among children exposed frequently to music than among children not so exposed.

Conclusion: Moore concluded that frequent exposure to music boosts the musical development of young children.

Note

Because frequent exposure to music is nearly universal in today's culture, either statement will lack meaning until the nature of the music and the nature of the exposure are defined.

EXERCISE 10

Original

She was assisted by the classroom teacher in distributing and collecting testing materials.

Revision

The classroom teacher helped her distribute and collect testing materials.

Note

Beware the temptation to use a fancy word where a plain word will do, especially when the fancy word is less precise. Assist and help are not synonymous: a surgeon's colleague assists with heart transplants; a surgeon's son helps clean the garage.

EXERCISE 11

R

Original

[Children in Trinidad grow up singing, dancing, and hearing music everywhere—at home, in school, and in the streets.] The sum total of all these musical experiences of a child in the Trinidadian culture can be expected to influence his music aptitude during the developmental years.

Revision

This musically-rich culture probably accelerates music aptitude development among Trinidadian children.

EXERCISE 12

R

Original

Second graders in three separate classes will be involved twice a week for approximately a six-month period.

Revision

Three classes of second-grade students will each meet twice weekly for six months.

EXERCISE 13

Original

Posters raise the level of awareness of students regarding research opportunities.

Revision

Posters alert students to research opportunities.

Note

This sentence reminds me why I wrote Appendix C: well-chosen verbs shorten and invigorate writing. (Alert is a versatile word, useful also as an adjective or a noun.)

EXERCISE 14

Original

At this present time, it is hopeful that we can achieve our goal.

Revision

I hope we can achieve our goal.

EXERCISE 15

R

Original

The problem of this study is to compare the effects of teaching a collegiate wind band quality literature with two different methods of instruction and investigate the level of musicianship attained with each method.

Revision

The problem of this study is to compare the levels of musicianship attained by use of two methods of collegiate wind band instruction.

Note

Two words commonly used where they are not needed are different (this exercise) and separate (Exercise 12). (See Chapter 2, Part 3, A Collection of Troublesome Words [different].)

EXERCISE 16

R

Original

Results of this study showed that firstly, Chinese test-retest reliabilities were lower than the American test-retest reliabilities. Secondly, American students' mean scores were slightly lower than the Chinese students' mean scores. However, the difference was not large enough to be statistically significant.

Revision

Test-retest reliability coefficients were .85 for American students and .79 for Chinese students. Mean scores were lower for American students than for Chinese students, but differences were not statistically significant.

Note

When you have concise, easily interpretable facts at hand for a research report (.85), give them to the reader rather than hide them behind a veil of verbal interpretation.

EXERCISE 17

Original

American music is often divided into periods with wars serving as convenient demarcations.

Revision

Music historians have categorized American music by time frame, using wars as reference points.

Note

Often is used too often when frequency is not the issue. (See Chapter 2, Part 3, A Collection of Troublesome Words [often].)

EXERCISE 18

R

Original

[Four judges each used a three-dimensional scale—precision, efficiency, and style—to rate the subjects' performances.] Test-retest correlation coefficients were calculated for each dimension and for the three dimensions combined for one judge to measure reliability.

Revision

The researcher, to estimate test-retest reliability for each dimension and the composite, had one judge rate performances twice.

Note

Confusion over research reports on the part of persons unfamiliar with research methods may be due to this kind of writing as much as to content.

EXERCISE 19

Original

[A comparison of standardized test scores between the groups will reveal whether there is a statistically significant difference between the two. Still, statistically significant differences do not necessarily indicate practical significance.] To assess the practical significance of the results, the means of the standardization sample can be used for comparison.

Revision

The researcher might assess practical significance by comparing mean scores of the subjects to mean scores of the standardization sample.

Note

One of the most common and most disruptive of all grammatical errors is failure to place the rightful subject of a participial phrase in its rightful position: immediately following that phrase. (See Appendix B, Part 2, Example B-5.)

EXERCISE 20

R

Original

[Madsen and Darrow's approach to investigating test validity for blind students, in contrast to Anderson's mixed-response approach, was to have students use a single method of response from beginning to end for each test.] They used two methods of recording responses. The oral response method was applied to MAT, but a Braille answer sheet was used with the Walker Test.

Revision

They asked subjects to respond orally to MAT, then had them use Braille answer sheets to respond to the Walker Test.

EXERCISE 21 (Note: Subjects of the study were hearing-impaired.)

R

Original

Limited research pertaining to the present study is available. However, research has been conducted with visually handicapped individuals and tests have been adapted for administration to specific handicaps.

Revision

Research related directly to this study is sparse, but some researchers have adapted tests from studies of visually handicapped students for use with hearing-impaired students.

Note

Notice how clearly and precisely the first phrase of the revision characterizes the message as compared to the first sentence of the original.

EXERCISE 22

R

Original

A total of 23 students participated. The sample represents a population of first graders, second graders, and third graders from a cross-section of socioeconomic backgrounds.

Revision

The subjects, 23 students in grades one through three, were selected from a cross-section of socioeconomic backgrounds.

Note

First graders is common language in research reporting, but the language of the revision is more precise: the subjects are not graders, they are students.

EXERCISE 23

R

Original

One week after group administration, each student was individually tested at Cedarbrook School.

Revision

Students at Cedarbrook School were tested first as a group, then a week later as individuals.

Note

The revision orients readers to the setting before launching into time frames. Also, the two key conditions, group and individuals, take emphasis from their positions at the ends of phrases and from the parallel construction.

EXERCISE 24

R

Original

The researcher obtained the means and standard deviations for the group administration and individual administration of MRT. The mean differences between Adapted MRT and MRT were calculated for each grade level and all grades combined. Results are shown in Figure 7.

Revision

Means and standard deviations for MRT (individual administration) and Adapted MRT (group administration) are shown by grade level in Figure 7.

Note

Words like obtained and calculated are usually needless in statistical reports: any statistics presented have necessarily been calculated from information that was necessarily obtained.

EXERCISE 25

Original

[Still another threat to school funding needs to be taken seriously. An aging population is infusing each community with a growing percentage of "empty nesters," meaning older people who have no children at home.] Educators, administrators, and board members of public schools should be alarmed that seventy percent of their constituents are now "empty nesters" whose support is allegedly declining.

Revision

Educators, administrators, and board members of public schools should be alarmed that seventy percent of their constituents are now "empty nesters," persons whose willingness to support education-related tax referendums is likely to decline.

Note

The last clause in the original sentence needs to be nonrestrictive, and needs to reveal clearly whose support for what is about to decline.

EXERCISE 26

Original

[Public education will have to maintain excellence while coping with language barriers and conflicting values among various minority groups. The Bill of Rights, the branches of government, the Constitution, and our system of education were all formed on a monocultural basis.] Strategic planning is about being creative instead of adaptive during such a transition; thus, strategic planning means being proactive rather than reactive.

Revision

Reaction and adaptation are insufficient during such a period of social and institutional transition. We need a strategic plan that will help us solve problems proactively and creatively.

EXERCISE 27

Original

Shinichi Suzuki was born in Nagoya, Japan, in 1898. As a child, he grew up in an environment conducive to his becoming acquainted with the workings of stringed instruments. He worked in the first violin factory that was founded in Japan by his father.

Revision

For Shinichi Suzuki—born in Nagoya, Japan in 1898—acquaintance with the workings of stringed instruments was a natural outgrowth of his childhood environment. He worked in the first violin factory built in Japan, a factory founded by his father.

Note

The original has the feel of a junior-high report—stilted sentences by which the writer shows no sense of primary information as compared to secondary information.

EXERCISE 28

Original

[The final Inner Game skill is Trust. Trust in the Inner Game sense is not blind, but rather is preceded by well-laid groundwork through practice and hard work. Trust is essential to one's entering the requisite state of relaxed concentration.] Unfortunately, barriers to trusting exist; however, for ease of identification, Green has articulated three barriers to trust: worrying what others will think of you, the feeling of being out of control, and fears about your own ability.

Revision

Unfortunately, barriers to trust threaten Inner Game success. Green has identified three: worrying about what others think, feeling out of control, and fearing a lack of ability.

APPENDIX B

ENGLISH USAGE, GRAMMAR, AND PUNCTUATION:

A PRIMER

My purpose in writing this appendix is not to duplicate material presented in grammar books, but to offer a refresher course in basic terms and to present grammar and punctuation errors that I see commonly in student writing. There are three sections:

Section	Function
1. English Usage Review: Terms and Examples	—to refresh your knowledge of the basic components of English
2. Grammar	—to alert you to grammatical errors common in student writing
3. Punctuation	—to help you make good use of those little marks that many writers find troublesome and few use to full advantage

Refer to the BOOKMARK for principles shown in { }.

See the Introduction to this book for more details about using the BOOKMARK.

1. English Usage Review: Terms and Examples

Parts of Speech: A Skeletal View

The "parts of speech" are simply eight word functions labeled to make discussion about language possible. Seven will be useful to your thinking, talking, and reading about formal language.[14] The seven are exemplified in Figure 3, defined by number below Figure 3, and described in detail on subsequent pages.

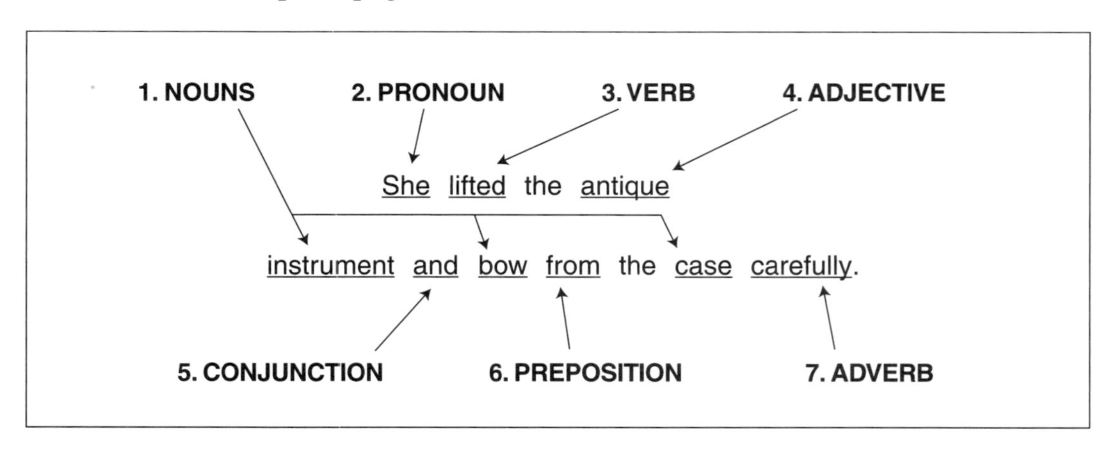

Figure 3. Parts of Speech Exemplified

Label	Function
1. NOUN:	—names a person, place, thing, or idea.
2. PRONOUN:	—used in place of or in reference to a noun or noun phrase (In Figure 3, she replaces, perhaps, Jane, or The violinist.)
3. VERB:	—expresses action or state of being.
4. ADJECTIVE:	—describes or modifies a noun or pronoun.
5. CONJUNCTION:	—connects words or groups of words.
6. PREPOSITION:	—usually introduces a phrase and shows the relationship between its object (object of the preposition) and another word in the sentence.
7. ADVERB:	—modifies a verb, adjective, or other adverb by telling how, when, where, why, how often, or to what extent.

The word the—like a and an—is called an *article;* though left unidentified in the parts-of-speech figure above to avoid clutter, articles are a type of adjective (the most common type).

[14] The interjection (Wow; Whew; Oh, no!) is rare in formal writing.

Parts of Speech: A More Detailed View

Nouns, verbs, adjectives, and adverbs are nearly infinite in number, making lists of examples impractical, but each has some characteristics worth noting.

NOUNS: (Nouns name a person, place, thing, or idea.)

Number:

Jim is a teacher who enjoys students.

(Jim, teacher → **SINGULAR**; students → **PLURAL**)

Gender:

MASCULINE	(brother, boar)	**NEUTER**	(rock, trumpet)
FEMININE	(aunt, mare)	**INDEFINITE**	(cook, pilot)

Case:

Neighbors broke the child's toy.

(Neighbors → **NOMINATIVE** (subject); child's → **POSSESSIVE** (shows ownership; functions as an adjective); toy → **OBJECTIVE** (object))

* *

VERBS: (Verbs express action or state of being.)

Number:

Joey runs because all healthy children run.

(runs → **SINGULAR**; run → **PLURAL**)

Tense:

I play better now than I played years ago, and will play better yet with practice.

(play → **PRESENT**; played → **PAST**; will play → **FUTURE**)

I have played since childhood. I had played in many tournaments by the time I was 21 years old, and will have played for 30 years by next Christmas.

(have played → **PRESENT PERFECT** (past merging with present); had played → **PAST PERFECT** (past's past); will have played → **FUTURE PERFECT** (past-to-be))

Voice: **ACTIVE** (The subject of the verb performs the action.)

The researcher found evidence.

PASSIVE (The subject of the verb is acted upon.)

Evidence was found by the researcher.

(Sometimes writers of passive voice leave the actor unidentified.)

Evidence was found.

Form: **TRANSITIVE VERB:** carries action to an object

Faith moves mountains.

INTRANSITIVE VERB: has no object receiving the action

Young children speak without inhibition.

LINKING VERB: a type of intransitive verb that links the subject to a noun or an adjective.

- I am a musician. (subject to noun)
- The runner looks tired. (subject to adjective)

GERUND: a verb form that ends in ing and functions as a noun.

Thinking is highly encouraged in this class.

INFINITIVE: a verb form introduced by to and used as noun, adjective, or adverb.

- To love is to live well. (noun)
- The president is a good person to know. (adjective)
- He left the meeting early to go home. (adverb)

Note about split infinitives

If you insert an adverb after the to, you will have split the infinitive. Example: *He will be told if he is to eventually go.* Teachers of grammar encourage students to avoid split infinitives. One possible solution would be this: *He will be told if he is eventually to go.* On rare occasions a split infinitive constitutes the least cumbersome construction; according to contemporary thought, you should accept the split in such cases—as we occasionally accept a preposition at the end of a sentence to avoid awkwardness. Caution: do not lean on recent acceptance of such alternate constructions as an opportunity to write carelessly; you will write best if you try first to conform to long-standing rules of grammar. Give in to an alternate construction only after your attempts to revise have confirmed the need for it.

PARTICIPLE: a verb form that ends in ing or ed and functions as the main verb of a clause (with a helping verb), or as an adjective.

- Because he is ignoring his studies, his grades have dropped. (verbs)
- Shredded cheese looks like peeling paint. (adjectives)

An entire phrase functioning as a participle is called a **PARTICIPIAL PHRASE.** The noun, pronoun, or noun clause immediately following it functions as the subject of the phrase.

- Moved by his tears, Susan consented.
- Running as fast as possible, he caught the train.

A common writing error is to follow a participial phrase with a noun, pronoun, or noun clause that does not perform the action of the phrase **{6}**:

NO Turning onto Elm Street, the view overwhelmed me.
YES Turning onto Elm Street, I was overwhelmed by the view.
OR . . . eliminate the participial phrase:

When I turned onto Elm Street, the view overwhelmed me.

(See also Example B-4 in Part 2 of this appendix.)

* *

ADJECTIVES: (Adjectives describe or modify a noun or pronoun.)

Form:		
	POSITIVE	The director is paid a large salary.
	COMPARATIVE	The vice president is paid a larger salary.
	SUPERLATIVE	The president is paid the largest salary of all.

* *

ADVERBS: (Adverbs modify a verb, adjective, or other adverb by telling how, when, where, why, how often, or to what extent.)

Form:		
	POSITIVE	Kenyatta writes well.
	COMPARATIVE	Maria writes better than Kenyatta.
	SUPERLATIVE	Of everyone in the class, Trina writes best.

* *

PRONOUNS: (Pronouns are used in place of or in reference to nouns and noun phrases.)

You will understand pronouns best by studying lists of examples. First note that nouns, pronouns, and verbs combine to make a context for language, called "person." **FIRST PERSON** language refers to the writer, **SECOND PERSON** to the person written to, and **THIRD PERSON** to the person written about, i.e., a third party. For more information, read Chapter 5, Part 1: "Person in Writing."

FIRST PERSON	I taught the classes.
SECOND PERSON	Did you teach the classes?
THIRD PERSON	The researcher taught the classes.

RELATIVE pronouns—who, whose, whom, which, and that—introduce dependent clauses. **PERSONAL** pronouns, the most numerous type, refer directly to persons or things. Study the examples in Figure 4, shown by person (first, second, third), number (singular, plural), and case (nominative, possessive, objective). Gender is also an important characteristic of pronouns; for more information about pronoun gender, read Chapter 5, Part 2: "Gender in Writing."

FIRST PERSON	Nominative Case	Possessive Case	Objective Case
Singular	I	my, mine	me
Plural	we	our, ours	us
SECOND PERSON			
Singular	you	your, yours	you
Plural	you	your,yours	you
THIRD PERSON			
Singular	he, she, it	his, her(s), its	him, her, it
Plural	they	their, theirs	them

Figure 4. Personal Pronouns Organized by Person, Number, and Case

The word to which a pronoun refers is called its **ANTECEDENT**. In the sentences below, the first underlined word is the antecedent and the second is the corresponding pronoun:

- The researcher lost all the data. He is distraught.
- Chantel is the wealthiest person in her neighborhood.

Antecedents are important because they help you determine the type of pronoun to use, e.g., the number or gender. If the antecedent to which a pronoun refers is nonspecific (anything, nothing, everyone) or generic (teacher, athlete), you will have a choice to make. Turn to Chapter 5, Part 2 for information about the treatment of gender. For a thorough treatment of other issues regarding pronoun use, including pronouns other than relative pronouns and personal pronouns, refer to a grammar book, e.g., Kramer, et al. (1995) or Hacker (1997).

* *

PREPOSITIONS: (A preposition usually introduces a phrase and shows the relationship between its object [object of the preposition] and another part of the sentence.)

The phrase introduced by a preposition is called a prepositional phrase. A prepositional phrase consists of the preposition, the object of the preposition, and commonly one or more modifiers.

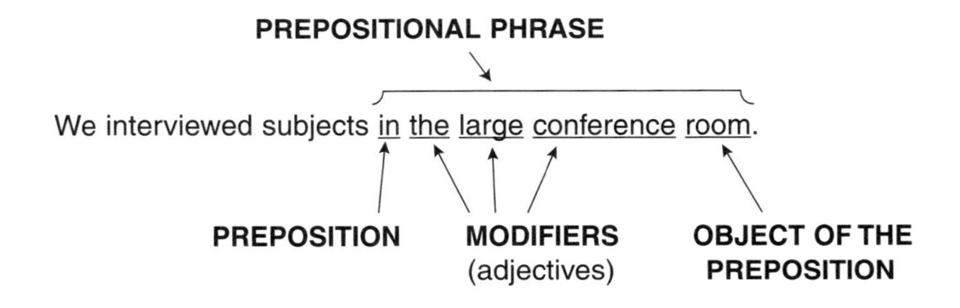

A short list of prepositions is shown in Figure 5; longer lists can be found in grammar books.

about	below	except	near	through
after	beside	for	of	to
against	between	from	off	toward
among	but	in	on	under
around	by	inside	out	until
at	considering	instead of	over	up
before	down	into	past	with
behind	during	like	since	within

Figure 5. A Partial List of Prepositions

A common characteristic of wordy, tiresome writing is an overabundance of prepositional phrases. Avoid sentences that look and feel like this:

> The most alarming aspect of the news from the organization of parents from the neighborhood was about the girl under suspicion of lying during the questioning of witnesses.

Some words can function as either a preposition or an adverb. To be a preposition, the word must refer to an object. The underlined words in these sentences refer to no object; therefore, they are adverbs.

> The train will be coming <u>through</u>. Do not let the children move <u>around</u>.

* *

<u>CONJUNCTIONS</u>: (Conjunctions connect words or groups of words.)

COORDINATING: <u>for</u>, <u>and</u>, <u>nor</u>, <u>but</u>, <u>or</u>, <u>yet</u>, and <u>so</u> [meaning therefore] connect grammatically *equal* words or clauses.

- We had only bread <u>and</u> water to sustain us.
- Our choice was clear: act wisely <u>or</u> die quickly.

CORRELATIVE: connect grammatically *equal* words and clauses *in pairs*.

> The crew had been toughened by <u>both</u> faint praise <u>and</u> cruel criticism. They decreed that everyone must <u>either</u> help <u>or</u> leave.

SUBORDINATING: <u>before</u>, <u>after</u>, <u>because</u>, <u>rather than</u>, and many other subordinating conjunctions double as prepositions and connect grammatically *unequal* clauses.

- We must pack well <u>before</u> we go.
- I will wait <u>until</u> you are ready.
- The photographer stood <u>near</u> the doorway.

* *

Parts of a Sentence: A Skeletal View

The basic parts of a sentence are exemplified in Figure 6 and defined by number below Figure 6. Three other terms important to understanding a sentence are shown at the bottom.

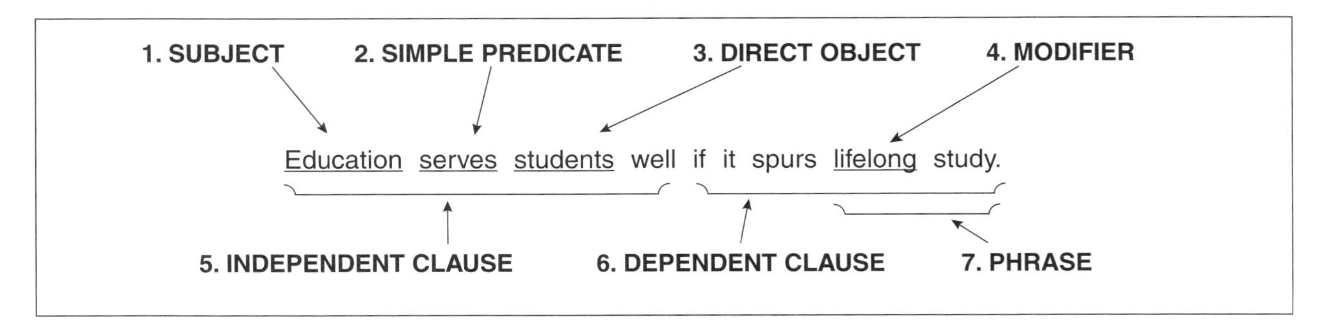

Figure 6. Parts of a Sentence Exemplified

Label	Description
1. SUBJECT	—the noun or pronoun around which the sentence is focused.
2. PREDICATE	—whatever is said about the subject (above, everything following the subject). The verb is called the simple predicate.
3. DIRECT OBJECT	—receiver of action (in an active-voice sentence).
4. MODIFIER	—a word or group of words that limits the meaning of another word or group of words.
CLAUSE	—a group of related words having both subject and predicate.
5. INDEPENDENT CLAUSE	—a clause that can function as a complete sentence.
6. DEPENDENT CLAUSE	—a clause that cannot function as a complete sentence.
7. PHRASE	—a group of related words lacking subject, predicate, or both.

Here are three other terms important to understanding a sentence:

8. RESTRICTIVE CLAUSE	—a descriptive clause essential to the meaning of the independent clause in which it is embedded.
9. PARENTHETIC EXPRESSION	—an aside (single word, phrase, or clause), enclosed by commas, parentheses, or dashes.
10. NONRESTRICTIVE CLAUSE	—a descriptive clause that gives extra information.

(Addendum to Figure 6)

The student who did best, by the way, was John, who is very bright.

8. RESTRICTIVE CLAUSE — 9. PARENTHETIC EXPRESSION — 10. NONRESTRICTIVE CLAUSE

Parts of a Sentence: A More Detailed View

You may understand better some of the options available to you in sentence construction if you know a little more about the characteristics and functions of phrases and clauses.

PHRASES:

Phrases function as parts of speech. They can do no more, because they lack the subject/predicate combination needed to express a complete thought. The three parts of speech that may be expressed as a phrase are shown in Figure 7.

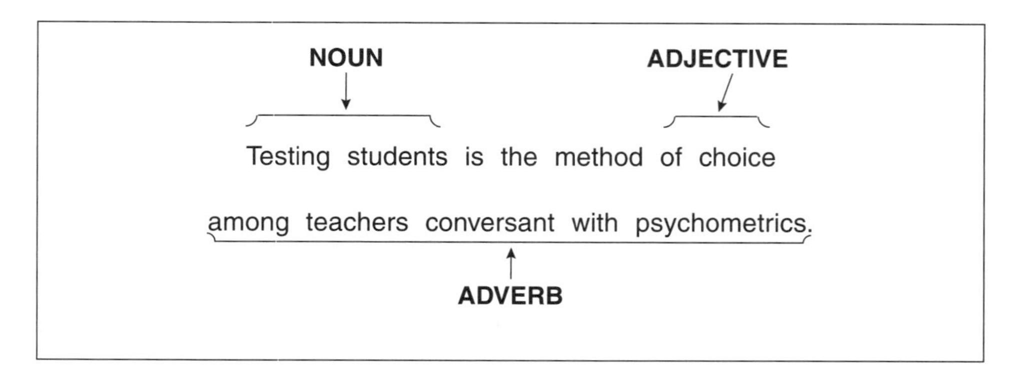

Figure 7. Examples of the Three Parts of Speech that May Be Expressed as a Phrase

Long phrases can be expected to have multiple short phrases embedded within them, as you can see by looking at the adverb phrase in Figure 7 (among teachers; with psychometrics).

Phrases can be categorized further by type: verbal, prepositional, or absolute (and still further by subtype, but not within the scope of this appendix). The first phrase in Figure 7 is a verbal phrase, because it is derived from a verb form. The second and third phrases are prepositional phrases, a type of phrase described in some detail in a previous section—Parts of Speech: A More Detailed View; Prepositions. No absolute phrase is shown in Figure 7. An absolute phrase modifies the whole sentence rather than just another word or phrase. I will finish this sentence with an underlined absolute phrase, having written all that I intend to write here about phrases. For greater detail about phrases, see Kramer, et al. (1995) or Hacker (1997).

CLAUSES:

Clauses contain a subject and a predicate, so they do express complete thoughts. Of the two principal types of clauses—independent (main) and dependent (subordinate)—the independent clause is easiest to understand: it amounts to a sentence within a sentence. The sentence below consists of two independent clauses joined by a comma and a conjunction, a typical construction.

> The poorly prepared teacher entered the classroom as usual at 10:00 a.m., and by 10:05 the students were ready to leave.

The writer could have chosen to put a period after 10:00 a.m., eliminated the comma and conjunction, and capitalized by to make a separate sentence of the second independent clause. Such writing judgments have to do primarily with how closely related the writer wants separate thoughts to be.

Dependent clauses, three of which are bracketed in Figure 8, cannot function as complete sentences; they depend on independent clauses to make their meaning clear. In the first and third sentences in Figure 8, the dependent clause follows the independent clause on which it depends. In the second sentence, the dependent clause precedes the independent clause on which it depends.

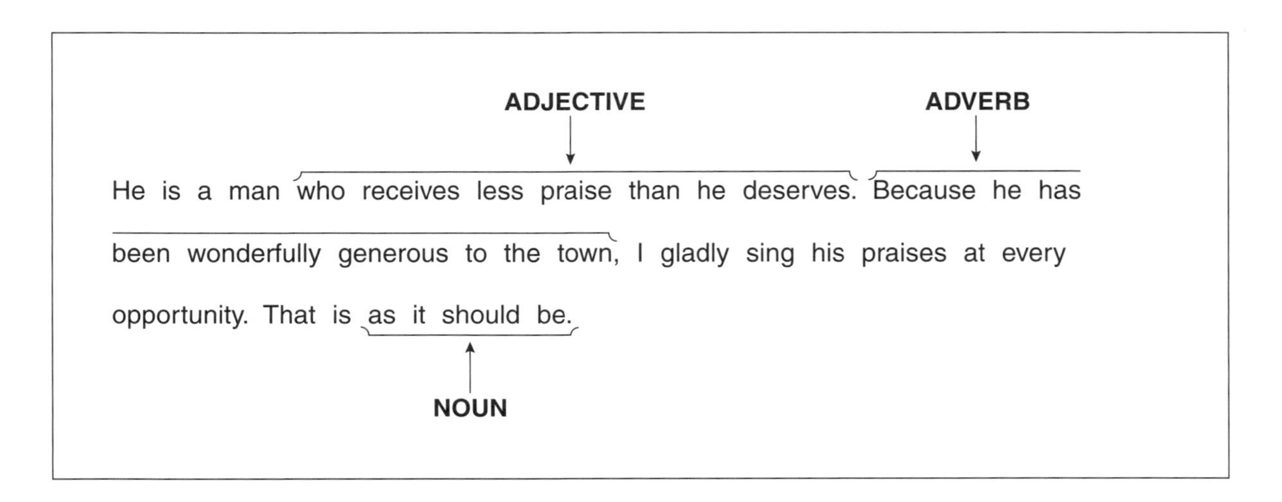

Figure 8: Three Examples of Dependent Clauses, Labeled by Function

As with phrases, dependent clauses carry a noun function, an adjective function, or an adverb function. The first dependent clause in Figure 8, for example, is an adjective clause that describes the man in the preceding independent clause; the second is an adverb clause that tells why the person who wrote the sentence sings praises; the third is a noun clause that functions as the object of its sentence.

Notice that dependent clauses are introduced by a relative pronoun (<u>who</u> in the first sentence) or by a subordinating conjunction (<u>because</u> in the second sentence and <u>as</u> in the third). That introductory word is all that keeps some dependent clauses from being independent; the second and third sentences in Figure 8 are cases in point.

You will notice also that some dependent clauses are set off by commas and some are not. Lack of a comma shows a close relationship between the clause and the rest of the sentence— specifically, that the clause is restricting or defining something. Such a clause is known as a restrictive clause or defining clause. In the first sentence below, by making <u>who I know to be honest</u> restrictive (no comma), I imply that—unlike some of my neighbors—this is a neighbor who I know to be honest. In the second sentence, by making <u>who I know to be honest</u> nonrestrictive (comma), I am identifying the person as a neighbor, then adding the fact that I know her to be honest. In short, restrictive clauses (no comma) qualify other information in the sentence in some way, and nonrestrictive clauses (comma) simply add information.

- She is a neighbor who I know to be honest.
- She is a neighbor, who I know to be honest.

Of all the ways in which misused commas damage writing, the most common may be to mislead readers about whether information is restrictive or nonrestrictive. You will find some treatment of that issue in the punctuation section of this appendix. For greater detail about all kinds of clauses and related issues, see Kramer, et al. (1995) or Hacker (1997).

<u>STYLE</u>:

In Chapter 3 I described style as simply "a particular way of doing something." When you choose one form of phrase or clause over another, you alter the style of your writing. For example, here are three similar messages, each featuring a different phrase function. The phrases in question are bracketed.

NOUN PHRASE	[Testing students] is the method of choice among teachers conversant with psychometrics.
ADJECTIVE PHRASE	The teachers [testing students] are those conversant with psychometrics.
ADVERB PHRASE	The teachers conversant with psychometrics have decided [to test students].

Bonus Tidbit:

The three phrases—if I may allude to the subtypes of phrases that I said are beyond the scope of this appendix—may also be described as a gerund phrase, a participial phrase, and an infinitive phrase respectively. If you are interested in more detail, consult Kramer, et al. (1995) or Hacker (1997).

Notice that the choices you make in putting a sentence together alter not only its style and feel, but its emphasis. In the noun-phrase sentence above, emphasis is on the method; in the adjective-phrase sentence, emphasis is on the subset of teachers choosing that method; in the adverb-phrase sentence, emphasis is on the decision made by that particular subset of teachers.

When you want to show the relationship of a sentence to the preceding sentence—or in the case of a topic sentence, to the preceding paragraph—introductory adverb phrases are particularly useful **{4}**.

- By comparison, . . .
- In contrast, . . .
- Looking from a different perspective, . . .
- In support of Cratz, . . .
- In opposition to Cratz, . . .
- Along the same line of thought, . . .
- For all other purposes, . . .
- Lacking regard for his predecessors, . . .

These eight are but a few grains of sand in a mountain of possibilities. Judicious use of introductory adverb phrases will help readers immensely, but two cautions are in order:

1. Frequent use of introductory phrases will damage style and tire readers.
2. The first noun following the phrase must be the grammatical subject of that phrase. (See this appendix, Part 2, Example B-4.)

Just as choosing one type of phrase over another alters the style, feel, and emphasis of a sentence, so does choosing one type of clause over another. Here are three similar messages, each featuring a different clause function.

NOUN CLAUSE	[A recipient of less praise than he deserves], he is an unfortunate man.
ADJECTIVE CLAUSE	He is an unfortunate man [who receives less praise than he deserves].
ADVERB CLAUSE	[Having received less praise than he deserves], he is an unfortunate man.

The differences among these sentences are in the weight each clause carries relative to the rest of the sentence. In both the noun clause and the adjective clause, the emphasis is clearly on the fact that the man is unfortunate. The writer implies in both cases that a lack of deserved praise bears on the man's misfortune, but leaves open the possibility that other factors play as great or greater a role. The most important difference between the noun clause and the adjective clause is placement: the man's status as unfortunate is given more weight in the first case than in the second by its placement at the end of the sentence. Finally, the emphasis in the adverb clause is on the cause of the man's misfortune. Unlike the other sentences, the sentence containing the adverb clause implies that the greatest cause of the man's misfortune is his having been deprived of deserved praise.

No doubt you are less conscious of types of phrases and types of clauses when you write than you are of the type of message or impression you want to give the reader. That is as it should be. Just as you achieve your destination by automobile more by being able to steer the car where you want it to go than by understanding the parts of an engine, you achieve your destination with a sentence or paragraph more by being able to steer the writing where you want it to go than by understanding the parts of speech. That having been said, there is still some value in knowing a spark plug wire from a radiator hose—or an adverb phrase from a noun phrase—when you want to diagnose a problem and get back on the road.

A Few Other Terms You Will Encounter In This Book

ABBREVIATION: a shortened version of a word

- equiv. for equivalent
- abbrev. for abbreviation

ALLITERATION: commencement of two or more words of a word group with the same letter

- He laughed loudly and leapt away.
- Ants abound.

APPOSITIVE: a noun or noun clause that refers to the same entity as the noun preceding it.

- I told you, Jim, that I would be absent.
- Paula Hansen, the researcher in charge, administered all tests.

COLLOQUIALISM: provincial usage, as opposed to standard usage

colloquial	standard
• We waited on him.	• We waited for him.
• It was hard.	• It was difficult.
• The tests turned out negative.	• The test results were negative.
• I have a problem with that.	• I disagree.
• They tuned him out.	• He lost their attention.

CONTRACTION: a speech-related combining of words

- don't for do not
- you're for you are

CONJUNCTIVE ADVERB: an adverb that connects parts of a sentence in the way that conjunctions connect words and phrases

- however
- therefore
- consequently
- nevertheless

NOMINALIZATION: use of a noun-form where a verb-form is the more natural construction

Verb Form: We have considered that.
Nominalization: We have had that under consideration.

2. Grammar

I will leave this topic to grammar books, except for five grammatical errors so common in the writing I see that I want to highlight them:

1. Subject/Verb Disagreement
2. Antecedent/Pronoun Disagreement
3. Wrong Verb Tense
4. Wrong Pronoun Case
5. Misplaced Subject

Example B-1: Subject/Verb Disagreement

A singular subject needs a singular verb; a plural subject needs a plural verb. To make your study of these examples easier, I have underlined subjects and verbs in the revisions.

Original

R

B-1a. (Subject/Verb Disagreement)

Experimental and investigative studies involving overt and covert tactile learning in a classroom environment has been conducted by several researchers.

Revision

(First Version)

Experimental and investigative studies involving overt and covert tactile learning within a classroom environment have been conducted by several researchers.

(Second Version)

Several researchers have conducted experimental and investigative studies of overt and covert tactile learning via classroom instruction.

To choose the verb has been in **B-1a**, the writer probably looked back to learning or environment rather than to the plural subject studies, which requires have been. Be careful not to let intervening material induce you to choose a verb that disagrees in number with the subject.

B-1a Bonus Tidbit

The second revision is stronger than the first because it is active **{14}**, precise (of rather than involving) **{18}**, and shorter **{9}**. Also, the subject and verb are closer together **{3}**.

Original

R

B-1b. (Subject/Verb Disagreement)

Psychometric analyses (Simon, 1993) of the MMCT results was based on data from 26 classrooms.

B-1c. (Subject/Verb Disagreement)

Of paramount importance in the hierarchy of musical understanding is the structural elements of pitch and duration.

Revision

(First Revision)

Psychometric analyses (Simon, 1993) of the MMCT results were based on data from 26 classrooms.

(Second Revision)

Psychometric analysis (Simon, 1993) of the MMCT results was based on data from 26 classrooms.

Of paramount importance in the hierarchy of musical understanding are the structural elements of pitch and duration.

The writer of **B-1b** may have failed to use a singular verb (first revision), or may have mistakenly written the plural noun analyses (second revision). In **B-1c**, placement of the verb ahead of the subject may have made subject-verb disagreement easier to overlook. I think the writer heard importance or hierarchy or understanding as the subject, wrote a singular verb, then failed to adjust after writing the plural subject elements. This sentence presents a strong case for rereading material after some time has passed.

Example B-2: Antecedent/Pronoun Disagreement

A singular antecedent needs to be referred to by a singular pronoun. This fundamental principle of grammar is being violated more each year as writers, fleeing from generic masculine pronouns, duck into the first sanctuary they see.

Original	Revision
B-2a. (Antecedent/Pronoun Disagreement) If a child is loved unconditionally, they will feel secure.	(First Revision) If a child is loved unconditionally, he or she will feel secure. (Second Revision) A child who is loved unconditionally will feel secure.
B-2b. (Antecedent/Pronoun Disagreement) When an NBA player refuses to work for millions of dollars per year, the general public sees them as arrogant and spoiled.	When an NBA player refuses to work for millions of dollars per year, the general public sees him as arrogant and spoiled.

Even where gender is not an issue, as in **B-2b**, this violation seems on the rise. One theory is that sensitivity to gender-neutral writing—or more accurately, a deluge of ill-advised responses to that sensitivity—has spawned a corresponding insensitivity to antecedent/pronoun disagreement. For an extensive treatment of gender-neutral writing—background, problems, and solutions—see Chapter 5, Part 2, Gender in Writing.

Example B-3: Wrong Verb Tense

Think clearly about time frames when you write. You need more than past, present, and future tense to maintain proper temporal relationships among events. You may want to read about verb tenses in the first section of this appendix under Part 1, Parts of Speech: A More Detailed View, or in a basic grammar book. To make these example easier to read, I have underlined words and phrases that relate to verb tense.

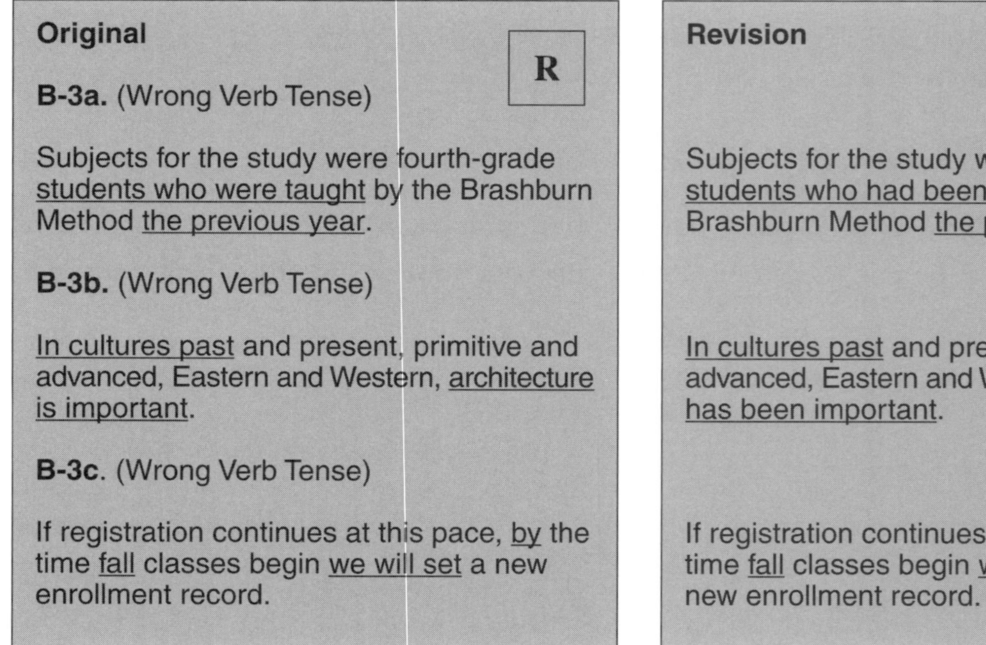

Original	Revision
B-3a. (Wrong Verb Tense)	
Subjects for the study were fourth-grade students who were taught by the Brashburn Method the previous year.	Subjects for the study were fourth-grade students who had been taught by the Brashburn Method the previous year.
B-3b. (Wrong Verb Tense)	
In cultures past and present, primitive and advanced, Eastern and Western, architecture is important.	In cultures past and present, primitive and advanced, Eastern and Western, architecture has been important.
B-3c. (Wrong Verb Tense)	
If registration continues at this pace, by the time fall classes begin we will set a new enrollment record.	If registration continues at this pace, by the time fall classes begin we will have set a new enrollment record.

The writer of **B-3a** should not have referred to the past and to the past-of-the-past with the same simple past-tense verb, were; past perfect (had been) is needed in the second case. Intervening material in **B-3b** may have caused the writer to forget about cultures past, for which music cannot be important (present tense); present perfect tense, on the other hand (has been), works well for both past and present. The writer of **B-3c** is describing the enrollment record as a past-to-be, a circumstance that will have occurred by fall; the verb tense needed is present perfect (will have set).

Example B-4: Wrong Pronoun Case

Refer to Figure 4, earlier in this chapter, to review the three cases of personal pronouns: nominative, possessive, and objective. The most common pronoun case errors I see in student writing are 1) use of objective case for nominative, and 2) use of objective case for possessive. To make these example easier to read, I have underlined the pronouns.

Original	**Revision**
B-4a. (Objective for Nominative)	
At the interview, Laura admitted that it was her.	At the interview, Laura admitted that it was she.
B-4b. (Objective for Possessive)	
The subjects said they did not mind me filming them.	The subjects said they did not mind my filming them.

You will hear an objective-for-nominative error if you try the pronoun as a subject: in **B-4a**, she admitted or she was is the obvious choice over her admitted or her was. The object in **B-4b** is filming, a verb-form functioning as a noun (gerund). Filming is what subjects did not mind. Whose filming? My filming (possessive case). Did not mind me sends another message altogether. Might a similar sentence be written in which the objective case (me) would be correct? Yes, so long as the pronoun itself is the object: The subjects said they did not see me filming them. Filming in this case is a verb-form functioning as a verb (participle), and the pronoun becomes the object: Did not see who? Did not see me.

B-4a Bonus Tidbit

As communication has become more casual, even in so-called formal writing, it was she has come to sound a bit stodgy. One reaction to the stodginess is to ignore grammatical correctness; a better reaction is to avoid this type of construction altogether by replacing it with specific information: "At the interview, Laura admitted that she was the informant."

Example B-5: Misplaced Subject

A common grammatical error is to misplace the subject of a sentence that begins with a participial phrase, causing another noun to function erroneously as the subject **{6}**. For more information about participial phrases, see the detailed information about verbs in Part 1 of this appendix.

I saw a blatant public display of this error when police in a major city placed copies of this notice on windshields of parked cars.

If left unlocked, a thief would now have your vehicle!

My response was, "I agree; please don't unlock the thieves." When a sentence begins so, the first noun or noun clause following the participial phrase becomes the implied subject of the phrase. What the police meant to tell citizens was this.

If left unlocked, your vehicle would now be in the possession of a thief!

The revised version is no more true than the original, but it is at least grammatically correct.

To make these examples easier to read I have underlined the subject in each sentence—the erroneous subject in the originals and the intended subject in the revisions.

Original	Revision
B-5a. (Misplaced Subject) R After taking the *Ernst Pattern Recognition Test (EPRT)*, the investigator gave 10 minutes of perceptual flexibility instruction twice a week for 17 weeks to two intact groups of second-grade students.	(Passive) After taking the *Ernst Pattern Recognition Test (EPRT),* two intact groups of second-grade students were given 10 minutes of perceptual flexibility instruction twice a week for 17 weeks. (Active) The investigator administered the *Ernst Pattern Recognition Test (EPRT)* to two intact groups of second-grade students, and subsequently gave 10 minutes of perceptual flexibility instruction to each group twice a week for 17 weeks.

The investigator cited in **B-5a** did not take EPRT: the students did. The first revision shows a clear repair of the grammatical problem, but the second revision—converted to active voice—is stronger.

Original	Revision
B-5b. (Misplaced Subject) Having discussed basic learning associations and the possible outcomes of learning behaviors, processes by which humans learn should be described as well.	(First Revision) Having discussed basic learning associations and the possible outcomes of learning behaviors, I should now describe processes by which humans learn.

Original	Revision
B-5c. (Misplaced Subject) R	(Second Revision) This discussion of basic learning associations and the possible outcomes of learning behaviors leads to a description of processes by which humans learn.
In an effort to reduce high intercorrelations among the dimensions of the rating scale, the judges evaluated each performance on three separate occasions.	In an effort to reduce high intercorrelations among the dimensions of the rating scale, the researcher had the judges evaluate each performance three times at one-week intervals.

Sometimes a writer, as subject, tries to stay out of the action by writing passive structures; that increases the risk of misplacing the subject. In **B-5b**, the writer—not the processes—discussed basics of learning. The second revision shows a way to avoid the original grammatical violation and still keep the writer-as-actor in the background, but it is not as strong and clear as the first revision. Similarly, in **B-5c**, the writer/researcher—not the judges—made the effort to reduce intercorrelations. This type of faulty construction is particularly hazardous—and all too common—in research writing, where readers are easily misled simply because they are up to their necks in details.

B-5c Bonus Tidbit

1. The researcher (third person) could be written I (first person). (See Chapter 5, Part 1)
2. The specificity added at the end of the revision is critical to the reporting of research. Three separate occasions could refer to morning, afternoon, and evening of the same day.

3. Punctuation

Punctuation marks separate thoughts in some places and combine thoughts in others, helping readers to understand relationships among pieces of material. Skillful use of punctuation by a writer is important to readability and correct interpretation. I will assume that you know how to use capital letters and sentence-enders (. ? !) correctly. Other marks are presented by section; the section about commas is longest by far.

Commas

Within a sentence, the most fundamental and frequently used punctuation mark is the comma. Important and numerous as they are, commas are probably thrown about by guesswork more than any other mark in the English language. Some comma decisions are subjective, but most follow well-conceived rules.

Example B-6: Overuse of Commas

Like words, commas should be used only if their presence helps the reader. Otherwise they become a kind of visual baggage that slows the reader down without benefit.

Original	Revision
B-6a. He ran, without hesitation, to the student's aid.	He ran without hesitation to the student's aid.
B-6b. After the argument, he returned to his study.	After the argument he returned to his study.
. . . but **B-6c.** does need a comma.	
B-6c. After the argument with his partner and friend of twenty years, he returned to his study. Why? --------->	Introductory phrases reach a critical length, beyond which a comma helps the reader read more efficiently. Rule of thumb: Use a comma after a string of prepositional phrases eight words or longer.
B-6d. A student, bold enough to ask for extra help from a teacher, will probably receive it, but, a shy student, suffering confusion, may be lost for the school year.	A student bold enough to ask for extra help from a teacher will probably receive it, but a shy student suffering confusion may be lost for the school year.

Aside from rules, let the meaning of a sentence guide you when you are tempted to spray it with commas. To know which commas to omit from **B-6d**, the writer needed to diagnose bold enough to ask . . . and suffering confusion as restrictive, i.e., essential to the meaning of the independent clauses in which they are embedded. (See Part 1 of this appendix.) Reading aloud can help you make such decisions.

<u>Example B-7</u>: Commas to Set Off Introductory Words or Word Groups

You need to place a comma after an introductory word group that contains a verb form (gerund, participle, infinitive), and after an introductory adverb or adverb clause that modifies the whole sentence. Note that the lack of a comma may alter meaning, as in **B-7b**.

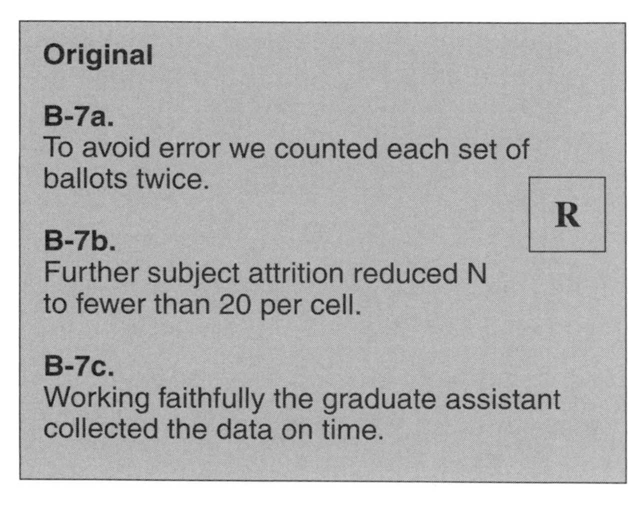
Original

B-7a.
To avoid error we counted each set of ballots twice.

R

B-7b.
Further subject attrition reduced N to fewer than 20 per cell.

B-7c.
Working faithfully the graduate assistant collected the data on time.

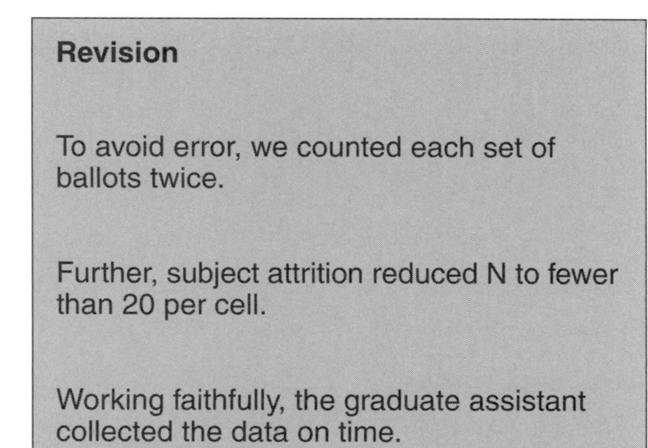
Revision

To avoid error, we counted each set of ballots twice.

Further, subject attrition reduced N to fewer than 20 per cell.

Working faithfully, the graduate assistant collected the data on time.

<u>Example B-8</u>: Commas to Set Off Nonrestrictive Clauses

Proper use of commas tells the reader where a clause begins or ends and whether it is restrictive (defining) or nonrestrictive (nondefining). (For definitions and examples of restrictive and nonrestrictive clauses, see Part 1 of this appendix.) Without comma clues, the reader may be left to choose which of two or more possible meanings is correct.

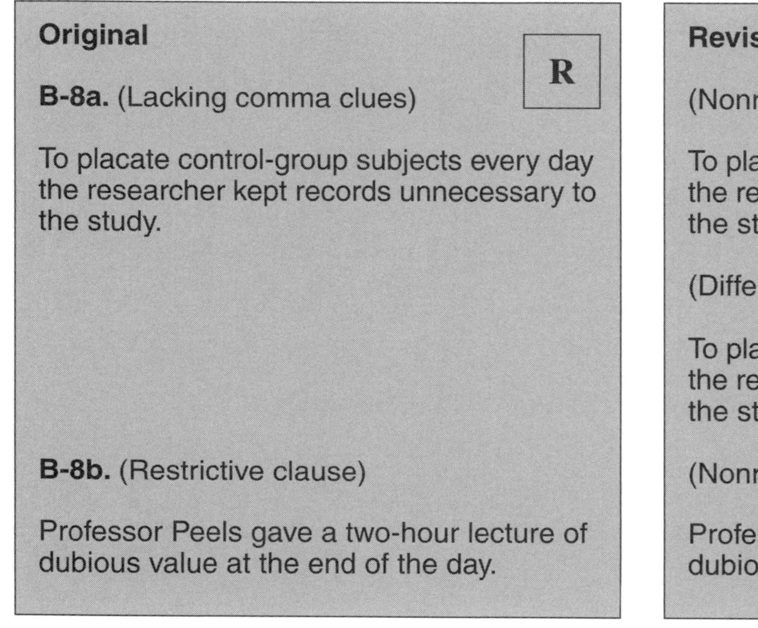
Original

R

B-8a. (Lacking comma clues)

To placate control-group subjects every day the researcher kept records unnecessary to the study.

B-8b. (Restrictive clause)

Professor Peels gave a two-hour lecture of dubious value at the end of the day.

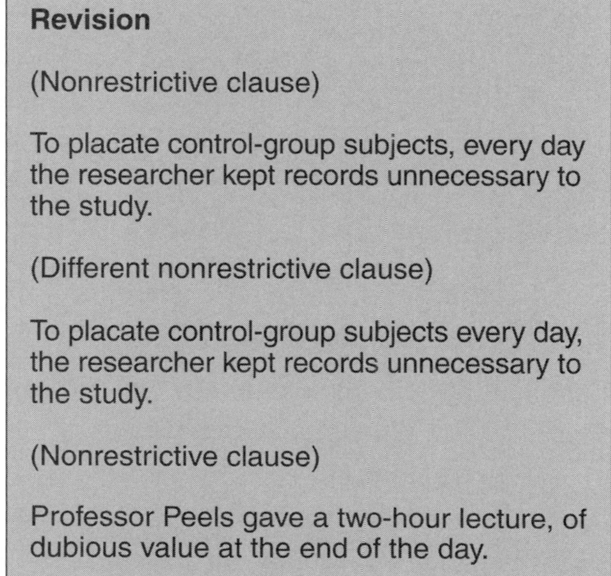
Revision

(Nonrestrictive clause)

To placate control-group subjects, every day the researcher kept records unnecessary to the study.

(Different nonrestrictive clause)

To placate control-group subjects every day, the researcher kept records unnecessary to the study.

(Nonrestrictive clause)

Professor Peels gave a two-hour lecture, of dubious value at the end of the day.

Was the lecture cited in **B-8b** inherently of dubious value (restrictive), or did giving it at the end of the day cause it to be of dubious value (nonrestrictive)? The original may be correct. One comma makes the difference.

Original	**Revision**
B-8c. (Restrictive clause)	(Nonrestrictive clause)
I used the audiometer which the school provided.	I used the audiometer, which the school provided.

A writer who intends the message of **B-8c** would do well to avoid which as the relative pronoun, because the reader's only clue to meaning (the school's audiometer was chosen over others) is absence of the comma. The reader is forced to depend on the writer's having omitted the comma purposely, an unnecessary burden on both reader and writer. Introduce a nonrestrictive clause (revision) with which, then precede it with a comma; introduce a restrictive clause with that, or by reconstructing the sentence so as to eliminate the relative pronoun. Strunk and White (1979, p. 59) and Fowler (1996, p. 774) both recommend such distinctive uses of which and that. (See also Chapter 2, Part 3, A Collection of Troublesome Words: [that, which].)

Original	**Revision**
B-8d. (Restrictive clause, using which)	(Restrictive clause, using that)
I used the audiometer which the school provided.	I used the audiometer that the school provided.
	OR
	I used the audiometer provided by the school.

See also Chapter 2, Part 3, A Collection of Troublesome Words (that, which).

Example B-9: Commas (and Parentheses) to Set Off Words that Interrupt the Flow of a Sentence

Long sentences contain primary and secondary information. A good writer identifies which is which by wise use of punctuation **{20}**.

Original	Revision
B-9a. (Secondary material separated, but not marked)	
A good musical environment especially in the home enhances the musical development of young children.	A good musical environment, especially in the home, enhances the musical development of young children.
B-9b. (Secondary material wholly unidentified)	(Emphasis 1)
The Association for Supervision and Curriculum Development is a well-respected professional organization housed near the nation's capitol.	The Association for Supervision and Curriculum Development, a well-respected professional organization, is housed near the nation's capitol.
	(Emphasis 2)
	The Association for Supervision and Curriculum Development, housed near the nation's capitol, is a well-respected professional organization.

While the writer of **B-9a** has simply left the reader to separate the secondary material visually, the writer of **B-9b** has left the reader to decide entirely where emphasis belongs and what the true message is. To write Emphasis 1 is to make the association's reputation parenthetical and emphasize housed near the nation's capital; to write Emphasis 2 is to make the association's location parenthetical and emphasize well-respected professional organization.

B-9a and b Bonus Tidbit

When secondary material is an aside to the function of the sentence, use parentheses: "The Association for Supervision and Curriculum Development (ASCD) is a well-respected professional organization."

Original	Revision
B-9c. (Comma missing after the interruptive clause) **R**	
Beck and Wong, using a Manipulation Performance Test found that English children ages 10–15 have better spatial perception than Ugandan children.	Beck and Wong, using a Manipulation Performance Test, found that English children ages 10–15 have better spatial perception than Ugandan children.

Original	Revision
B-9d. (Comma missing before the interruptive clause) **R**	
Rhythmic phrases from all three compositions will be recorded on the evaluation tape consecutively as will the tonal phrases and harmonic phrases, allowing judges to rate all of one dimension before proceeding to another.	Rhythmic phrases from all three compositions will be recorded on the evaluation tape consecutively, as will the tonal phrases and harmonic phrases, allowing judges to rate all of one dimension before proceeding to another.

Think of commas surrounding an interruptive expression as an inseparable pair. Readers will be made uncomfortable by a comma before the expression and not after, as in **B-9c**, or by a comma after the expression and not before, as in **B-9d**.

B-9c and d Bonus Tidbit

"Interruptive expression" is non-technical language. The interruption in **B-9c**, for example, is a nonrestrictive participial phrase placed appositively. Because I want to retain the flavor of a writing guide rather than a grammar book, I use technical terms sparingly. You will need to know the parts of speech and parts of a sentence shown at the beginning of this appendix to read about and talk about writing and to think about written construction in detail, but intimate knowledge of more advance terms may be only marginally useful to the art of writing.

Be careful not to miscast thoughts in a sentence by enclosing information between commas erroneously. When enclosed information is removed, the remaining material should form the core meaning of the sentence.

Original	Revision
B-9e. (Misidentified Interruptive Expression)	
Russians came to gawk at, and debate, what the new McDonald's restaurant means.	Russians came to gawk at the new McDonald's restaurant and to debate what it means.

Errant commas in **B-9e**, taken from a newspaper story, create a nonsensical message: <u>Russians came to gawk at what the new McDonald's restaurant means.</u>

B-9 Bonus Tidbit

Whether to use parentheses or commas to set off an interruption is subjective. Commas are the norm; parentheses are stronger: "The students were quiet, orderly, and cooperative (but not diffident) when they came to take the test." Advice about a third option, the dash, can be found near the end of this appendix.

Example B-10: Commas to Introduce Independent Clauses

Two independent clauses joined by a conjunction to form a compound sentence are each capable of standing alone as a simple sentence. A comma preceding the conjunction alerts the reader to that condition at the midway point, leading the reader to interpret the whole correctly without perhaps having to reread it.

Original	Revision
B-10a. Some of the more basic elements have already been incorporated but objective research would help discern appropriate techniques.	Some of the more basic elements have already been incorporated, but objective research would help discern appropriate techniques.
B-10b. **R** The researcher identified two contaminating variables immediately and he took proper steps to neutralize them.	The researcher identified two contaminating variables immediately, and he took proper steps to neutralize them.
B-10c. The buses will transport students and teachers will drive their own cars.	The buses will transport students, and teachers will drive their own cars.
B-10d. The researcher observed the third-grade classroom last Monday and Wednesday she met with the teacher and principal.	The researcher observed the third-grade classroom last Monday, and Wednesday she met with the teacher and principal.

Sentences **B-10c** and **d** are obviously confusing; you are not likely to omit the comma. Let them sensitize you to the help a comma gives readers when sentences are less confusing but similarly constructed (**B-10a** and **b**). Make exceptions for very short sentences containing two independent clauses: "I went there and Jack came here." (For more about clauses, see Parts of Speech: A More Detailed View in Part 1 of this appendix.)

Example B-11: Commas to Mark a Series

In a series of words or phrases, place a comma before the conjunction introducing the last word or phrase.

Original	Revision
B-11a. The taxpayer must pay the bill for elaborate buildings, governmental offices and officers hired to work in them.	The taxpayer must pay the bill for elaborate buildings, governmental offices, and officers hired to work in them.
B-11b. To work with young children successfully, one must be attuned to their propensities, tolerant of their incongruities, understanding about their innate selfishness and strong drive and enduring in the face of days that sometimes seem interminable.	To work with young children successfully, one must be attuned to their propensities, tolerant of their incongruities, understanding about their innate selfishness and strong drive, and enduring in the face of days that sometimes seem interminable.

To use a comma before the final conjunction in a series of three or more terms or phrases was once an ironclad rule. A movement for elimination of the final comma decades ago gained substantial support, causing the practice to become a question of style. In many cases a sentence is clear without a comma preceding the final conjunction:

All you need is notebook, paper and pencil.

In most cases, as seen in **B-11a** and **b**, loss of the final comma makes the sentence more difficult to read. That is especially so when the series is long or the phrases complex. An interesting example can be seen on a rest area plaque near Edison's New Jersey laboratory site:

> From this West Orange laboratory came patents for moving pictures, talking pictures, the fluoroscope, dictating machine, mimeograph, storage battery, phonograph records, the magnetic separation of iron and cement manufacturing processes.

No matter the reader's cognizance that magnetic separation of iron and cement is impossible, lack of a comma before and leads most persons to read the phrase that way. Then the reader needs to double back and mentally insert the comma. Writers have a choice of three approaches to the comma before the final conjunction in a series:

1. Omit the comma in all cases and let the reader untangle ambiguities.
2. Omit the comma in simple series, use it in complicated series, and ignore the inconsistency.

3. Use the comma in all cases to achieve both clarity and consistency.

I strongly recommend the third approach. Clarity is essential and consistency puts the reader's mind at ease. As I was about to send the final version of this book to the publisher, a student submitted this sentence to me in a chapter of his dissertation:

> Among the factors used to judge leadership effectiveness, group productivity and follower satisfaction are dominant—especially in field studies.

The sentence is a good one, but had the writer subscribed to either of the first two approaches above, group productivity would have looked like the second in a series of three terms. I read the sentence efficiently only because the writer had established, as a consistent characteristic of his writing style, the use of final commas in sentence series.

Semicolons

Semicolons simultaneously divide and link. At the same time a semicolon divides pieces of material into distinct units, it shows mutuality by containing them within one sentence.

Example B-12: Semi-colons to Join Independent Clauses

Sometimes commas and periods are not adequate to characterize the true relationship between two independent clauses.

Original	Revision
B-12a. (Conjunction that Weakens) The children bring joy and hope to the nursing-home residents, and the nursing-home residents give love and attention to the children.	The children bring joy and hope to the nursing-home residents; the nursing-home residents give love and attention to the children.
B-12b. (Inappropriate Comma) The children bring joy and hope to the nursing-home residents, the nursing-home residents give love and attention to the children.	
B-12c. (Separate Sentences) The children bring joy and hope to the nursing-home residents. The nursing-home residents give love and attention to the children.	

Sometimes a conjunction weakens a compound sentence by separating two closely related thoughts (**B-12a**). A comma is insufficient without the conjunction (**B-12b**), and separate sentences leave the reader to infer a connection that the writer wants to make explicit (**B-12c**). In that circumstance, a semicolon becomes the mark of preference. Note that **B-12a** and **B-12c** are acceptable, but that each—for different reasons—is weaker than the revision. Use of a semicolon to join independent clauses is, more than anything, a device to invigorate writing **{20}**.

<u>Example B-13</u>: Semicolons Used with Connectors

Sometimes you want to make a complex relationship clear among groups of thoughts. One tool you may use is a semicolon in partnership with either a coordinate conjunction (and, but, . . .) or a conjunctive adverb (however, nevertheless, consequently . . .).

Original	Revision
B-13a. (Thoughts Needing a Relationship Shown)	(Semicolon Coupled with a Coordinate Conjunction)
The teacher blamed the principal while the principal blamed the teacher. The problem persisted for another year.	The teacher blamed the principal while the principal blamed the teacher; and the problem persisted for another year.
B-13b. (Thoughts Needing a Relationship Shown)	(Semicolon Coupled with a Conjunctive Adverb)
The art teacher, the music teacher, and the dance teacher tried to coordinate their schedules and curriculums, but failed. The children's artistry grew rapidly because of each teacher's competence and dedication.	The art teacher, the music teacher, and the dance teacher tried to coordinate their schedules and curriculums, but failed; nevertheless, the children's artistry grew rapidly because of each teacher's competence and dedication.

B-13b Bonus Tidbit

Notice that <u>nevertheless</u> is set off from the subsequent independent clause by a comma. Everything following the semicolon functions grammatically as a separate sentence, invoking the rule exemplified in Example **B-7**.

Example **B-13c** shows the erroneous use of a comma in place of a semicolon when joining two independent clauses with the conjunctive adverb however. This is a particularly common and confusing practice.

Original	Revision
B-13c. Most school track coaches are burdened by a heavy meet schedule, however, the magnitude of the problem varies from state to state. **Note** Other conjunctive adverbs are sometimes mistreated in this way; therefore and nevertheless come to mind, but however takes the greatest abuse by far.	(First Revision) Most school track coaches are burdened by a heavy meet schedule; however, the magnitude of the problem varies from state to state. (Second Revision) Most school track coaches are burdened by a heavy meet schedule. The magnitude of the problem, however, varies from state to state.

In the original, however might modify either the first or second clause; in the first revision, the semicolon links however clearly to the second clause. When however does modify the first clause, as in the second sentence of the second revision, surrounding commas work well. For more on this subject, see Chapter 2, Part 3, A Collection of Troublesome Words (however).

B-12b and B-13c Bonus Tidbit

The poor construction shown in **B-12b**, joining two sentences by a comma, is called a *comma splice*. The underlying problem in **B-13c** is also a comma splice. The writer has simply masked it by inserting *however*.

Sometimes the however problem cited above is most easily resolved by simply changing however, a conjunctive adverb that requires a preceding semicolon, to but, a conjunction that requires only a preceding comma.

Original	Revision
B-13d. Females received similar physical fitness training in their own gymnasiums, however, they were not removed from their homes.	Females received similar physical fitness training in their own gymnasiums, but they were not removed from their homes.

Example B-14: Semicolons in a Series

Semicolons are used also to separate series that contain commas. Sometimes they separate series in a complicated sentence (**B-14a**) and sometimes they separate series in a list (**B-14b**).

> **B-14a.** (Semicolons separating series in a sentence)
>
> We were slowed by the equipment we had to carry; the muddy, unpaved, pock-marked roads; the ancient, ailing trucks, prone to breakdowns and short of spare parts; the outdated maps that showed no new roads—and worse, roads that had once been passable but now were not.

> **B-14b.** (Semicolons separating series in a list)
>
> Contemporary researchers agree (Anderson, 1992; Schmidt, 1994; Kim, 1994; Slackowitz, 1995; Brady, 1996; Yu, 1999; Wong, 1999).

Colons

Too many writers are unclear about similarities and differences in the use of a colon and a semicolon. Both link pieces of related material, but the material following a colon bears a specific type of relationship to preceding material: it describes, illustrates, or amplifies. By using a colon, the writer is saying to the reader, "let me explain in detail."

Except for circumstances shown in **B-14a** and **b**, material to the right of a semicolon usually contains a subject and a verb; material to the right of a colon, on the other hand, may be as short as one word or as long as a list, and often does not contain a subject and a verb.

Example B-15: A Colon to Introduce an Illustration

> The human animal is not necessarily swayed by fact: drunk driving kills, yet people drive drunk; smoking damages health and takes lives, yet people smoke; drug abuse ruins lives in hellish ways, yet people abuse drugs.

Example B-16: A Colon to Introduce an Amplification

> After three years of work, one emotion dominates: frustration. We have gathered all the anecdotal evidence and library evidence available, and we are now left without choices if we want to solve the puzzle: only a trip to Africa will enable us to see the project to completion.

B-16 Bonus Tidbit

I contrived this example to give two uses of the colon within a small space. Such heavy use of colons is not recommended.

Example B-17: A Colon to Introduce a List

> Kratz has identified three effective approaches to separating fact from fiction in an interview:
>
> 1. . . .
> 2. . . .
> 3. . . .

B-17 Bonus Tidbit

Numbers in a list should be aligned at the periods, meaning that the 0 in number 10 should align with the 9 above it.

Each entry in a list as shown in **B-17** should consist of a complete sentence, begun with a capital letter and ended with a period or question mark. If list entries together constitute a series in a sentence begun by the preceding stem, 1) no colon should be used after the stem, 2) entries should begin with lower case letters, 3) each entry except the last should be followed by a comma or a semicolon, 4) the comma or semicolon preceding the last entry should be followed by a conjunction (and; or), and 5) the last entry should be followed by a period or a question mark. For examples of two approaches to lists, see Chapter 1, Part 4, Disjointedness—Disjointed Insert.

You should **not** place a colon where it will separate a verb from its complement, e.g., subject or object, or where it will separate a preposition from its object(s):

Do Not Separate . . .	Misuse of Colons
verb from subject:	Participants will: listen to three lectures, make one short presentation, and submit three preliminary drawings.
verb from object:	Participants will need: a pencil, a ruler, and a compass.
preposition from object:	He divided them into: high, moderate, and low.

A Final Thought About Commas, Semicolons, and Colons

Whenever you relate two ideas (or more) to each other within a sentence, you have decisions to make. You may decide that one idea is less important than the other, but still related to it. In that case you are likely to subordinate the less important idea within a dependent clause, introduced perhaps by a subordinating conjunction (because in the example below) that indicates its relationship to the main idea:

> Because he wrote his lesson plans with attention to every detail, the next day he taught exceptionally well.

On the other hand, you may want to present the ideas to the reader as independent clauses. When you relate independent clauses to each other you have three punctuation options from which to choose: comma, semicolon, or colon. What you use will depend on the nature of the message and the type of emphasis you want. The most common link between independent clauses, by far, is a comma followed by a conjunction.

> He wrote his lesson plans with attention to every detail, and the next day he taught exceptionally well.

Still, semicolons and colons offer you chances to clarify and strengthen your writing.

> He wrote his lesson plans with attention to every detail; the next day he taught exceptionally well.

> The next day he was rewarded for having written his lesson plans with attention to every detail: he taught exceptionally well.

Hyphens, Dashes, and Slashes

A hyphen, which joins, is a short horizontal line (big-boned). A dash, which interrupts, is either a long horizontal line—made by a professional printer or by a computer with the dash-character capability—or two consecutive short horizontal lines--made by a typewriter or by a computer lacking the dash-character capability. A slash, which offers a choice, is a diagonal line (issue/category). Notice that all of these marks are made with no space on either side.

Misuse of hyphens, dashes, and slashes can have a disastrous effect on meaning. Study the function of each and use them properly.

Example B-18: Hyphens

One use of hyphens, of course, is to join two parts of a single word carried from one line to another. You can find rules for word hyphenation in standard grammar books. In brief form, hyphenate between syllables, as you see between the previous line and this line, or hyphenate between double letters, as you see at the end of this line. When you break words in other places, your communication suffers.

A more common use of hyphens is to create compound words, thousands of which have become standard. Here are a few.

Nouns	Verbs	Adjectives
front-runner	quick-freeze	fun-filled
also-ran	deep-fry	big-hearted

You will need a dictionary to know which standard compound words are to be hyphenated, which have evolved into single words (benchmark, watershed, software), and which remain separate (riot squad, high school, dress rehearsal). You need not limit your use of hyphenated words to those found in the dictionary. My desire for brevity, clarity, and energy tempt me to create hyphenated compound adjectives frequently, nouns less frequently, and verbs infrequently.

Original	**Revision**
B-18a.	(compound noun)
The person who wielded the club spoke.	The club-wielder spoke.
B-18b.	(compound adjective)
One rough ride and the pain it inflicted increased my respect for accomplished equestrians.	One painfully-rough ride increased my respect for accomplished equestrians.

The choice of original or revision in **B-18a** and **b** is not a matter of right and wrong, but a matter of what tone you want to set. Compound words shorten writing, deliver meaning in a more compact package, and energize sentences. I generally like those effects.

B-18a and b Bonus Tidbit

Avoid overuse. Like cherry chocolates, compound words in great number become too rich.

Be careful not to write hyphens where dashes are needed. The effect is visually disorienting.

Original	**Revision**
B-18c. (Hyphen for Dash)	
Her greatest fear-though fear was not typical of her-was that he had died.	Her greatest fear—though fear was not typical of her—was that he had died. OR Her greatest fear--though fear was not typical of her--was that he had died.

<u>Example B-19</u>: Dashes

The dash is a mark of self-interruption that sets off material more dramatically than commas or parentheses.

Original	Revision
B-19a. (Use of Commas) Artistic power carries classical music across centuries, yet most of the population, for lack of background alone, is shut out of the gratification it has to offer. **B-19b.** (Use of Parentheses) Artistic power carries classical music across centuries, yet most of the population (for lack of background alone) is shut out of the gratification it has to offer.	(Strengthened with Dashes) Artistic power carries classical music across centuries, yet most of the population—for lack of background alone—is shut out of the gratification it has to offer.

The commas in **B-19a** hide the parenthetic expression in a sea of other phrases. The parentheses in **B-19b** call more attention to the phrase, but cast it as an aside. In contrast to both, the dashes in the revision are like a spotlight shown on the star of the show, or like a voice raised in spoken communication. Dashes are a bold and unusual tool of writing. Use them with good judgment, and use them sparingly. Like the little boy who cried wolf, you can condition people to ignore your boldness if it becomes too common.

Example B-20: Slashes

Slashes are used sometimes as a quick-fix substitute for a better form of expression. They seem to mean either or or and, and the reader may need to guess which. If you use a slash, do it with deliberation, not as a substitute for a writing decision.

Original	Revision
B-20a. (Slash-Induced Ambiguity) English/education majors may find the book interesting.	(One possible meaning) English majors and education majors may find the book interesting. (A second possible meaning) Students carrying a double major in English and education may find the book interesting.

Be particularly careful how you use slash-words in combination with other words.

Original	Revision
B-20b. (Errant Column Heading)	
Blood/Body Fluid Collection	Blood/Body-Fluid Collection

The **B-20b** column-heading from a data sheet means—unintentional as it may be—"blood fluid collection (which is nonsense) and (or?) body fluid collection." The creator of the form meant "blood collection and (or?) body-fluid collection." The hyphen added to the revision creates a compound adjective that modifies collection, enabling readers to see the intended meaning immediately.

A Closing Note

Short sentences are generally more readable than long sentences (see Chapter 1, Part 1), but you can make long sentences optimally readable by having command of writing mechanics. I offer the monster-sentence below only to demonstrate that point: a sentence this long should be expected perhaps once in a thousand pages.

> Plainly and simply, the student clarinetist needs to hear a good clarinet sound to produce a good clarinet sound; needs to hear a classical style or a jazz style to perform musically in a classical style or a jazz style; needs to play in small ensembles that expose individual roles and foster musical cooperation (woodwind quintet, jazz ensemble) to become musically independent and mature; and finally, needs to add many hours of playing in solo—putting sounds into the aural-feedback loop—to become what a student clarinetist ostensibly aspires to become: an accomplished musician.

A high-level use of punctuation marks divides this monster-sentence into units that function almost as sentences themselves. The whole is a single sentence only in that it begins with a capital letter and ends with a period.

Certainly you can raise the readability of your writing with wise use of punctuation marks. Learn particularly the advantages of the semicolon, colon, and dash. Warning: do not use clever punctuation as a rationale for throwing sentence length to the wind. As long as readability is one of your aims, you should—as pointed out in Chapter 1, Part 1—avoid overstuffed sentences, monitor the average length of your sentences, and write sentences of varying length.

That last point is more important than many writers realize. Just as mile after mile of driving dulls a driver's senses if the terrain lacks variety, so page after page of reading dulls a reader's senses if sentence length lacks variety. Both drivers and readers need peaks and valleys to stay alert and stimulated. Look at the contrasting examples below (see also Chapter 3, Example **13e**).

Sentences of Similar Length

The second-grade curriculum is slated for revision beginning next month. The third-grade curriculum was revised during the previous school year. Our plan is to eventually revise and link curriculums for all grades. This process has been under way for a little more than three years. The target date for completion is still another three years away.

Revised to Sentences of Varying Length

The third-grade curriculum was revised last school year, and the second-grade curriculum will be revised this year. We will begin next month. Eventually we will link the curriculums of all grades by carrying out a long-range plan adopted a little more than three years ago. Completion is expected in another three years.

The dull, staid feeling of the first example as compared to the second stems primarily from lack of variety in sentence length. The five sentences of the first example carry a word count of 11, 11, 12, 13, and 11; the four sentences of the revision carry a word count of 19, 5, 23, and 7. Notice also a variety in the way sentences begin in the revision as compared with the original.

Sentence Openers: Original

- The second-grade . . .
- The third-grade . . .
- Our plan . . .
- This process . . .
- The target date . . .

Sentence Openers: Revision

- The third-grade . . .
- We begin . . .
- Eventually we will have . . .
- Completion is expected . . .

Facile use of various kinds of phrases and clauses leads to still greater variety in sentence openings and endings, all of which keeps the writing fresh and the reader attentive. To refresh your mind to the possibilities, reread "Parts of a Sentence: A More Detailed View," early in this appendix. Read particularly the subsection about style.

You probably know the condition of your writing mechanics better now than before you read this appendix. You should not agonize over deficiencies, but neither should you ignore them. I offer four pieces of advice.

1) Continue systematic study of this appendix to whatever extent you need it, even as you work with the rest of the book.
2) Supplement that study with other sources that you find helpful. I recommend highly the first chapter of *The Elements of Style* (Strunk and White).
3) Create a check-off system so you know when you have assimilated a feeling for each rule in this appendix and in *The Elements of Style*, or whatever text you use. ***The system I offered in Chapter 2, Part 3, would work as well for rules and principles as it does for word use.***
4) Persist until your new writing habits become second nature.

Make freedom your goal—the freedom to express yourself fully on paper. That is a tool of inestimable importance, not only in academic work but in whatever professional career you choose.

APPENDIX C

A RESERVOIR OF VERBS

A noun or pronoun with no other word to activate it is like an automobile without fuel: it goes nowhere. To activate nouns and pronouns, writers use some form of the verb *be* (*be, am, is, are, was, were, being,* and *been*)—sometimes involving nominalizations and passive structures (There *is opposition* to the project, but it *will be approved*)—or they use either a noun pressed into service as a verb (The two parties should *dialogue*) or an active verb (The Board *opposes* the project, but voters *will approve* it). Of all these choices, active verbs are the premium-grade fuel. Active verbs invigorate writing. Feel the difference between the original statements below and the revisions.

Originals	**Revisions**
He was uncooperative when we asked him to go.	He refused to go.
Accepting the blame for his wife's accident has become Harold's mantle. He is experiencing agony because of her debilitating injuries, and has made a commitment to fill her every need.	Harold blames himself for his wife's accident. He agonizes over her debilitating injuries and bends to her every need.

Sometimes you will use forms of *be,* passive structures, or nominalizations purposely—and for good reason. Those forms have legitimate functions. Still, strong writing depends on a high percentage of active verbs. So does concise writing: note differences in length in the examples above. I have written this appendix because I know everyone uses weaker than necessary verb forms unintentionally at times for lack of a ready storehouse of alternatives. The two alphabetical lists of active verbs in this appendix provide that storehouse. Meanwhile, each list carries its own function. The list titled *Reminders* contains about 1,100 commonly used verbs that you probably know well. The list titled *Mind Provokers* contains about 2,000 more challenging verbs that will help you express yourself broadly, and at the same time precisely. The two lists together offer a wide range of active verbs for you to explore, and they allow experienced and inexperienced writers alike to make good use of the appendix: less experienced writers may use *Reminders* as their primary prompter; more experienced writers may use *Mind Provokers.*

The reason *Mind Provokers* is the longer of the two lists is that I have included common words having imaginative uses beyond their usual context. A few words you might not expect to find on the *Mind Provokers* list, for example, are *buckle, stock, shield, bathe,* and *capture*, but they are there because of their potential for expansive use:

> I expected all research subjects to *buckle* under the last few questions, but one young lady had *stocked* her mind with ready answers and *shielded* her pride with willful indifference.

> He *bathed* himself in unrealistic expectations, ignoring the truth that to *capture* her heart he must first *capture* her attention.

Judgments about which words belong on which list could occupy a lifetime, as there are no correct answers. While the placements of dozens of words are contestable, each list as a whole generally serves its purpose. Trying not to strangle you with too many entries, I have excluded four types of active verbs from the lists, as described in the following paragraphs.

First, in keeping with the purpose of this book, I have excluded verbs that seem suited more to fiction than to formal writing. Some are useful within formal writing, but as a whole their value is too slight to warrant inclusion. A few examples are *belch, clang*, and *slosh.*

Second, I have excluded verbs that will be minimally useful because of their obscurity. Most are valuable in the right circumstance, but as a whole they yield too small a return for the time needed to learn them. Your path to these verbs is more likely to be through a thesaurus, in response to a specific, narrow need. Here is a small sample of ***obscure verbs:***

adumbrate	elinguate	manducate	nidificate	perigrinate	recrudesce	urticate
cadge	inculpate	mizzle	oppilate	prate	repugn	vellicate
cohobate	lucubrate	nesslerize	oppugn	ratriocinate	sparge	wintle

Third, I have excluded verbs having so singular an application that you are likely to bring them to mind when you need them. Here is a small sample of ***specifically applied verbs:***

blink	debate	faint	molt	picket	solder	trawl
breed	dismount	italicize	neuter	redistrict	stitch	triage
cremate	elope	lisp	oxidize	refract	sublet	void

Finally, I have excluded verbs so common that you can call them up at will. Here is a small sample of ***extremely common verbs.***

ask	eat	listen	open	ride	smile	teach
come	give	look	pick	run	stand	think
cry	go	move	read	see	take	understand
drive	hear	need	rest	sit	talk	write

Other judgments I have made in compiling this appendix are to exclude *ize* words unless I consider them nearly indispensable *(epitomize, itemize, ostracize)* and to exclude fancy versions of more common verbs *(orientate = orient; pacificate = pacify; systematize = systemize).* I have eliminated some verbs that can be constructed easily by adding a prefix to another verb *(de-emphasize),* but I must tread lightly in that territory; many such words belong on the list *(degrade; disengage; retrace).* I have included some words that are more common as nouns than as verbs, but only if they double as active, uniquely useful verbs *(cloak, frame, label).*

I have missed some verbs that should be on these lists and included some that should not; having felt difficulty and uncertainty along the way, I have no question of that. Still, I think you will find the lists valuable if your aims are to enlarge your vocabulary of verbs and to write more active sentences. (Read about writing principles 12 and 14 in "Writing Principles Described.")

Do not run through columns of words quickly, as that will only discourage you. Rather, use the lists a small portion at a time, and perhaps create a system of marks similar to those I recommended in Chapter 2 to keep yourself informed of your level of familiarity with each entry. That will help you accumulate a rich store of active verbs. Stop just long enough on each word to sense its usefulness, and maybe form a tentative sentence. You will need a good dictionary to introduce yourself to unfamiliar words and find deeper meanings and wider uses for familiar words.

You may find some unfamiliar words less than useful, but others you will want to study and incorporate into your vocabulary. Be adventurous. While you generally want to attune your writing vocabulary to your intended audience, there is nothing wrong with stretching readers' vocabularies here and there. Context usually illuminates meaning. Just be sure your purpose is not to impress or to baffle, but rather to say what you have to say as efficiently and precisely as possible.

Where common use calls for a verb to be combined with another word or words, those words are shown in parentheses, e.g., hole (up); piece (together); stave (off).

REMINDERS

Easily Recalled Active Verbs: An Alphabetical List of About 1,100

abbreviate
abide
abolish
absorb
abstain
acclaim
accelerate
accom-
modate
accomplish
accumulate
acquaint
acquire
acquit
activate
adapt
adjust
administer
admire
adopt
adore
advance
allege
alter
alternate
ambush
analyze
annoy
anticipate
appeal
applaud
appoint
approximate
arbitrate
articulate
assemble
assert
assess
assign
assist
associate
assume
assure
attach
attack
attempt
attend
attract
attribute
auction
audit
authenticate
authorize
automate
avoid
await
awaken
award
✦✦✦✦✦
babble
backfire
backslide
backstab
bail
balance
band
bank
baptize
bar
barbecue
bargain
bark
barnstorm
bat
battle
bawl
bear
beautify
beg
behave
behold
behoove
believe
belong
bend
benefit
beware
bid
bide
bite
blackmail
blame
blast
blat
blaze
bleach
bleed
blend
bless
blind
block
bloom
blow
bluff
board
boil
bombard
borrow
bother
bounce
bow
box
brag
braid
brainwash
brake
branch
brawl
break
breathe
breed
breeze
bribe
brighten
bring
broadcast
broaden
broil
bruise
brush
bubble
bump
burst
bury
button
buy
buzz
✦✦✦✦✦
cage
calculate
calm
cap
capitalize
capsize
carve
catalog
caucus
caution
cease
celebrate
cement
censor
center
certify
chain
chatter
challenge
chant
characterize
charge
charm
chart
chase
cheapen
cheat
cheer
chew
chill
chime
chip
chirp
choke
chop
chronicle
circulate
claim
clamp
clang
clank
clap
clatter
clash
clasp
classify
claw
clean
clear
clench
click
clinch
cling
clump
clip
clock
clog
clothe
cluck
coagulate
coast
cock
coil
collate
collide
combine
command
commem-
orate
commence
commend
complicate
compliment
compromise
conceive
condense
confide
confine
confirm
conquer
consent
conserve
consult
contain
contest
contract
contradict
contrast
convene
convert
coordinate
cope
corrupt
counsel
counterfeit
crackle
cram
craze
creak
crease
creep
criticize
croak
crop
crouch
cuddle
cuff
✦✦✦✦✦
dam
damage
dart
dash
deactivate
debrief
decay
decline
decompress
decree
dedicate
deduct
deepen
deface
deform
defy
degrade
delegate
delete
delight
depreciate
depress
deprive
descend
desert
designate
despise
destine
detach
detain
defect
devise
devote
dictate
diddle
dignify
dilate
diminish
dimple
direct
disassemble
disband
disburse
discard
disclose
discolor
discount
discourage
disgrace
disguise
disgust
dishonor
disillusion
disinfect
disinherit
dislocate
dislodge
dismiss
disorient
display
dispute
disqualify
disregard
disrespect
disrobe
disrupt
dissatisfy
dissect
distinguish

distract
distress
distribute
distrust
disturb
diversify
divorce
donate
doodle
doom
double-check
double-cross
double-dip
doze
drain
dramatize
drape
drawl
dread
drizzle
drown
duck
dun
duplicate
✦✦✦✦✦
eavesdrop
egg (on)
elect
eliminate
embezzle
emigrate
emphasize
enable
enact
enclose
endanger
endeavor
energize
enforce
engage
engrave
enlarge
enlighten
enslave
envy
equalize
equate
equip
erase
escape
escort
estimate
evacuate
evaluate
evaporate
evict
exaggerate
excavate
exceed
excel
except
exchange
exclaim
exclude
exhume
exile
expedite
expel
expend
expire
expose
extend
externalize
extort
extradite
✦✦✦✦✦
facilitate
fade
fake
falsify
familiarize
fantasize
fascinate
fatigue
feast
fetch
finagle
finesse
fizzle
flabbergast
flake
flank
flatten
flavor
flick
flimflam
flip
float
flock
flood
flop
flow
flush
foam
focus
fold
foliate
foot
forecast
foreclose
forerun
forfeit
formalize
free-lance
freewheel
freeze
frighten
frost
froth
frustrate
fulfill
function
fuss
✦✦✦✦✦
gag
gain
gallop
gamble
gargle
gash
generalize
gesture
gibber
giggle
glad-hand
glamorize
glance
glare
glaze
glitter
gnash
gobble
goof
gore
gorge
govern
grab
grade
graduate
graft
graph
grease
greet
grieve
grin
grind
grip
gripe
grit
groan
group
grunt
guarantee
guard
guide
gulp
gust
guzzle
gyp
✦✦✦✦✦
hack
halt
handcuff
handicap
hanker
hash
haul
heal
heft
hemorrhage
hesitate
hex
hibernate
hightail
hijack
hike
hire
hiss
hole (up)
holler
honk
hook
hoot
horse-trade
howl
huff
hulk
hull
humidify
hunt
husk
hydrate
hydroplane
hypnotize
✦✦✦✦✦
identify
ignore
illustrate
imagine
imitate
immigrate
immunize
impersonate
implement
imply
import
impress
improve
inbreed
include
inconvenience
increase
indent
indicate
individualize
influence
inform
inherit
initiate
inject
inlay
insist
inspect
instruct
insult
insure
intend
interbreed
interfere
interrupt
interview
irrigate
irritate
itch
itemize
✦✦✦✦✦
jerk
jiggle
jingle
jinx
jitter
join
jot
judge
junk
justify
✦✦✦✦✦
kibitz
kink
✦✦✦✦✦
land
launder
lease
lecture
legislate
license
limit
link
litigate
litter
load
lob
locate
lust
✦✦✦✦✦
maintain
manage
manufacture
march
mark
master
match
mate
materialize
mature
maximize
measure
mechanize
medicate
melt
mention
miff
minimize
miscopy
miscount
miscue
misdate
misdeem
misemploy
misfile
misfire
misinterpret
misjudge
mislabel
mislay
mislead
misplace
misplay
misprint
mispronounce
misquote
misread
misspell
mistrust
misunderstand
modernize
mooch
motivate
motorize
munch
✦✦✦✦✦
nationalize
navigate
necessitate
neglect
negotiate
nip
nitpick
nod
nominate
normalize
notice
notify
✦✦✦✦✦
obey
object
obligate
observe
obtain
occupy
occur
offend
offer
officiate
offset
omit
operate
oppose
orient
originate
outargue
outbid
outbluff
outdate
outdo
outdraw
outfit
outflank
outlast

outlive
outplay
outrank
outrun
outsell
outshine
outshoot
outsing
outsit
outsleep
outsmart
outstare
outstay
outstrip
outstroke
outswear
outtalk
outtell
outthrow
outvote
outwait
outwalk
outwear
outweep
outweigh
outwork
overbid
overbuild
overbuy
overcharge
overcome
overcompen-
sate
overcrowd
overdevelop
overdo
overdraw
overdress
overestimate
overexcite
overexert
overexpose
overfeed
overfill
overflow
overhang
overhaul
overhear
overheat
overlap
overlay
overload
overlook
overmatch
overorganize
overpay
overpopulate
overpower
overproduce
overrule
oversell
overshoot
oversleep
overspend
overspill
overspread
overstate
overstay
overstep
overstock
overstudy
overstuff
oversub-
scribe
oversupply
overthrow
overuse
overweigh
overwork
✦✦✦✦✦
pack
package
panic
park
participate
pat
pause
paw
peek
peel
penalize
perceive
perch
perfect
perform
permit
personalize
persuade
pertain
phase (in;
out)
philosophize
phrase
pin
pinch
pity
place
plaster
please
pledge
plop
plot
plow
pluck
plug
poke
police
polish
pop
popularize
populate
position
possess
post
postdate
postpone
pound
pour
practice
praise
preach
prearrange
predict
prefer
prepackage
pressure
pretend
pretest
prevent
preview
proceed
process
procrastinate
profit
progress
promote
pronounce
prop
propel
propose
prorate
prosecute
prosper
protect
protest
provide
publicize
pump
punish
pursue
puzzle
✦✦✦✦✦
qualify
quarantine
question
quiet (down)
quiz
quote
✦✦✦✦✦
race
raise
rate
ration
rationalize
rattle
react
realize
reason
reassure
rebel
recalculate
recite
reclassify
reconsider
reconstruct
recover
recruit
recycle
redevelop
redirect
refer
refine
reflect
refresh
refund
refuse
regain
register
regret
regulate
reject
relax
relay
release
relieve
remain
remake
remark
remove
renegotiate
renew
repay
repeat
replace
reply
report
represent
reproduce
request
require
rescue
research
reserve
resign
resist
respect
respond
restore
restrain
restrict
resume
reveal
reverse
review
revise
reward
rinse
rip
risk
rub
ruin
rule
✦✦✦✦✦
sag
sail
sample
satisfy
scare
schedule
score
scrap
scratch
screw
scribble
scrub
seal
search
seat
secure
seek
segregate
select
sense
sentence
separate
settle
shake
shape
share
shine
shock
shrink
simplify
sip
skip
slam
slap
slice
slide
slip
slit
slop
slope
slosh
slug
slurp
smash
sniff
snoop
snort
soak
soar
sob
socialize
soil
solve
sort
sound
spare
sparkle
specialize
specify
spill
spin
splash
split
spoil
sponsor
spot
sprain
spray
spread
spring
sprinkle
spy
squash
squeak
squeeze
squirt
stab
stabilize
stack
stain
stall
stamp
stampede
standardize
stare
station
steal
steer
stereotype
stockpile
strain
strangle
strap
stretch
strip
struggle
stuff
stump
subcontract
subdivide
subscribe
subsidize
substitute
subtitle
subtract
suck
suffer
suffocate
suggest
summarize
supervise
support
suppose
surrender
surround
survey
survive
suspect
suspend
swear
sweat

sweep
swing
✦✦✦✦✦
table
tack
tackle
tag
tap
tattle
tear
tease
testify
theorize
threaten
tickle
tighten
tip
title
toast
tolerate
toot
top
torture
toss
tow
trade
train
transcribe
transfer
transform
translate
transplant
transport
treat
trespass
trim
trip
trot
tuck
tug
✦✦✦✦✦
uncover
underbid
underbuy
undercharge
undergo
underpay
underprice
underquote
underrate
undertake
undervalue
unfasten
unfold
unite
unload
unplug
unroll
unscrew
unseal
undress
unsnap
unstick
untangle
untie
untune
untwist
unwind
unwrap
unwrinkle
unzip
upgrade
uphold
uplift
upset
upstage
✦✦✦✦✦
vacate
vaccinate
value
vandalize
value
vandalize
vanish
vary
verbalize
verify
veto
vibrate
victimize
view
violate
visit
visualize
vocalize
volunteer
voyage
✦✦✦✦✦
wad
waddle
wade
wag
wake
warn
wave
wed
welcome
whine
whip
whisper
whistle
whiten
widen
wiggle
wine (and dine)
wink
winterize
wipe
withdraw
withhold
wonder
worry
worship
wrap
wreck
wrestle
wring
wrinkle
✦✦✦✦✦
yank
yawn
yell
✦✦✦✦✦
zip
✦✦✦✦✦

MIND PROVOKERS

Less Easily Recalled Active Verbs: An Alphabetical List of About 2,000

abandon
abate
abet
abhor
abjure
abort
abridge
abscond
absolve
abuse
abut
accede
accentuate
acclimate
accost
accrue
acquiesce
adhere
adjoin
admonish
adorn
adulterate
advocate
affiliate
affirm
affix
afflict
afford
affront
aggravate
aggrandize
agitate
agonize
alert
alienate
alight
align
allay
alleviate
allocate
allot
allude
amalgamate
amass
amble
ambulate
ameliorate
amend
amplify
anchor
animate
annihilate
annotate
anoint
antagonize
appall
appease
append
apprehend
apprise
arouse
array
arrest
ascend
ascertain
ascribe
aspire
assail
assault
assimilate
assuage
astonish
astound
atone
attain
attenuate
attest
attune
augment
avail
avenge
avert
✦✦✦✦✦
backpedal
badger
baffle
balk
balloon
ban
banish
banter
barge
barricade
bask
batch
bathe
batten
batter
bedazzle
bedevil
befall
befit
befog
beget
begrudge
belabor
belie
belittle
bemoan
bemuse
benumb
beseech
beset
besmirch
bestow
betray
bewail
beweep
bewilder
bicker
bilk
bind
bisect
blanch
blaspheme
blazon
blemish
bloat
blot
bludgeon
blunder
blunt
blur
blurt
boast
bob
bode (evil; well)
boggle
bolster
bolt
bond
boost
bore
bound
boycott
brace
bracket
brand
brandish
breach
brew
bridge
bristle
broach
brood
browse
buckle
budge
bundle
bungle
buoy
burden
burnish
bustle
butcher
buttress
bypass
✦✦✦✦✦
cajole
calcify
camouflage
canvass
capacitate
capitulate
captivate
capture
careen
carom
carouse
carp
cast
castigate
catapult
censure
chafe
champion
char
cherish
chide
churn
circumscribe
circumvent
cite
clamber
clamor
cleanse
cleave
cloak
cloister
cloud
clutch
coalesce
coax
coddle
codify
coerce
cogitate
cohabit
cohere
coincide
collaborate
collapse
collude
commingle
commiserate
compel
compensate
compile
complement
comply
compound
comprehend
compress
conceal
concede
conciliate
concoct
concur
condescend
confer
confiscate
conform
confound
confute
congeal
congest
conjure
conjoin
connive
connote
consecrate
consign
console
consolidate
consort
conspire
consternate
constrain
constrict
construe
consume
consummate
contaminate
contemplate
contend
contort
contrapose
contravene
controvert
convalesce
converge
convey
correlate
correspond
corroborate
corrode
countermand
counter-reply
countervail
covet
cower
cradle
craft
crave
crest
crimp
cringe
cripple
crisscross
crucify
crumble
crusade
crystallize
cull
culminate
cultivate
curb
curry (favor)
curtail
cushion
cycle
✦✦✦✦✦
dab
dabble
dampen
dangle
daub
daunt
dawdle
dazzle
debase
debauch
debilitate
debunk
decelerate
decimate
decipher
decry
deduce
defame
defer (to)
defile
deflate

deflect
defraud
defray
degenerate
degrade
deign
deject
deliberate
delineate
delude
deluge
delve
demean
demolish
demonize
demur
denigrate
denote
denounce
denude
deprave
depict
deplete
deplore
deploy
depose
deprecate
depredate
derange
deride
derive
derogate
desiccate
desecrate
desist
despair
despoil
despond
deter
deteriorate
detest
detract
devastate
deviate
devolve
devour
differentiate
diffuse
digress
dilapidate
dilute
disable
disabuse (of)
disaffect
disallow
disarm
disassociate
disavow
discern
discharge
disclaim
discomfit
disconcert
discredit
discriminate
disdain
disembark
disenchant
disencumber
disenfranchise
disengage
disentangle
disenthrall
disestablish
disfigure
disgruntle
dishabituate
dishearten
dishevel
disincline
disintegrate
disinter
disjoin
dismantle
dismay
disparage
dispatch
dispel
dispense
disperse
dispirit
displace
dispossess
disprove
disseminate
dissent
disserve
dissipate
dissociate
dissuade
distend
distill
distort
diverge
divert
divest
divine
divulge
dodder
dodge
doff
dole (out)
dominate
don
dote
douse
dredge
drench
dribble
drift
drone
droop
drub
drudge
dub
dwarf
dwell
dwindle
✦✦✦✦✦
earmark
ease
ebb
echo
edge
edify
efface
effuse
eject
eke
elaborate
elapse
elate
elevate
elicit
elide
elongate
elucidate
elude
emaciate
emanate
emancipate
emasculate
embark
embed
embellish
embitter
emblazon
embody
embolden
embrace
embroil
emend
emerge
emit
emote
empathize
empower
emulate
encapsulate
encase
enchant
encircle
encompass
encounter
encroach
enculturate
encumber
endorse
endow
endure
enervate
enfold
engender
engross
engulf
enhance
enlist
enliven
enmesh
ennoble
enrage
enrapture
ensconce
enshrine
ensue
ensure
entail
entangle
enthrall
enthrone
enthuse
entice
entitle
entrap
entreat
entrench
entrust
entwine
enumerate
enunciate
envelop
envision
epitomize
equilibrate
equivocate
eradicate
erode
err
erupt
escalate
eschew
espouse
estrange
etch
evade
eventuate
eviscerate
evoke
evolve
exacerbate
exalt
exasperate
excise
excoriate
exculpate
exemplify
exert
exhaust
exhibit
exhilarate
exhort
exonerate
exorcize
expand
expatiate
expiate
explicate
exploit
expound
expropriate
expunge
extinguish
extirpate
extol
extract
extrapolate
extricate
extrude
exuberate
exude
✦✦✦✦✦
fabricate
falter
fare
fashion
fathom
favor
fawn
faze
feature
feign
fend (off)
ferry
fester
festoon
fetter
feud
fidget
filibuster
filter
flag
flail
flap
flare
flash
flaunt
flee
fleece
flesh (out)
flex
flinch
fling
flirt (with)
flit
flog
flounce (out; off; away)
flower
fluctuate
fluster
flutter
foil
foist (on; upon)
foment
fondle
forage
forbid
forebode
foredoom
forefeel
foreknow
foreordain
foresee
foreshadow
foreshow
forestall
foretaste
foretell
forewarn
forge
forgo
forejudge
formulate
forsake
forswear
fortify
foster
foul
founder
fracture
fragment
frame
frazzle
fret
fringe
fritter (away)
frolic
front
fulminate (against)
fumble
fume
funnel
furnish
fuse
✦✦✦✦✦
gall
gallivant
galvanize
gape
garble
garner
garnish
gasp (out; forth)
gather
gauge
gawk
gaze
gear
generate
genuflect

germinate
gerrymander
gestate
gesticulate
gild
gird
gladden
gleam
glean
glide
glimpse
glint
glisten
gloat
glorify
gloss (over)
glower
glut
gnarl
gnaw
goad
gouge
gradate
grant
grapple
grasp
grate (on)
gratify
gravitate
graze
grimace
groom
grope
grouse
grovel
grumble
gurgle
gush
gyrate
✦✦✦✦✦
habituate
haggle
hail
hallucinate
hammer
hamper
harangue
harass
harbor
harden
harness
harp
harry
harvest
hasten
hatch
haunt
heap
heave
hedge
heed
hem (& haw)
herd
hew
highlight
hinder
hinge
hint
hitch
hoard
hobble
hobnob (with)
hoist
hone
honor
horrify
hose
hound
house
hover
huddle
hug
hum
humble
humiliate
hunker (down)
hurdle
hurl
hurtle
hush
hustle
hypothesize
✦✦✦✦✦
idealize
idle
idolize
ignite
ill-treat
illuminate
image
imbibe
imbrue
imbue
immerse
immobilize
immortalize
impair
impale
impart
impeach
impede
impel
impend
impinge
implant
implicate
implode
implore
impose
impound
impoverish
impregnate
imprint
improvise
impugn
impute
incapacitate
incarcerate
incense
inch
incinerate
incise
incite
incline
incorporate
incriminate
incubate
inculcate
indemnify
indict
indispose
induce
induct
indulge
inebriate
infect
infer
infest
infiltrate
inflame
inflate
inflect
inflict
infringe
infuriate
infuse
ingrain
ingratiate
inhabit
inhere
inhibit
innervate
inoculate
insinuate
inspire
install
instigate
instill
institute
insulate
integrate
intensify
intercede
intercept
interchange
interconnect
interject
interlace
interlock
interlope
intermingle
intermit
intermix
interpolate
interpose
interrelate
interrogate
intersect
intersperse
intertwine
intervene
interweave
intimate
intimidate
intone
intoxicate
intrigue
introspect
intrude
inundate
inure (to)
invade
invalidate
inveigh (against)
invert
invest
invoke
irk
irrupt
isolate
issue
iterate
✦✦✦✦✦
jab
jabber
jade
jam
jampack
jangle
jar
jaundice
jaunt
jeer
jell
jeopardize
jest
jibe
jilt
jockey
jog
jolt
jostle
journey
jubilate
juggle
jumble
jut
✦✦✦✦✦
key
kindle
knead
knit
knot
knuckle (down; under)
✦✦✦✦✦
label
labor
lace
lacerate
lack
lade(n)
lag
lambaste
lament
lance
languish
lap
lapse
lash
latch (onto)
laud
launch
lavish
layer
leach
leak
lean
leap
leash
leech (on to)
leer
legitimate
lend
level
levitate
levy
liberate
lilt
linger
lionize
liquefy
liquidate
loaf
loath
lobby
lodge
loft
log
loiter
loll
lollygag
loom
loop
loot
lop
lope
lounge
lubricate
lug
lull
lump
lunge
lurch
lure
lurk
luxuriate
lynch
✦✦✦✦✦
machinate
magnify
maim
malfunction
malign
malinger
malleate
manacle
mandate
maneuver
mangle
manifest
manipulate
map
mar
maraud
marinate
maroon
marvel
mash
mask
masquerade
massacre
massage
mastermind
mat
maul
maunder
meander
meddle
mediate
meld
memorialize
menace
mend
merge
merit
mesh
mesmerize
mete (out)
migrate
militate (for; against)
mill (around)
mimic
mince
mingle
minify
mire
misapply

misapprehend
misappropriate
misbehave
misbelieve
miscalculate
miscarry
miscast
mischoose
miscolor
misconceive
misconstrue
miscounsel
misderive
misdescribe
misdirect
misdo
misestimate
misgovern
misguide
mishandle
mishear
misinform
misknow
mislocate
mismanage
mismatch
misname
misremember
misreport
misrepresent
missend
misshape
misspeak
misspend
misstate
misteach
mistreat
misuse
misvalue
miswrite
mitigate
moan
mob
mobilize
mock
moderate
modify
modulate
moil
moisten
mold
molest
mollify
monitor
monopolize
moon
mortify
mound
mount
mourn
mow
muddle
muffle
mull (over)
multiply
mumble
murmur
muse
muster
mutate
mutilate
muzzle
mystify

✦✦✦✦✦

nag
nauseate
needle
negate
neologize
nestle
net
neutralize
nick
niggle
nominalize
nourish
nudge
nullify
numerate
nurse
nurture
nuzzle

✦✦✦✦✦

obfuscate
oblige
obliterate
obscure
obsess
obstruct
obtrude
obvert
obviate
occlude
ooze
opine
oppress
opt (for)
orate
ordain
ornament
oscillate
ossify
ostracize
oust
outdistance
outgrow
outmaneuver
outmatch
outmode
outrage
outreach
outsoar
outspan
outstretch
outthink
outwit
overarch
overawe
overbalance
overbear
overburden
overgrow
overindulge
overjoy
overrate
overreach
override
overrun
oversee
overtake
overtax
overtire
overturn
overwhelm
overwrite

✦✦✦✦✦

pace
pacify
pad
paint
pair
palaver
pale
palpitate
pamper
pander
pant
paraphrase
parlay
parley
parody
part
partition
patch
patronize
patter
pattern (after)
pave
peak
peal
peddle
peep
peer
peeve
pelt
penetrate
perambulate
perforate
percolate
perish
perk (up)
permeate
permute
perpetrate
perpetuate
persecute
persevere
persist
personify
perturb
peruse
pervade
pervert
pester
petrify
piddle (away)
piece (together)
pierce
pilfer
pillage
pioneer
pique
pit (against)
pitch
pivot
placate
plague
plateau
plead
plod
plumb
plummet
plunder
plunge
ply
poise
polarize
poll
pollute
pommel
ponder
pontificate
pool
pore (over)
portend
portray
pose
postulate
posture
pounce
pout
prance
prattle
precede
precipitate
preclude
preconceive
precondition
predate
predestine
predicate
predispose
predominate
preempt
preen
preexist
prefabricate
preface
prefigure
preform
preincline
preindicate
preinform
preinstruct
prejudge
prelimit
premeditate
preoccupy
preordain
prepossess
prerelease
prerequire
presage
prescribe
preselect
preserve
preside
press
presume
presuppose
prevail
prevaricate
prey
prime
primp
prize
probe
proclaim
procure
prod
profess
prognosticate
prohibit
project
proliferate
prolong
promenade
prompt
promulgate
propagate
prophesy
propitiate
propound
proscribe
protract
protrude
provoke
prowl
pry
puff
pulsate
pulverize
punctuate
purge
purify
purport
purvey
putrefy

✦✦✦✦✦

quaff
quake
quarrel
quaver
quell
quench
query
quibble
quicken
quip
quiver

✦✦✦✦✦

rack
radiate
rage
raid
rail (at; against)
rake (over; through)
rally
ram
ramble
ramify
rampage
ramrod
range
rank
rankle
ransom
rant
rap
rarefy
rasp
ravage
rage
raze
reactivate
ream
reanimate
reap
reapportion
rebound
rebuff
rebuke
rebut
recalcitrate
recant
recap
recapitulate
recapture

recede
recess
reciprocate
reclaim
recline
recoil
recompose
reconcile
reconstitute
recount
recoup
re-create
recreate
recriminate
rectify
recuperate
recur
redeem
redeploy
redouble
redress
reduce
reform
refrain
refurbish
refute
regale
regard
regenerate
regiment
regress
regurgitate
rehabilitate
rehash
reign
reimburse
rein (in)
reinforce
reiterate
rejoice
rejoin
rejuvenate
relegate
relent
relinquish
relish
remand
remedy
reminisce
remit
remonstrate
remunerate
rend
render
rendezvous
renege
renounce
renovate
repair
repatriate
repel
repent
rephrase
replenish
replicate
repose
repossess
reprehend
repress
reprieve
reprimand
reprise
reproach
reprove
repudiate
repulse
repute
requite
rescind
resemble
resent
reset
reshape
reside
resolve
resonate
resort
resound
respire
resurface
resurge
resurrect
resuscitate
retain
retaliate
retard
retire
retort
retrace
retract
retreat
retrench
retrieve
retroact
retrogress
revamp
revel
reverberate
revere
revert
revile
revive
revoke
revolt
revolve
rhapsodize
rid
ridicule
rigidify
rile
ring
riot
ripen
ripple
rise
rival
roam
roar
rob
rock
roister
romanticize
roost
romp
rot
rotate
root
rouse
rout
routinize
rove
ruffle
rumble
ruminate
rummage
rumple
rupture
rush
rustle

✦✦✦✦✦

sabotage
sack
sacrifice
sadden
saddle
salivate
salute
salvage
salve
sanctify
sanction
sanitize
sap
sate
satiate
satirize
saturate
saunter
savor
scale
scale
scamper
scan
scandalize
scar
scatter
scavenge
scheme
school
scintillate
scoff
scold
scoop
scorch
scorn
scour
scourge
scout
scowl
scramble
scrape
scrawl
screech
screen
scrimp
scroll
scrounge
scrunch
scrutinize
scuff
scuffle
sculpt
scurry
scuttle
sear
season
secede
seclude
secrete
secularize
sedate
seduce
seep
seesaw
seethe
segment
segue
seize
[self-govern]
[self-inflict]
[self-teach]
etc., though most compound words beginning with *self* are not verbs.
sensitize
sentimentalize
sequester
sermonize
sever
shackle
shade
shadow
shag
shame
shatter
shave
shear
shed
sheer
shelter
shelve
shield
shift
shimmer
shirk
shiver
shoo
shoulder
shove
shower
shriek
shroud
shrug
shutter
shuffle
shun
shunt
shuttle
side (with; against)
sideline
sideswipe
sidle
(lay) siege (to)
sift
sigh
sight
signal
signify
silence
simmer
simulate
singe
sinuate
siphon
situate
sketch
skew
skewer
skid
skim
skimp
skirt
skitter
skulk
slacken
slander
slant
slash
slate
slaughter
slay
slight
sling
slink
slither
slobber
slouch
slough (off)
sluice
slumber
slump
slur
smack
smear
smirk
smite
sneer
snicker
sniffle
snip
snipe
snivel
snub
snuggle
sock (in; away)
soft-pedal
sojourn
solemnize
solicit
solidify
souse
space
span
spar
spatter
spawn
spearhead
speculate
spew
spice
spiral
spite
splatter
splay
splice
splinter
splurge
sprawl
sprout
spruce (up)
spur
spurn
spurt
sputter
squabble
squall
squander
square (with)
squat
squawk
squeal
squelch
squint
squirm
stage
stagger
stagnate
stake

stalk
stammer
stanch
startle
stash
stave (off)
steel
steep
stem
stifle
stigmatize
stimulate
sting
stipulate
stock
stoke
stoop
storm
stow
straddle
strafe
straggle
strand
stratify
stray
streak
stream
stress
strew
stride
string
strive
stroke
stroll
structure
strut
stultify
stumble
stun
stupefy
stylize
stymie
subdue
subjugate
sublimate
submerge
submerse
submit
subordinate
subside
subsist
substantiate
subsume
subvert
succumb
suffuse
sulk
summon
superannuate
supercharge
supererogate
superimpose
superintend
supersaturate
superscribe
supersede
supplant
supplicate
suppress
surge
surmise
surmount
surpass
sustain
swagger
swamp
swap
swarm
swash
swat
sway
swell
swelter
swerve
swill
swindle
swirl
swish
switch
swivel
swoon
swoop
synchronize
syncopate
synthesize
systemize
✦✦✦✦✦
tabulate
tailor
taint
tally
tamp
tangle
tantalize
taper (off)
tarnish
tarry
tatter
taunt
tax
teem
telescope
temper
terminate
terrorize
thaw
thicken
thin (out)
thirst
thrash
thread
thresh (out; over)
thrill
thrive
throb
throng
throttle
thrust
thunder
thwart
tilt
tinge
tingle
tinker
tinkle
titillate
titter
toddle
toe (in)
topple
toil
toggle
torment
totter
tousle
tout
tower
toy
trace
track
traduce
trail
trample (on; upon; over)
tranquilize
transact
transcend
transfigure
transfix
transfuse
transgress
transmit
transpire
transpose
traumatize
traverse
tread
treasure
trek
tremble
trickle
trifle (away)
trifurcate
trigger
triplicate
trisect
triumph
trivialize
troop
trounce
trudge
trump (up)
trumpet
truncate
trundle
tumble
tussle
twinkle
twirl
twist
twitch
twitter
typify
tyrannize
✦✦✦✦✦
unbend
unbind
unblock
unbridle
unburden
unclog
undercut
underdevelop
underdo
under-estimate
under-expose
undergird
underlay
underlie
undermine
undernourish
underpin
underpraise
underscore
understate
undo
undulate
unearth
unfetter
unfurl
unglue
unhand
unhinge
unlearn
unleash
unloose
unmask
unmuzzle
unnerve
unpile
unravel
unreel
unruffle
unsaddle
unscramble
unseam
unseat
unsettle
unshackle
unsheathe
unshroud
unsnarl
unteach
unthink
untuck
unveil
upend
upheave
upraise
uprear
uprise
uproot
upsurge
upturn
urge
usher (in; out)
usurp
utter
✦✦✦✦✦
vacilate
validate
vanquish
vaporize
variegate
varnish
vault
vaunt
veer
vegetate
veil
venerate
ventilate
venture
vest
vex
vilify
vindicate
vitalize
vitiate
vivify
vociferate
vouch
vow
vulgarize
✦✦✦✦✦
waft
wage
wail
waive
waiver
waken
wall
wallop
wallow
waltz
wander
wane
wangle
ward (off)
warm
warp
warrant
water (down)
water-soak
waver
wax
weaken
wean
weasel
weather
weave
wedge
weep
weigh
weld
well (up; forth)
wend
wheedle
wheel (about; around)
whet
whiffle
while (away)
whimper
whirl
whisk
whitewash
whittle
whoop
wield
wile
will
wilt
wince
wind
winnow
wither
witness
wobble
worm
wrangle
wreak
wrench
wrest
wriggle
writhe
✦✦✦✦✦
yammer
yaw
yearn
yelp
yield
yowl
✦✦✦✦✦
zag
zig
zigzag
zing
zoom

REFERENCES

American Psychological Association. (1994). *Publication Manual of the American Psychological Association* (APA). (4th ed.) Washington, D.C.: American Psychological Association.

Bernstein, Theodore M. (1965). *Watch Your Language.* Great Neck, NY: Channel Press.

Flesch, Rudolf. (1974). *The Art of Readable Writing.* New York: Harper & Row.

Fowler, H. W. (1996). *The New Fowler's Modern English Usage.* Oxford University Press.

Hacker, Diana. (1997). *A Writer's Reference.* (3rd ed.) New York: Bedford Books of St. Martin's Press.

Kramer, Melinda G., Glenn Leggett, and C. David Mead. (1995). *Prentice Hall Handbook for Writers.* Englewood Cliffs, NJ: Prentice Hall.

Lanham, Richard A. (1991). *Revising Prose.* New York: Charles Scribner's Sons.

MLA. (1997). *Handbook for Writers of Research Papers.* New York: Modern Language Association of America.

Strunk, W., Jr., & White, E. B. (1979). *The Elements of Style* (3rd ed.) New York: Macmillan.

University of Chicago. (1993). *The Chicago Manual of Style* (14th ed.) Chicago: The University of Chicago Press.

Webster. (1997). *Webster's Encyclopedic Unabridged Dictionary of the English Language.* New York: Portland House, a division of Random House.

Zinser, William. (1994). *On Writing Well.* New York: HarperCollins.